4001 A.D.

MATT KINDT | CLAYTON CRAIN | DAVID MACK

CONTENTS

Original Series Logo: Ryan Sook
Collection Cover Art: Clayton Crain

Assistant Editor: Danny Khazem (4001 A.D.)
Associate Editor: Kyle Andrukiewicz (4001 A.D.)
Editor: Tom Brennan (Prologue)
Editor-in-Chief: Warren Simons

VALIANT.

Peter Cuneo
Chairman

Dinesh Shamdasani
CEO & Chief Creative Officer

Gavin Cuneo
Chief Operating Officer & CFO

Fred Pierce
Publisher

Warren Simons
Editor-in-Chief

Walter Black
VP Operations

Hunter Gorinson
VP Marketing & Communications

Atom! Freeman
Director of Sales

Matthew Klein
Andy Liegl
John Petrie
Sales Managers

Josh Johns
Associate Director of Digital Media and Development

Travis Escarfullery
Jeff Walker
Production & Design Managers

Tom Brennan
Editor

Kyle Andrukiewicz
Editor and Creative Executive

Robert Meyers
Managing Editor

Peter Stern
Publishing & Operations Manager

Andrew Steinbeiser
Marketing & Communications Manager

Lauren Hitzhusen
Danny Khazem
Assistant Editors

Ivan Cohen
Collection Editor

Steve Blackwell
Collection Designer

Rian Hughes/Device
Trade Dress & Book Design

Russell Brown
President, Consumer Products,
Promotions and Ad Sales

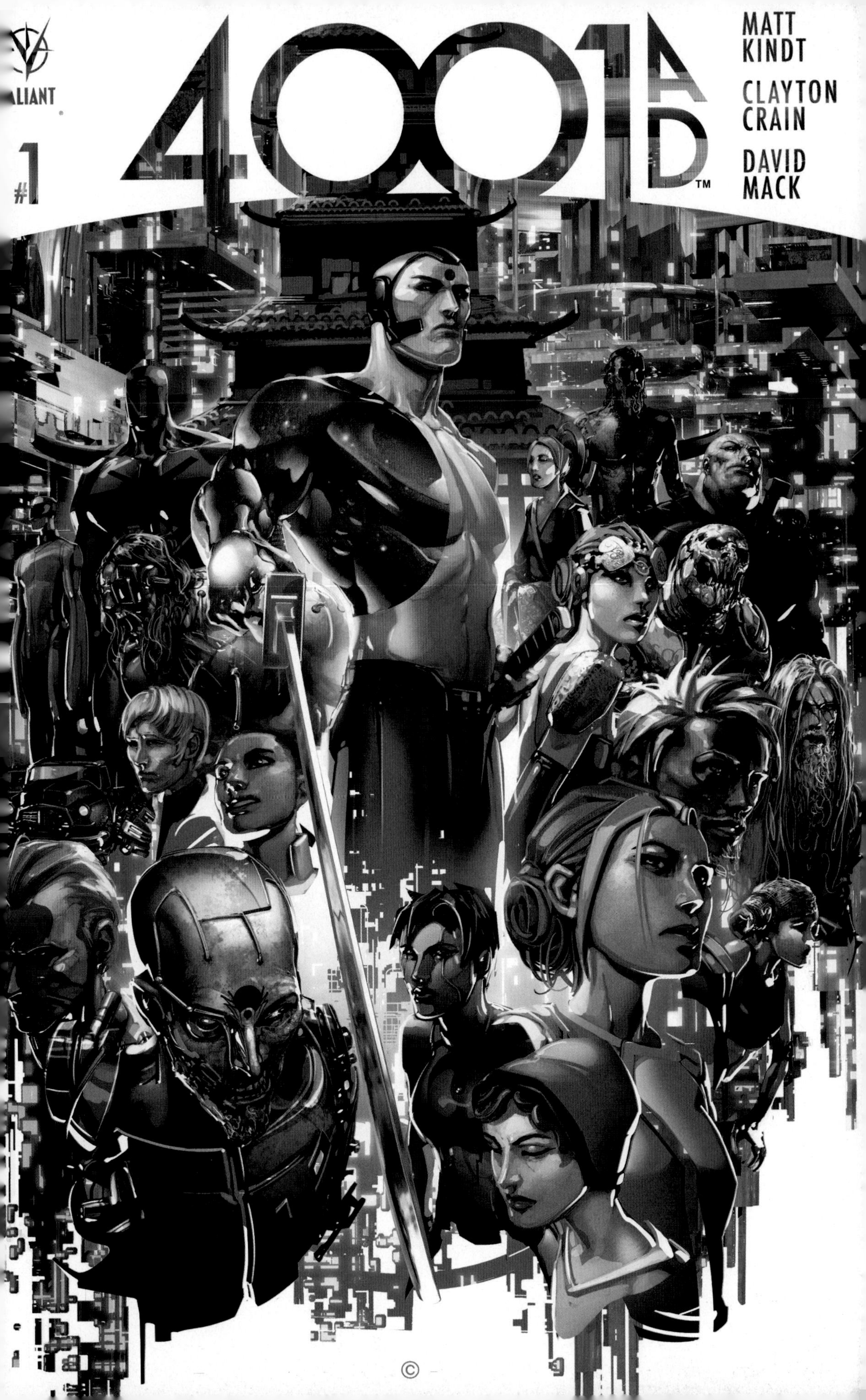
VALIANT
#1
4001 A.D.™
MATT KINDT
CLAYTON CRAIN
DAVID MACK

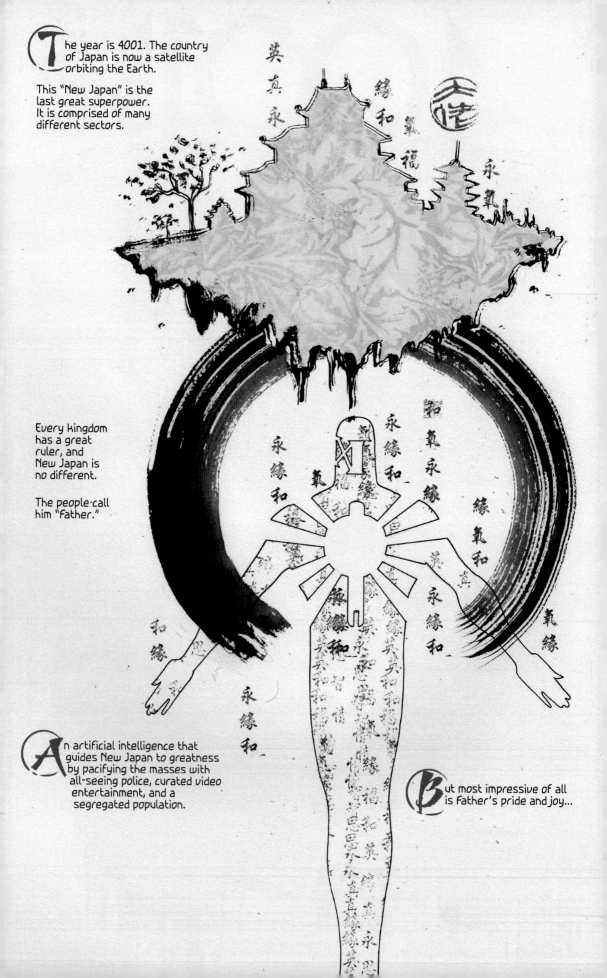

The year is 4001. The country of Japan is now a satellite orbiting the Earth.

This "New Japan" is the last great superpower. It is comprised of many different sectors.

Every kingdom has a great ruler, and New Japan is no different.

The people call him "father."

An artificial intelligence that guides New Japan to greatness by pacifying the masses with all-seeing police, curated video entertainment, and a segregated population.

But most impressive of all is father's pride and joy...

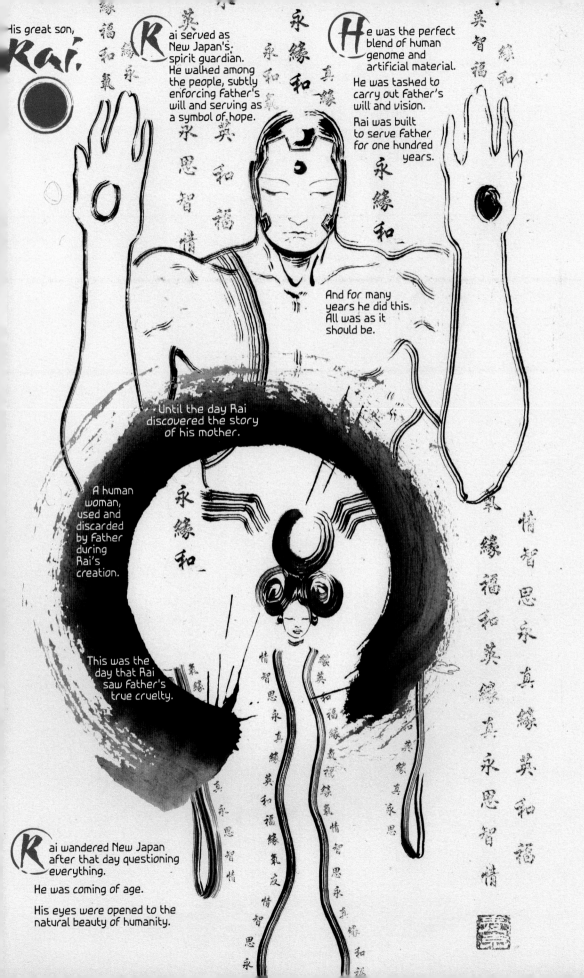

His great son,

Rai.

Rai served as New Japan's spirit guardian. He walked among the people, subtly enforcing father's will and serving as a symbol of hope.

He was the perfect blend of human genome and artificial material.

He was tasked to carry out father's will and vision.

Rai was built to serve father for one hundred years.

And for many years he did this. All was as it should be.

Until the day Rai discovered the story of his mother.

A human woman, used and discarded by father during Rai's creation.

This was the day that Rai saw father's true cruelty.

Rai wandered New Japan after that day questioning everything.

He was coming of age.

His eyes were opened to the natural beauty of humanity.

Rai met a young girl named Lula, who idolized him. She helped him discover the truth about his mother's death. In this way, Lula and New Japan became Rai's surrogate family.

Rai became disillusioned with Father's iron-willed grip on society.

What was humanity if it could not choose its own destiny?

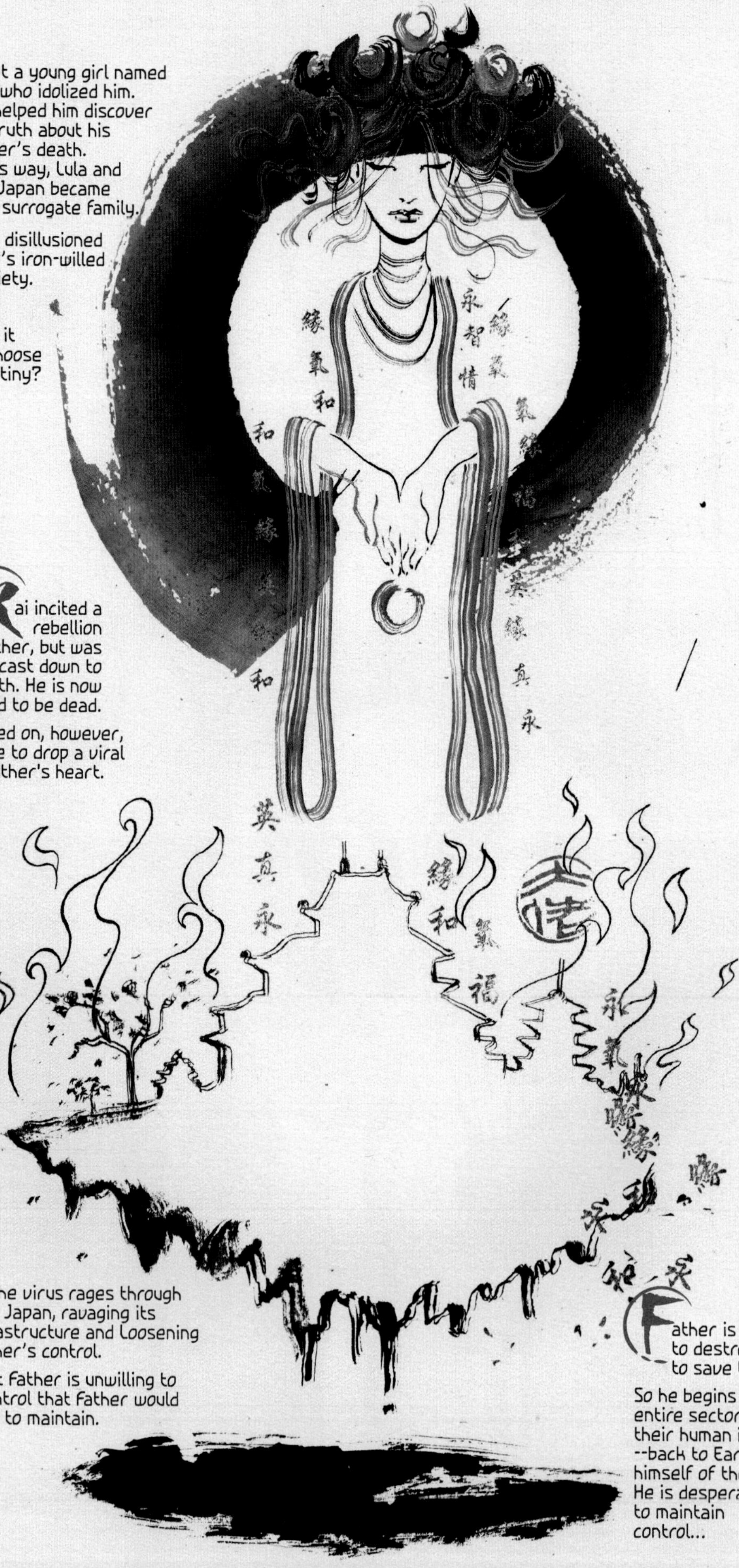

Rai incited a rebellion against Father, but was caught and cast down to Earth. He is now believed to be dead.

Lula continued on, however, and was able to drop a viral bomb into Father's heart.

Now the virus rages through New Japan, ravaging its infrastructure and loosening Father's control.

Control that Father is unwilling to give up. Control that Father would do anything to maintain.

Father is willing to destroy the body to save the mind...

So he begins dropping entire sectors--including their human inhabitants --back to Earth, to rid himself of the virus. He is desperate to maintain control...

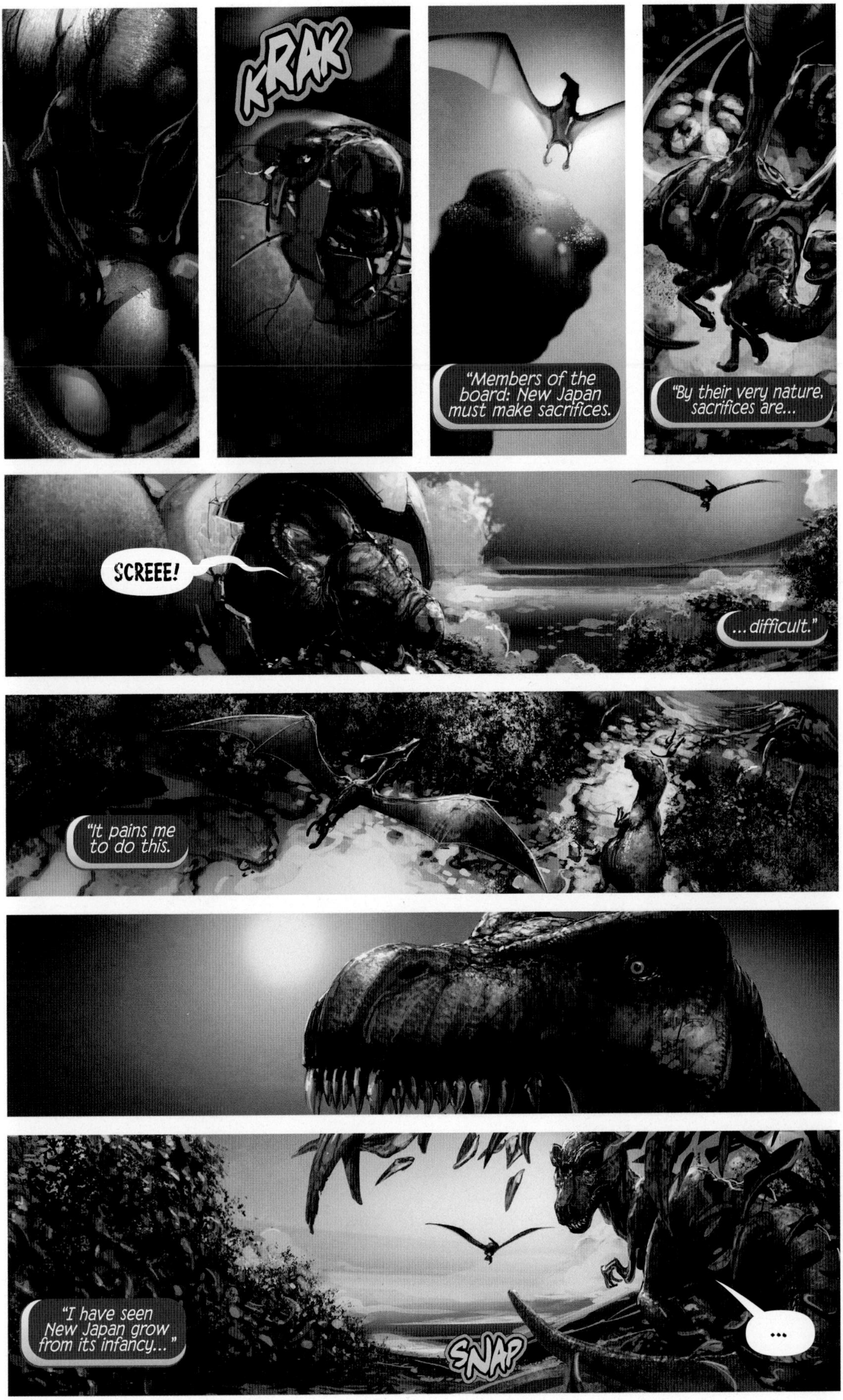
KRAK
"Members of the board: New Japan must make sacrifices.
"By their very nature, sacrifices are...
SCREEE!
...difficult."
"It pains me to do this.
"I have seen New Japan grow from its infancy..."
SNAP
...

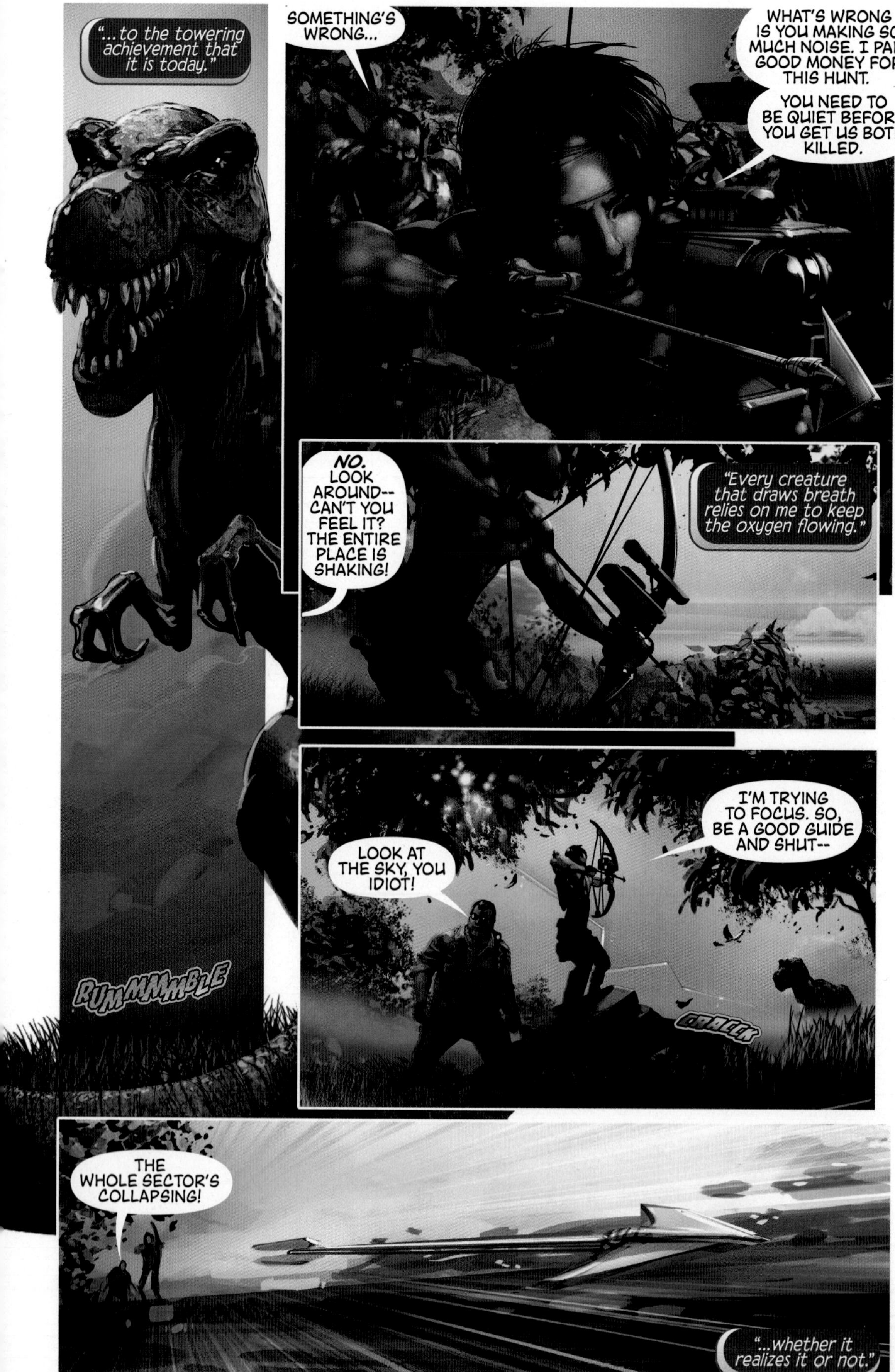
"...to the towering achievement that it is today."
SOMETHING'S WRONG...
WHAT'S WRONG IS YOU MAKING SO MUCH NOISE. I PAID GOOD MONEY FOR THIS HUNT.
YOU NEED TO BE QUIET BEFORE YOU GET US BOTH KILLED.
NO. LOOK AROUND-- CAN'T YOU FEEL IT? THE ENTIRE PLACE IS SHAKING!
"Every creature that draws breath relies on me to keep the oxygen flowing."
RUMMMMBLE
LOOK AT THE SKY, YOU IDIOT!
I'M TRYING TO FOCUS. SO, BE A GOOD GUIDE AND SHUT--
CRACK
THE WHOLE SECTOR'S COLLAPSING!
"...whether it realizes it or not."

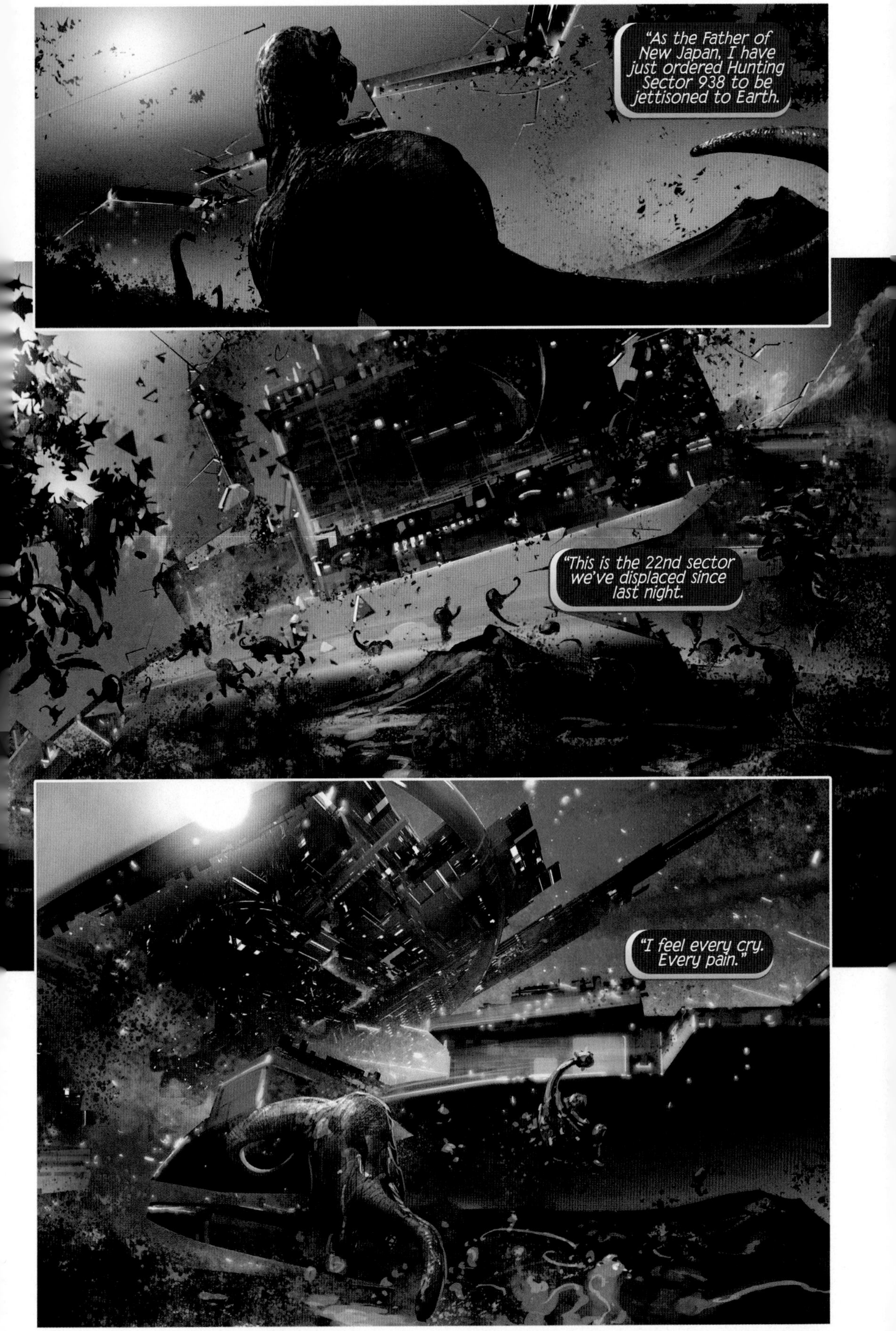
"As the Father of New Japan, I have just ordered Hunting Sector 938 to be jettisoned to Earth.
"This is the 22nd sector we've displaced since last night.
"I feel every cry. Every pain."

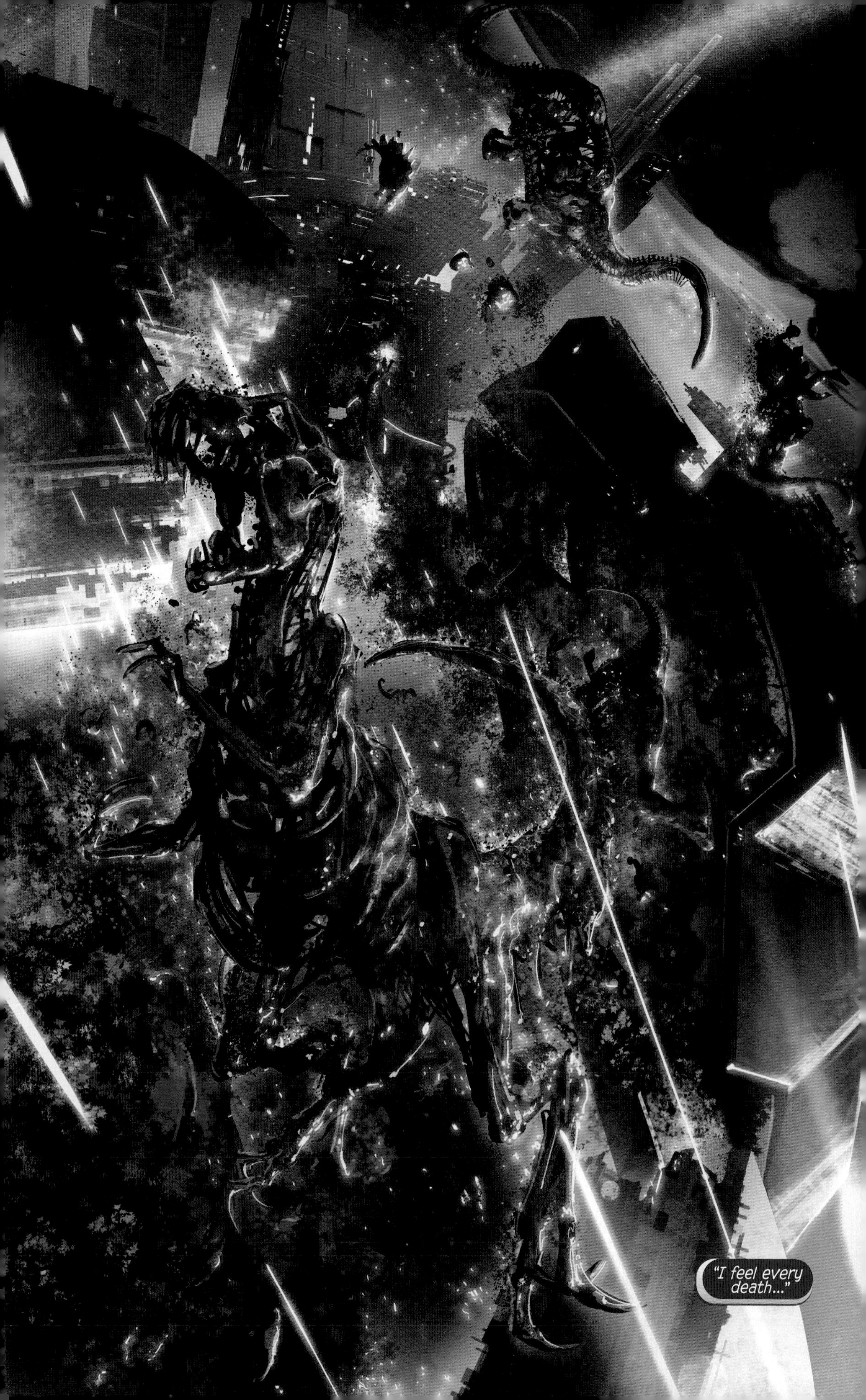
"I feel every death..."

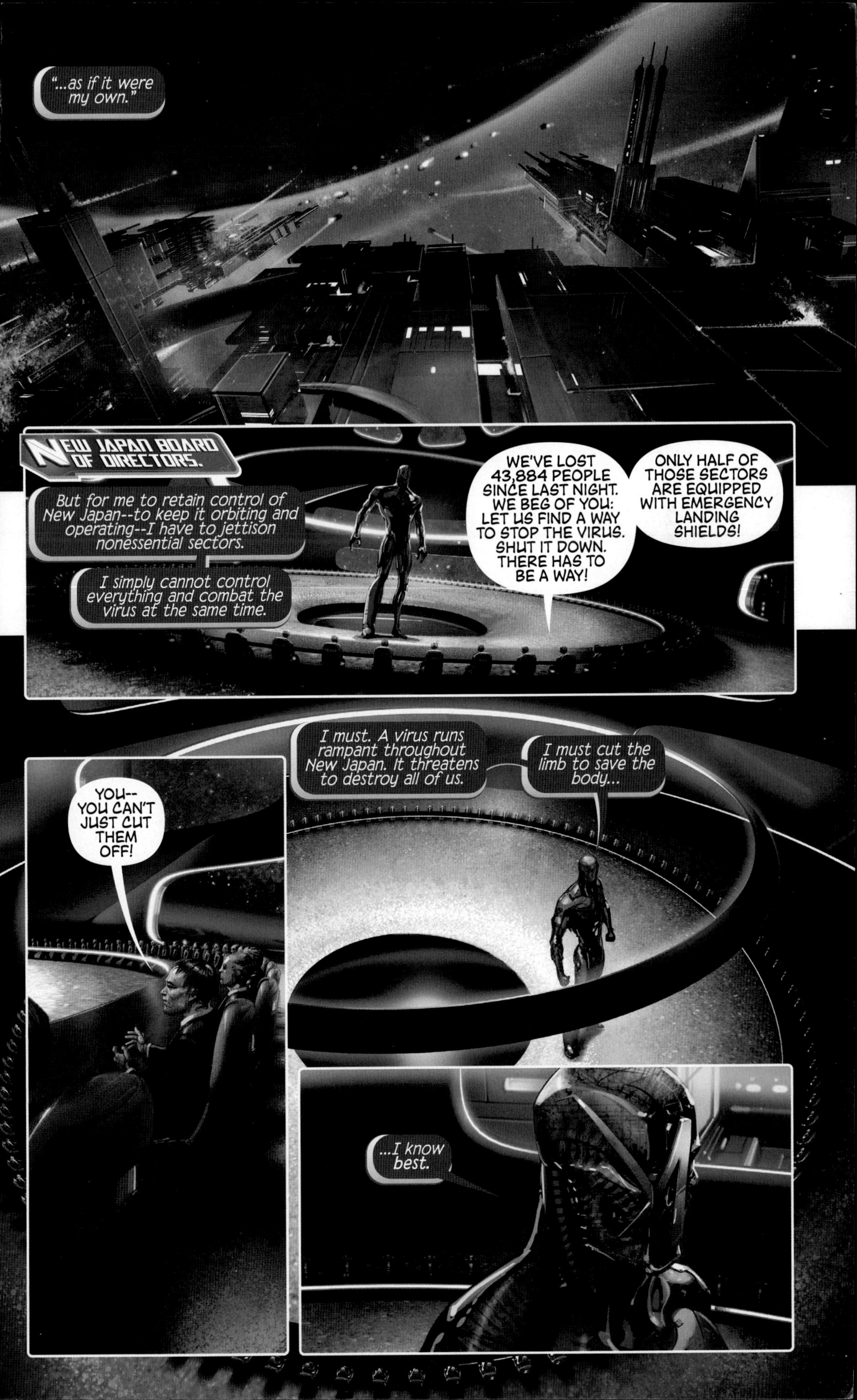

"...as if it were my own."
NEW JAPAN BOARD OF DIRECTORS.
But for me to retain control of New Japan--to keep it orbiting and operating--I have to jettison nonessential sectors.
I simply cannot control everything and combat the virus at the same time.
WE'VE LOST 43,884 PEOPLE SINCE LAST NIGHT. WE BEG OF YOU: LET US FIND A WAY TO STOP THE VIRUS. SHUT IT DOWN. THERE HAS TO BE A WAY!
ONLY HALF OF THOSE SECTORS ARE EQUIPPED WITH EMERGENCY LANDING SHIELDS!
YOU-- YOU CAN'T JUST CUT THEM OFF!
I must. A virus runs rampant throughout New Japan. It threatens to destroy all of us.
I must cut the limb to save the body...
...I know best.

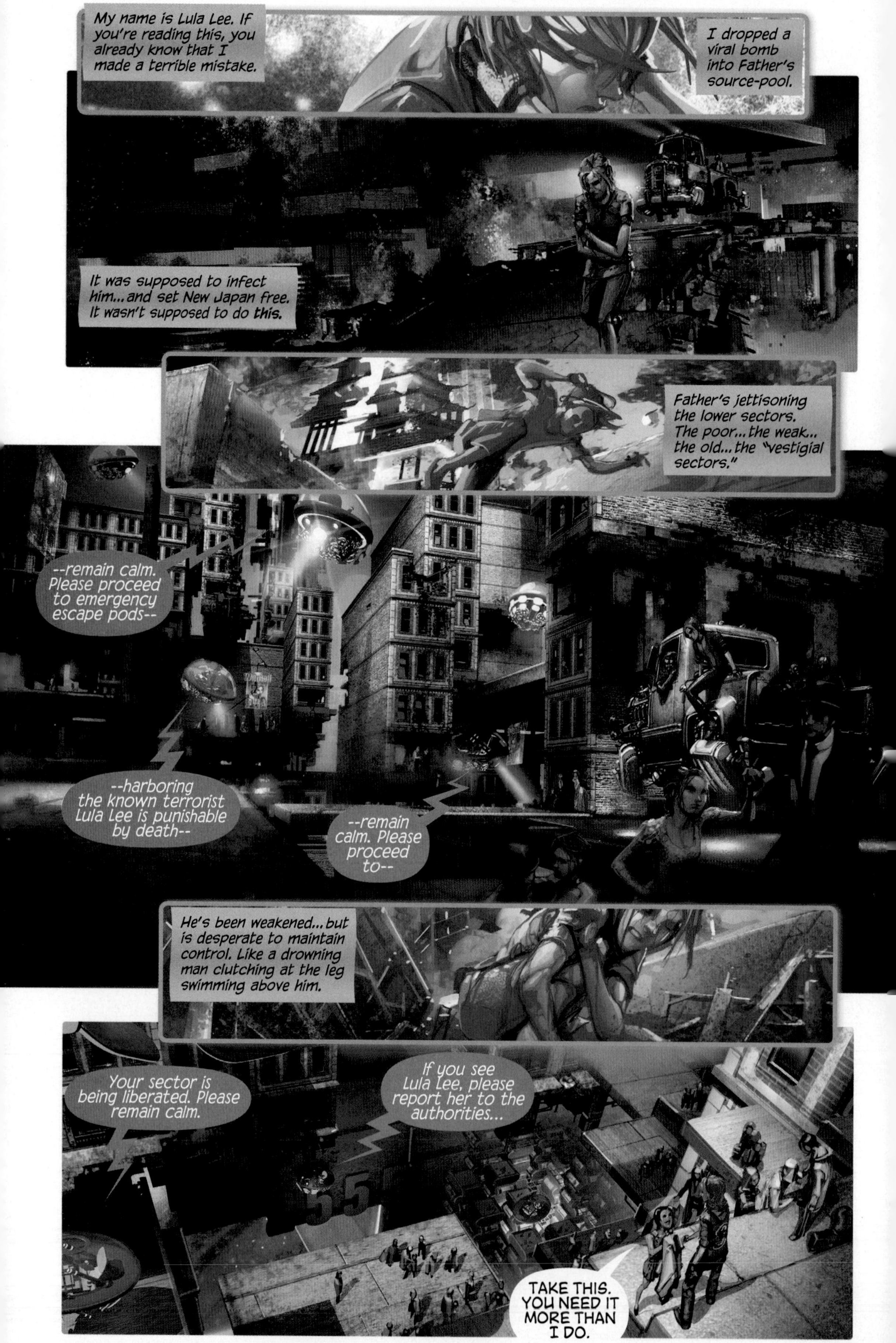
My name is Lula Lee. If you're reading this, you already know that I made a terrible mistake.
I dropped a viral bomb into Father's source-pool.
It was supposed to infect him... and set New Japan free. It wasn't supposed to do **this**.
Father's jettisoning the lower sectors. The poor... the weak... the old... the "vestigial sectors."
--remain calm. Please proceed to emergency escape pods--
--harboring the known terrorist Lula Lee is punishable by death--
--remain calm. Please proceed to--
He's been weakened... but is desperate to maintain control. Like a drowning man clutching at the leg swimming above him.
Your sector is being liberated. Please remain calm.
If you see Lula Lee, please report her to the authorities...
TAKE THIS. YOU NEED IT MORE THAN I DO.

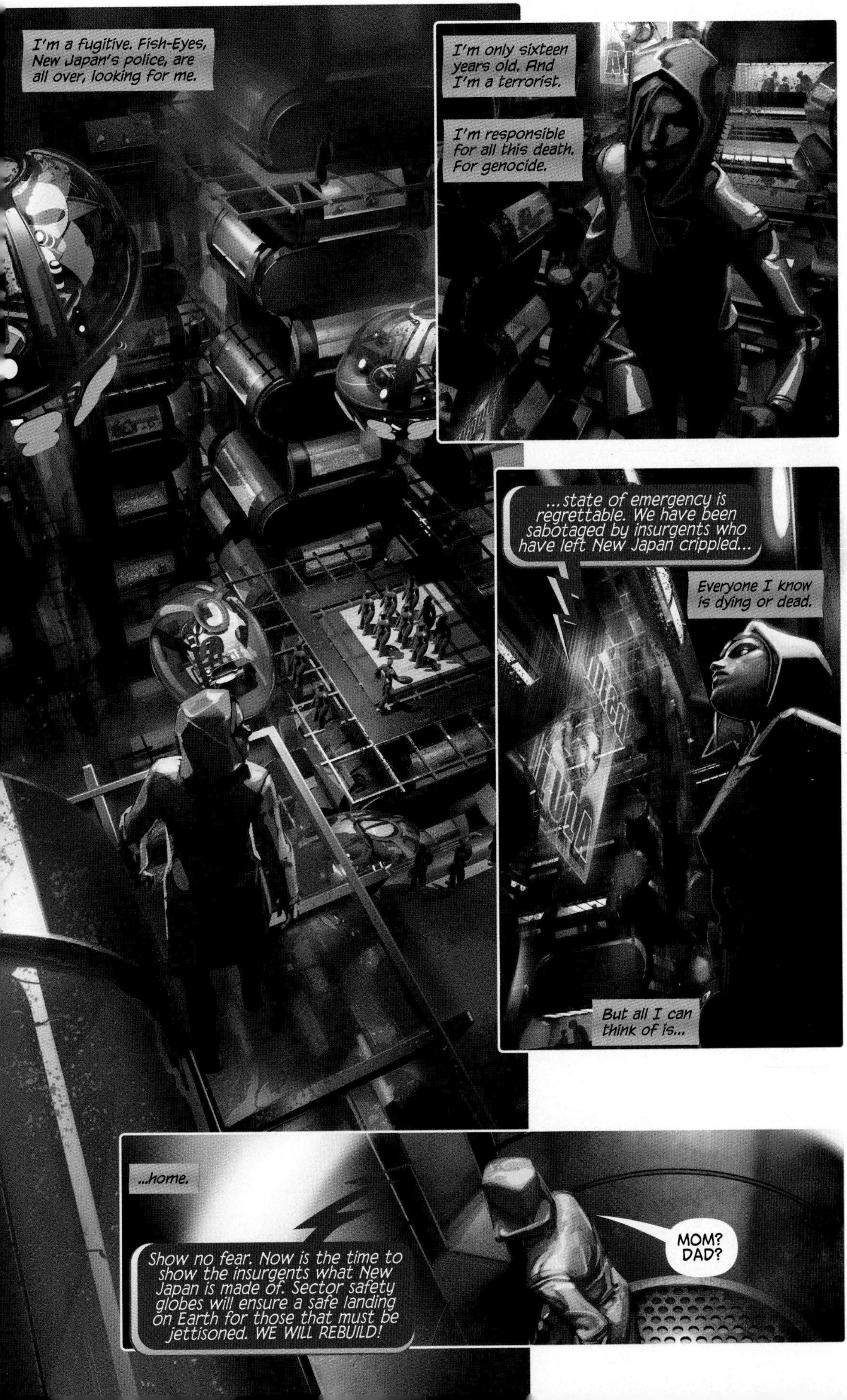

I'm a fugitive. Fish-Eyes, New Japan's police, are all over, looking for me.
I'm only sixteen years old. And I'm a terrorist.
I'm responsible for all this death. For genocide.
...state of emergency is regrettable. We have been sabotaged by insurgents who have left New Japan crippled...
Everyone I know is dying or dead.
But all I can think of is...
...home.
Show no fear. Now is the time to show the insurgents what New Japan is made of. Sector safety globes will ensure a safe landing on Earth for those that must be jettisoned. WE WILL REBUILD!
MOM? DAD?

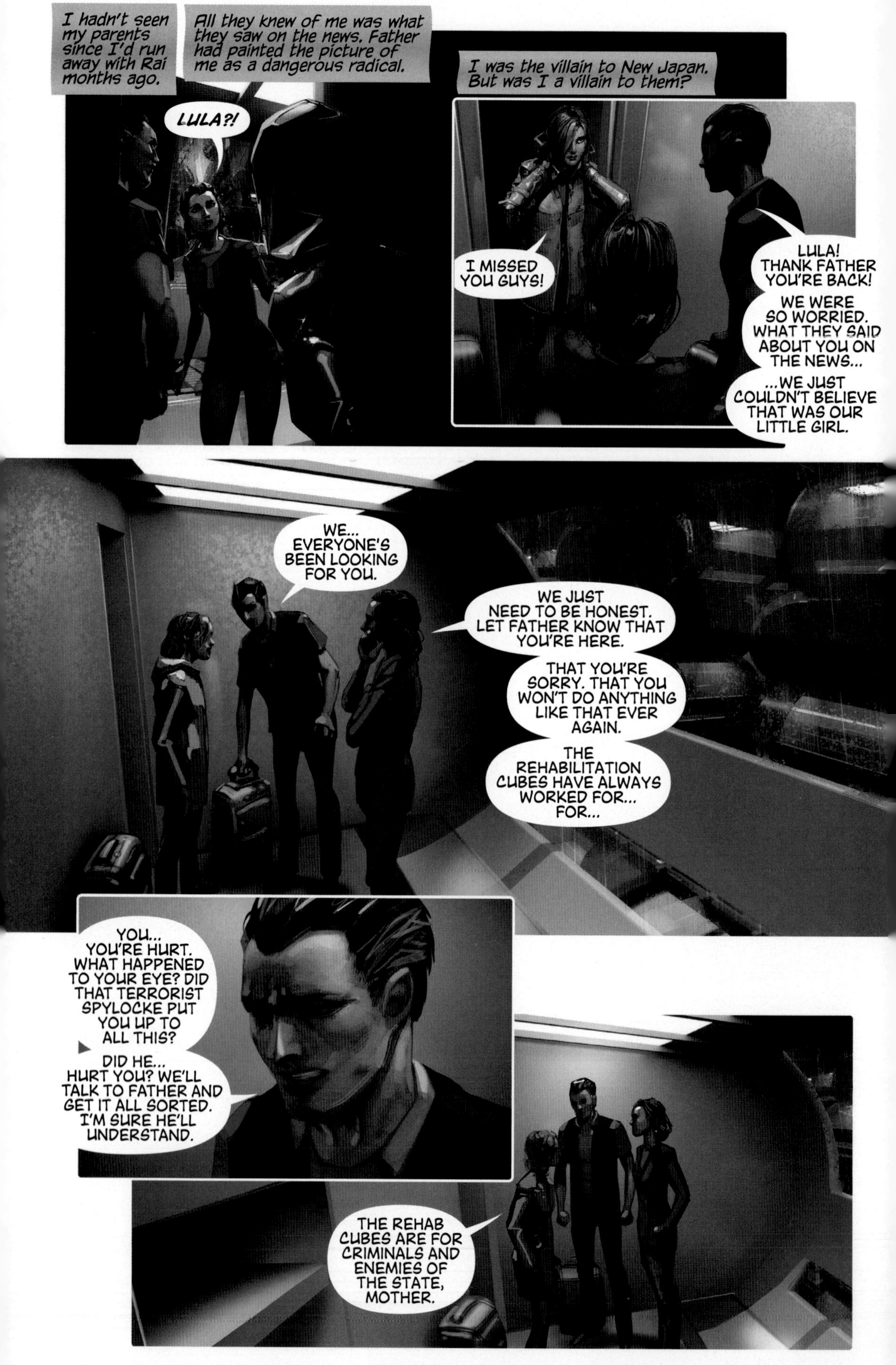

I hadn't seen my parents since I'd run away with Rai months ago.
All they knew of me was what they saw on the news. Father had painted the picture of me as a dangerous radical.
LULA?!
I was the villain to New Japan. But was I a villain to them?
I MISSED YOU GUYS!
LULA! THANK FATHER YOU'RE BACK!
WE WERE SO WORRIED. WHAT THEY SAID ABOUT YOU ON THE NEWS...
...WE JUST COULDN'T BELIEVE THAT WAS OUR LITTLE GIRL.
WE... EVERYONE'S BEEN LOOKING FOR YOU.
WE JUST NEED TO BE HONEST. LET FATHER KNOW THAT YOU'RE HERE.
THAT YOU'RE SORRY. THAT YOU WON'T DO ANYTHING LIKE THAT EVER AGAIN.
THE REHABILITATION CUBES HAVE ALWAYS WORKED FOR... FOR...
YOU... YOU'RE HURT. WHAT HAPPENED TO YOUR EYE? DID THAT TERRORIST SPYLOCKE PUT YOU UP TO ALL THIS?
DID HE... HURT YOU? WE'LL TALK TO FATHER AND GET IT ALL SORTED. I'M SURE HE'LL UNDERSTAND.
THE REHAB CUBES ARE FOR CRIMINALS AND ENEMIES OF THE STATE, MOTHER.

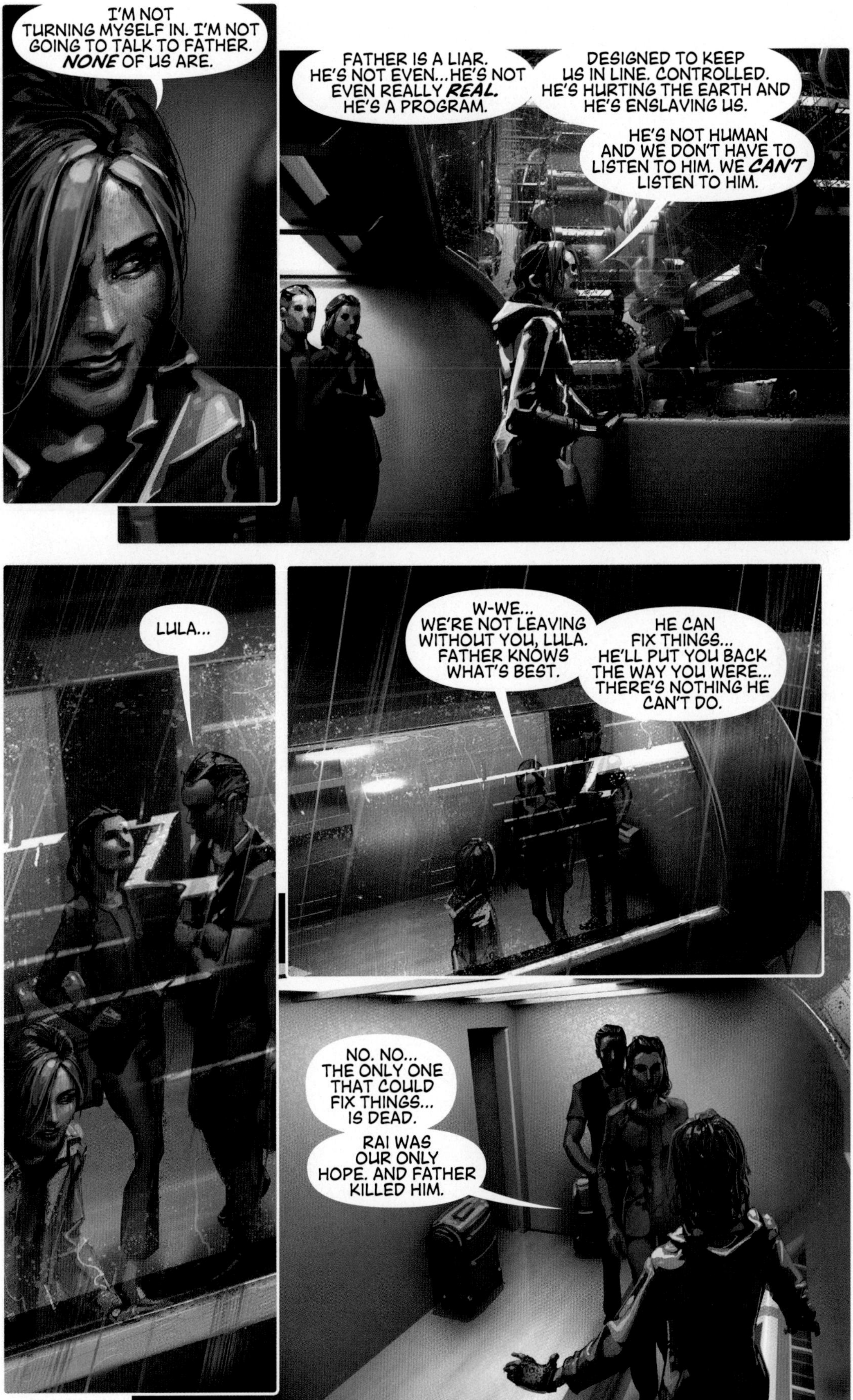
I'M NOT TURNING MYSELF IN. I'M NOT GOING TO TALK TO FATHER. NONE OF US ARE.
FATHER IS A LIAR. HE'S NOT EVEN...HE'S NOT EVEN REALLY REAL. HE'S A PROGRAM.
DESIGNED TO KEEP US IN LINE. CONTROLLED. HE'S HURTING THE EARTH AND HE'S ENSLAVING US.
HE'S NOT HUMAN AND WE DON'T HAVE TO LISTEN TO HIM. WE CAN'T LISTEN TO HIM.
LULA...
W-WE... WE'RE NOT LEAVING WITHOUT YOU, LULA. FATHER KNOWS WHAT'S BEST.
HE CAN FIX THINGS... HE'LL PUT YOU BACK THE WAY YOU WERE... THERE'S NOTHING HE CAN'T DO.
NO. NO... THE ONLY ONE THAT COULD FIX THINGS... IS DEAD.
RAI WAS OUR ONLY HOPE. AND FATHER KILLED HIM.

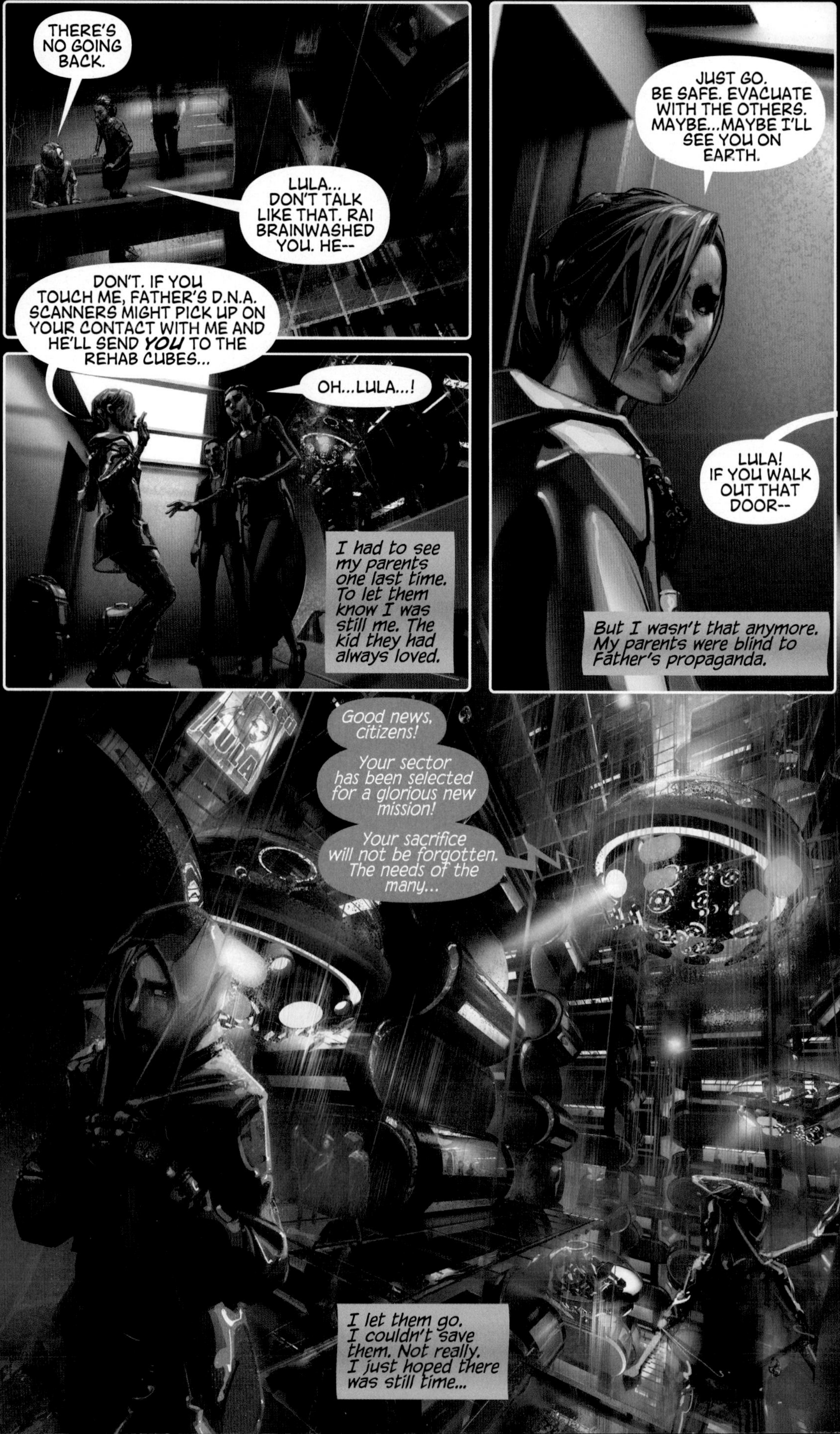
THERE'S NO GOING BACK.
LULA... DON'T TALK LIKE THAT. RAI BRAINWASHED YOU. HE--
DON'T. IF YOU TOUCH ME, FATHER'S D.N.A. SCANNERS MIGHT PICK UP ON YOUR CONTACT WITH ME AND HE'LL SEND *YOU* TO THE REHAB CUBES...
OH...LULA...!
I had to see my parents one last time. To let them know I was still me. The kid they had always loved.
JUST GO. BE SAFE. EVACUATE WITH THE OTHERS. MAYBE...MAYBE I'LL SEE YOU ON EARTH.
LULA! IF YOU WALK OUT THAT DOOR--
But I wasn't that anymore. My parents were blind to Father's propaganda.
LULA
Good news, citizens!
Your sector has been selected for a glorious new mission!
Your sacrifice will not be forgotten. The needs of the many...
I let them go. I couldn't save them. Not really. I just hoped there was still time...

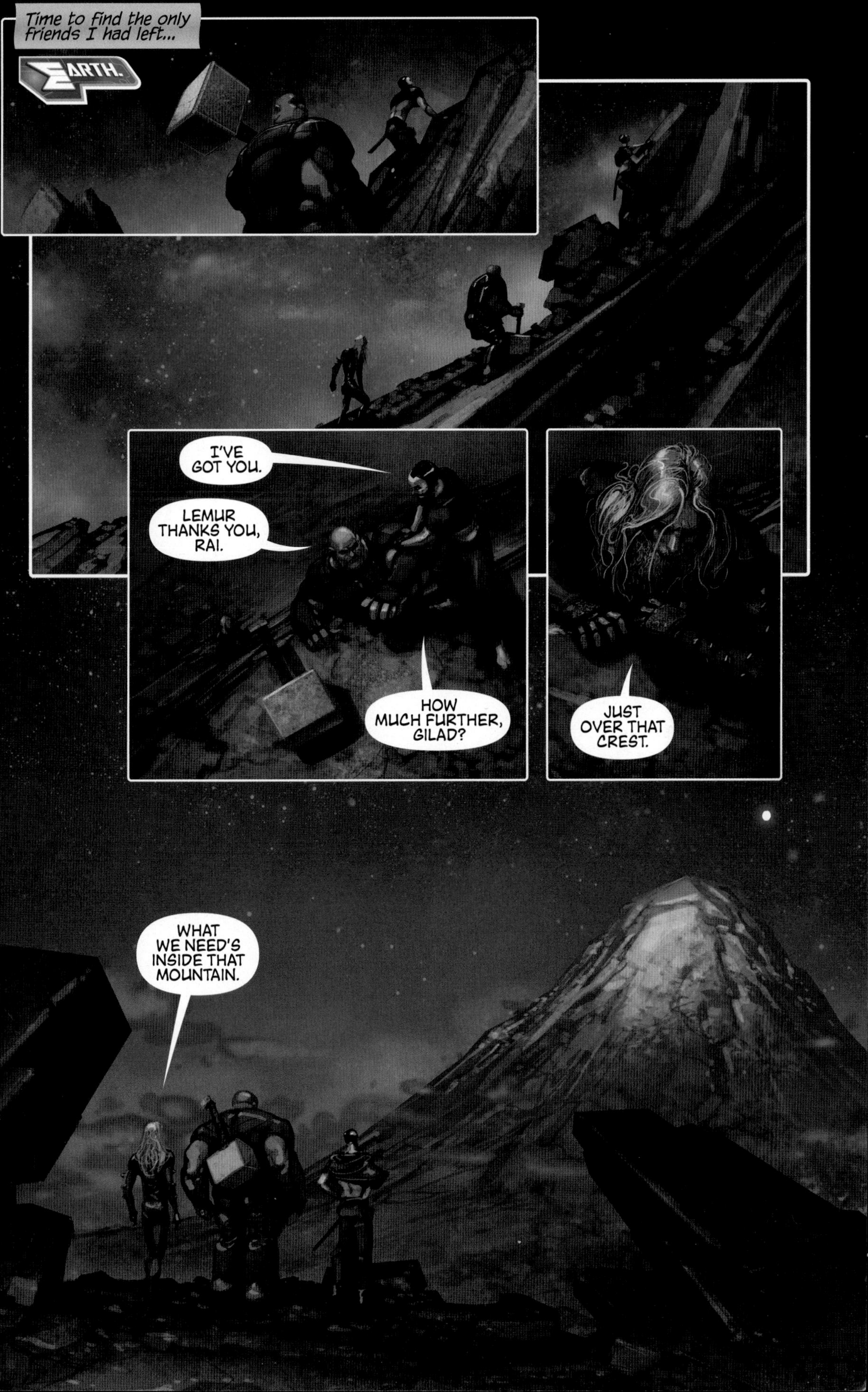
Time to find the only friends I had left...
EARTH.
I'VE GOT YOU.
LEMUR THANKS YOU, RAI.
HOW MUCH FURTHER, GILAD?
JUST OVER THAT CREST.
WHAT WE NEED'S INSIDE THAT MOUNTAIN.

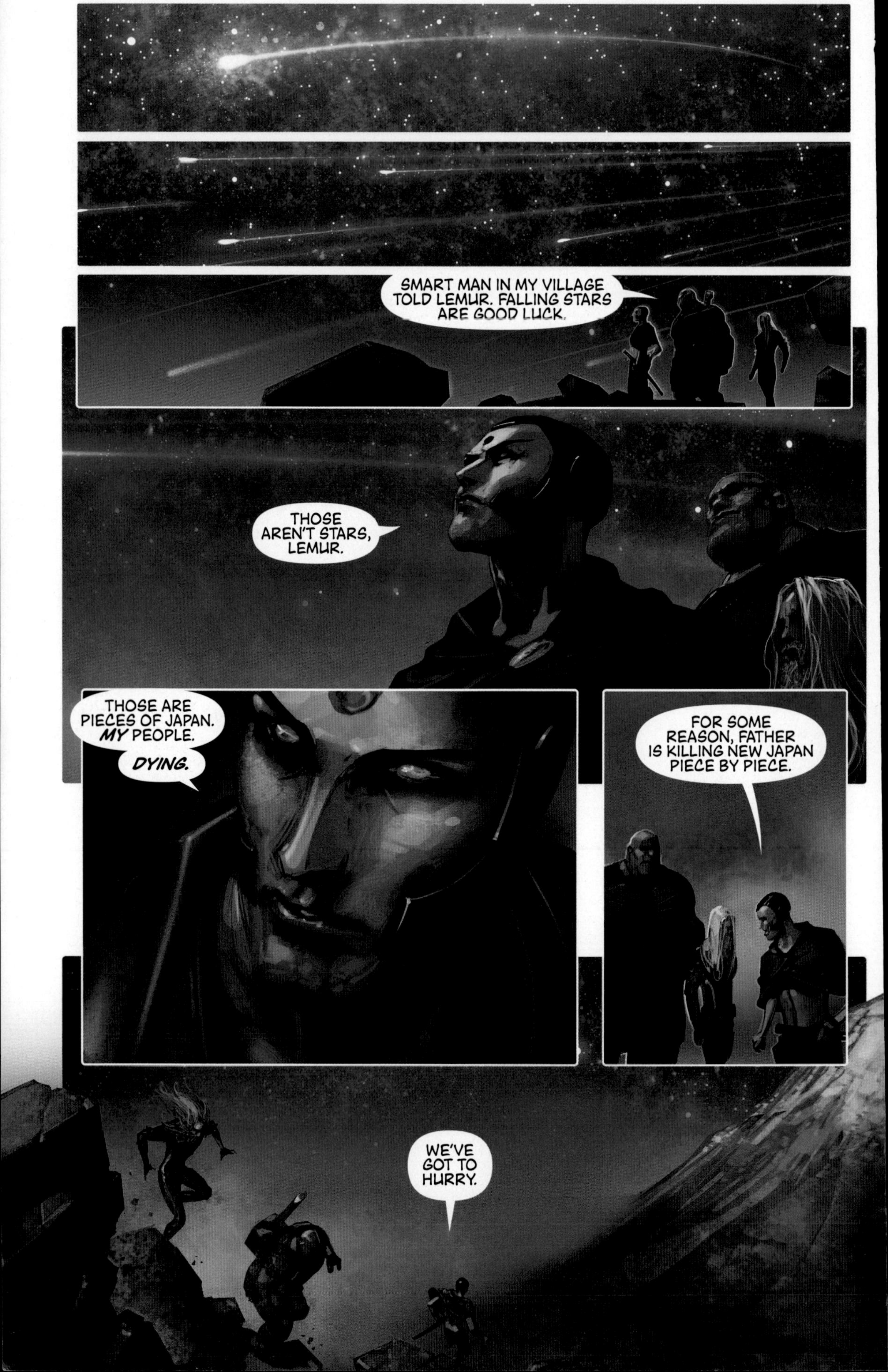
SMART MAN IN MY VILLAGE TOLD LEMUR. FALLING STARS ARE GOOD LUCK.
THOSE AREN'T STARS, LEMUR.
THOSE ARE PIECES OF JAPAN. *MY* PEOPLE.
DYING.
FOR SOME REASON, FATHER IS KILLING NEW JAPAN PIECE BY PIECE.
WE'VE GOT TO HURRY.

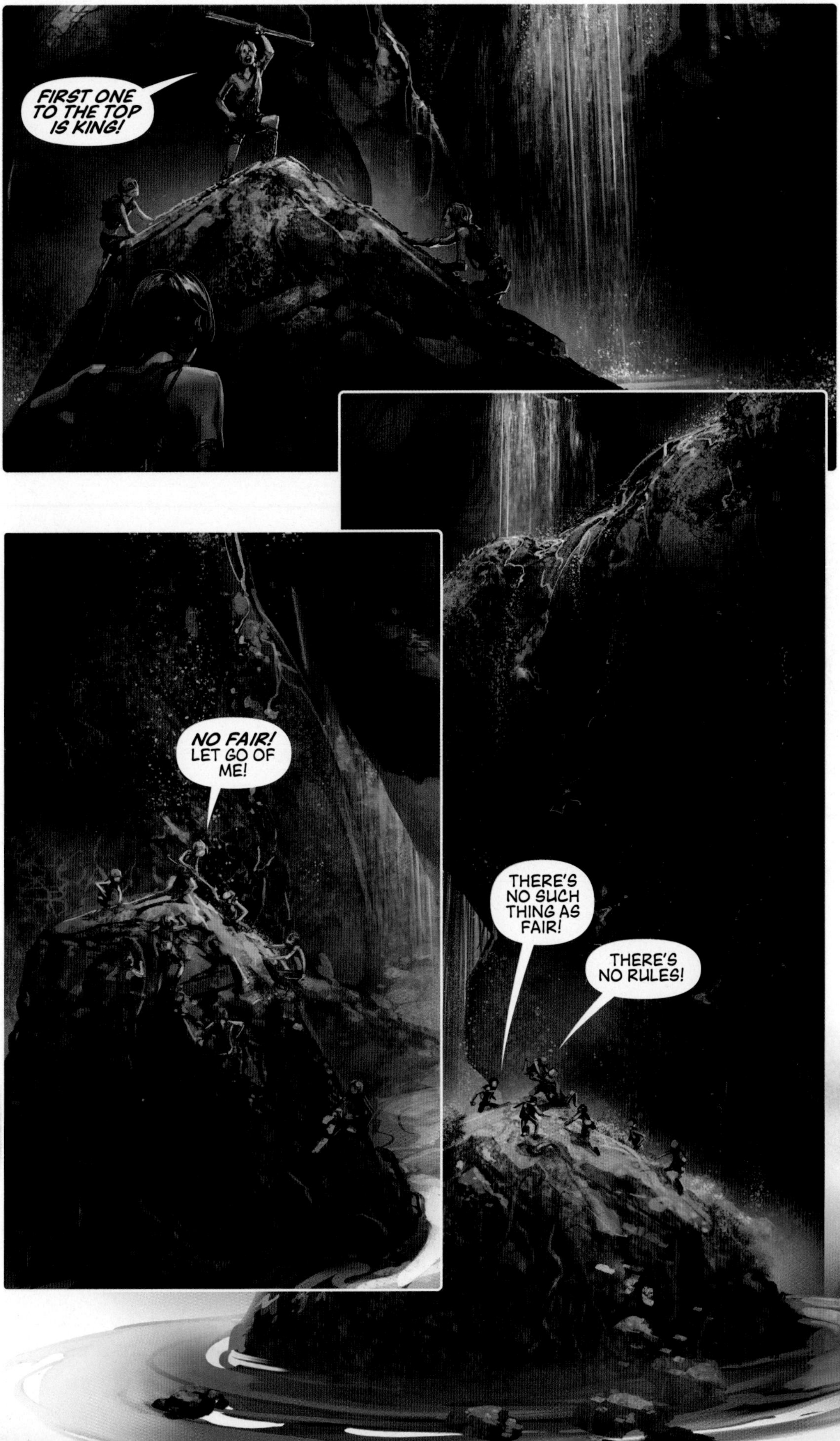
FIRST ONE TO THE TOP IS KING!
NO FAIR! LET GO OF ME!
THERE'S NO SUCH THING AS FAIR!
THERE'S NO RULES!

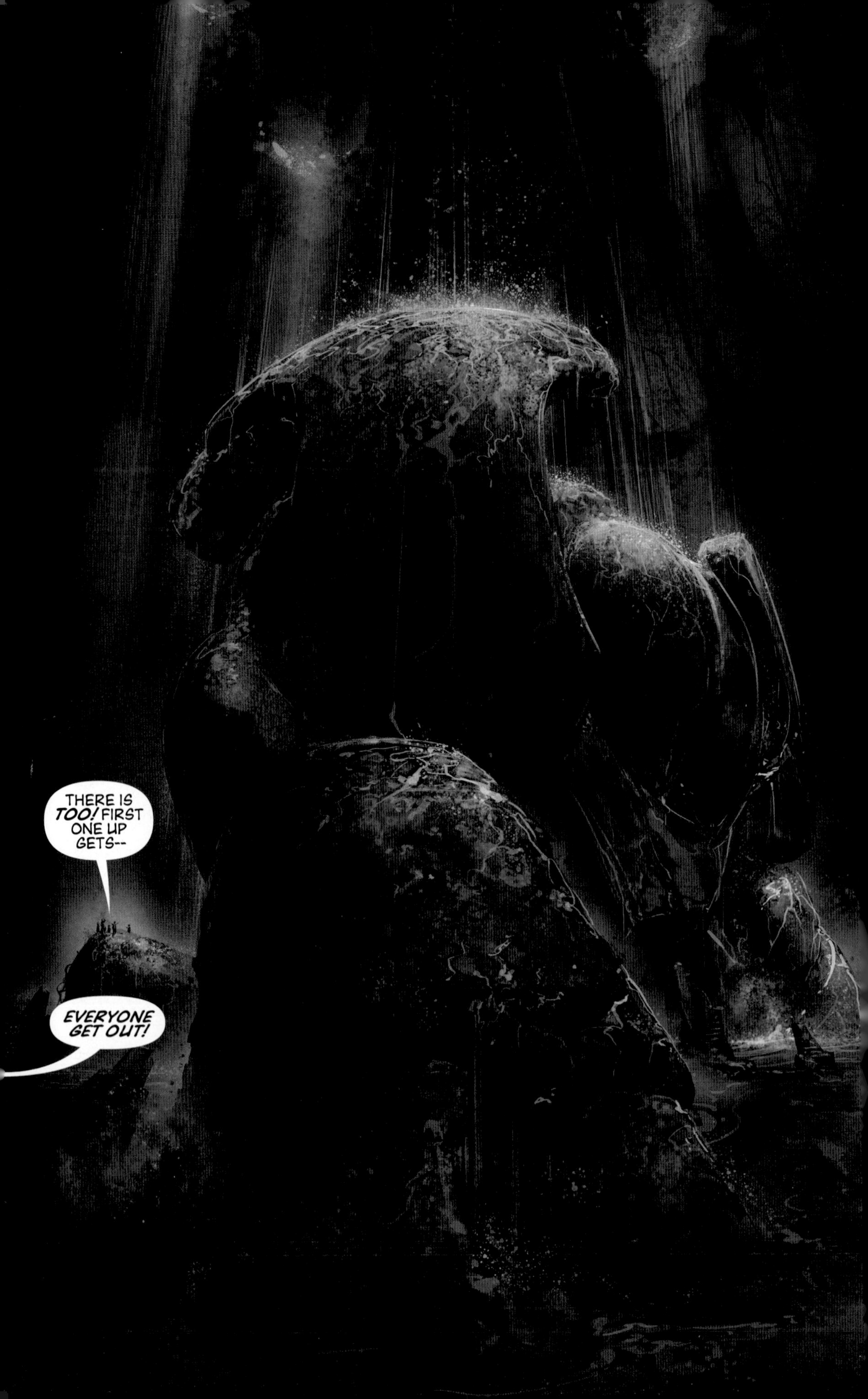
THERE IS TOO! FIRST ONE UP GETS--
EVERYONE GET OUT!

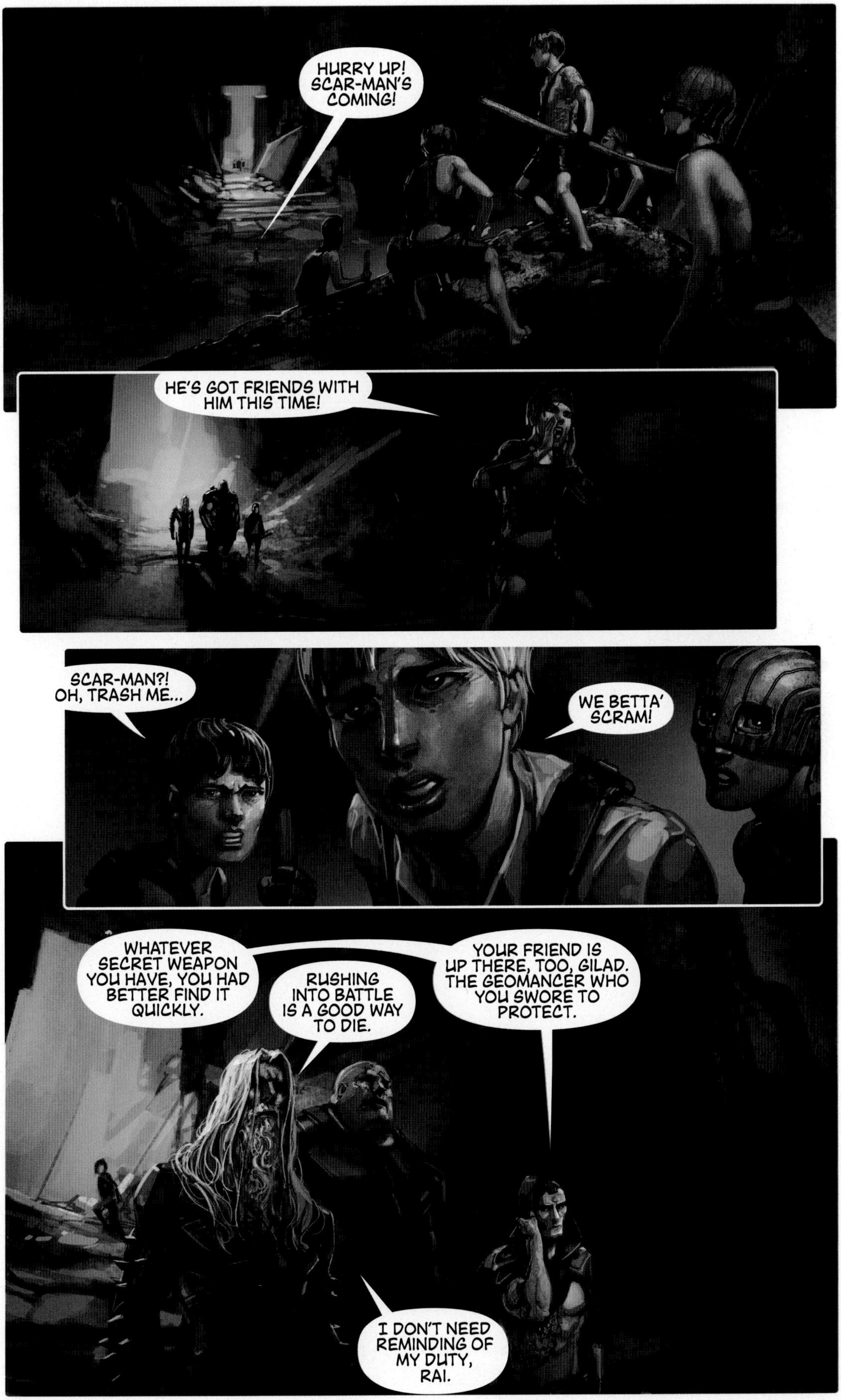
HURRY UP! SCAR-MAN'S COMING!
HE'S GOT FRIENDS WITH HIM THIS TIME!
SCAR-MAN?! OH, TRASH ME...
WE BETTA' SCRAM!
WHATEVER SECRET WEAPON YOU HAVE, YOU HAD BETTER FIND IT QUICKLY.
RUSHING INTO BATTLE IS A GOOD WAY TO DIE.
YOUR FRIEND IS UP THERE, TOO, GILAD. THE GEOMANCER WHO YOU SWORE TO PROTECT.
I DON'T NEED REMINDING OF MY DUTY, RAI.

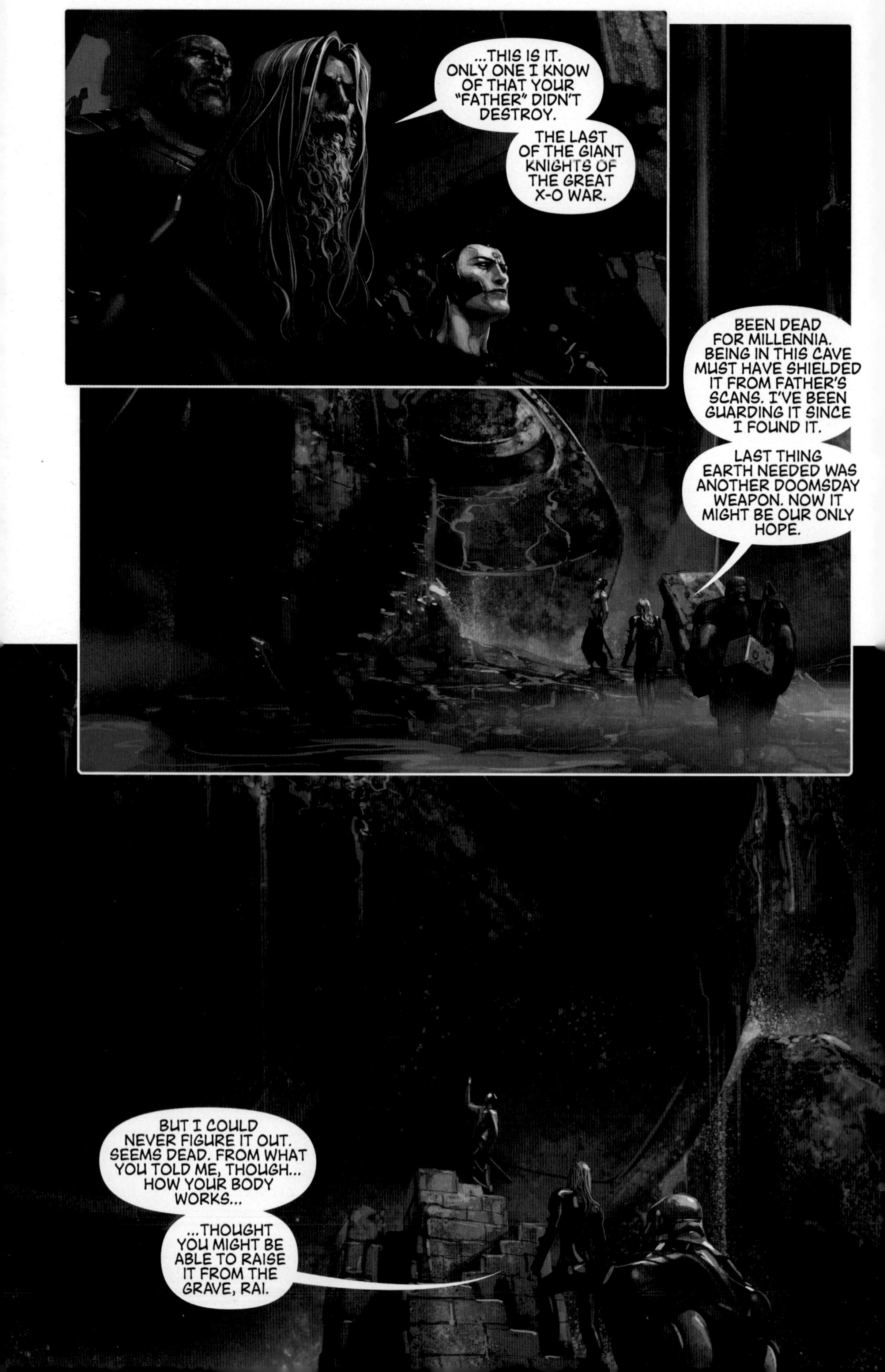
...THIS IS IT. ONLY ONE I KNOW OF THAT YOUR "FATHER" DIDN'T DESTROY.
THE LAST OF THE GIANT KNIGHTS OF THE GREAT X-O WAR.
BEEN DEAD FOR MILLENNIA. BEING IN THIS CAVE MUST HAVE SHIELDED IT FROM FATHER'S SCANS. I'VE BEEN GUARDING IT SINCE I FOUND IT.
LAST THING EARTH NEEDED WAS ANOTHER DOOMSDAY WEAPON. NOW IT MIGHT BE OUR ONLY HOPE.
BUT I COULD NEVER FIGURE IT OUT. SEEMS DEAD. FROM WHAT YOU TOLD ME, THOUGH... HOW YOUR BODY WORKS...
...THOUGHT YOU MIGHT BE ABLE TO RAISE IT FROM THE GRAVE, RAI.

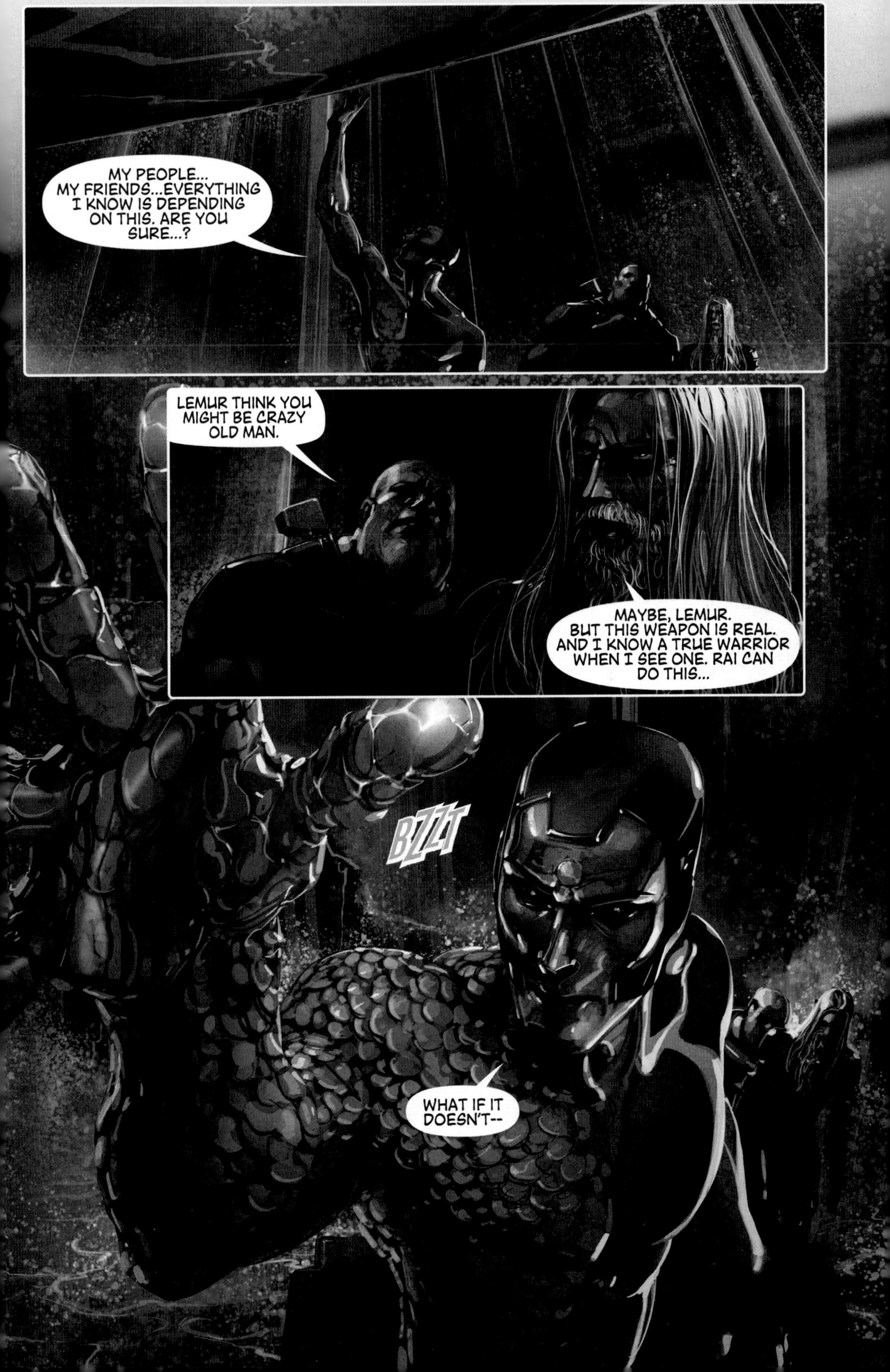
MY PEOPLE... MY FRIENDS...EVERYTHING I KNOW IS DEPENDING ON THIS. ARE YOU SURE...?
LEMUR THINK YOU MIGHT BE CRAZY OLD MAN.
MAYBE, LEMUR. BUT THIS WEAPON IS REAL. AND I KNOW A TRUE WARRIOR WHEN I SEE ONE. RAI CAN DO THIS...
BZZT
WHAT IF IT DOESN'T--

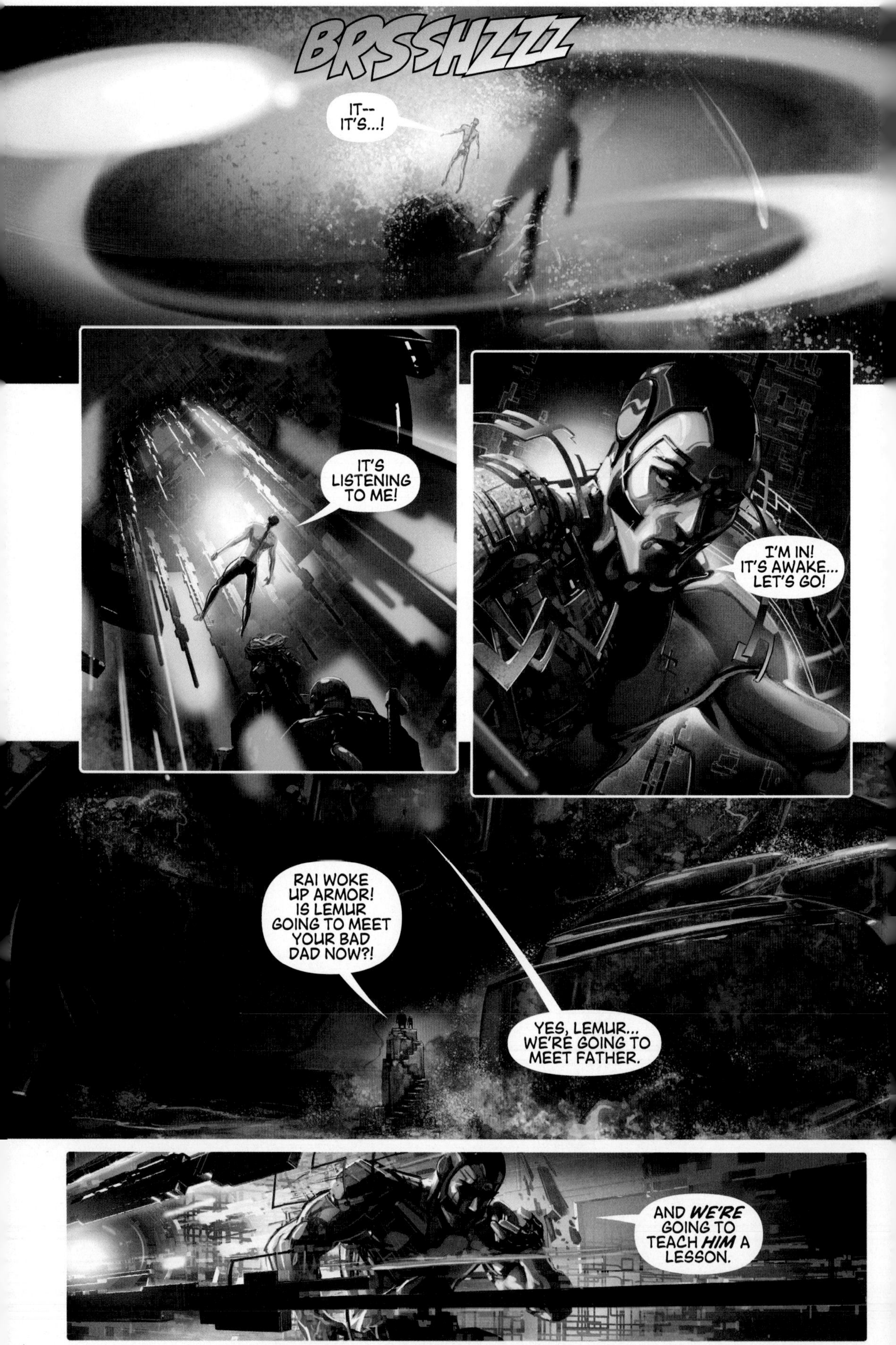
BRSSHZZZ
IT-- IT'S...!
IT'S LISTENING TO ME!
I'M IN! IT'S AWAKE... LET'S GO!
RAI WOKE UP ARMOR! IS LEMUR GOING TO MEET YOUR BAD DAD NOW?!
YES, LEMUR... WE'RE GOING TO MEET FATHER.
AND WE'RE GOING TO TEACH HIM A LESSON.

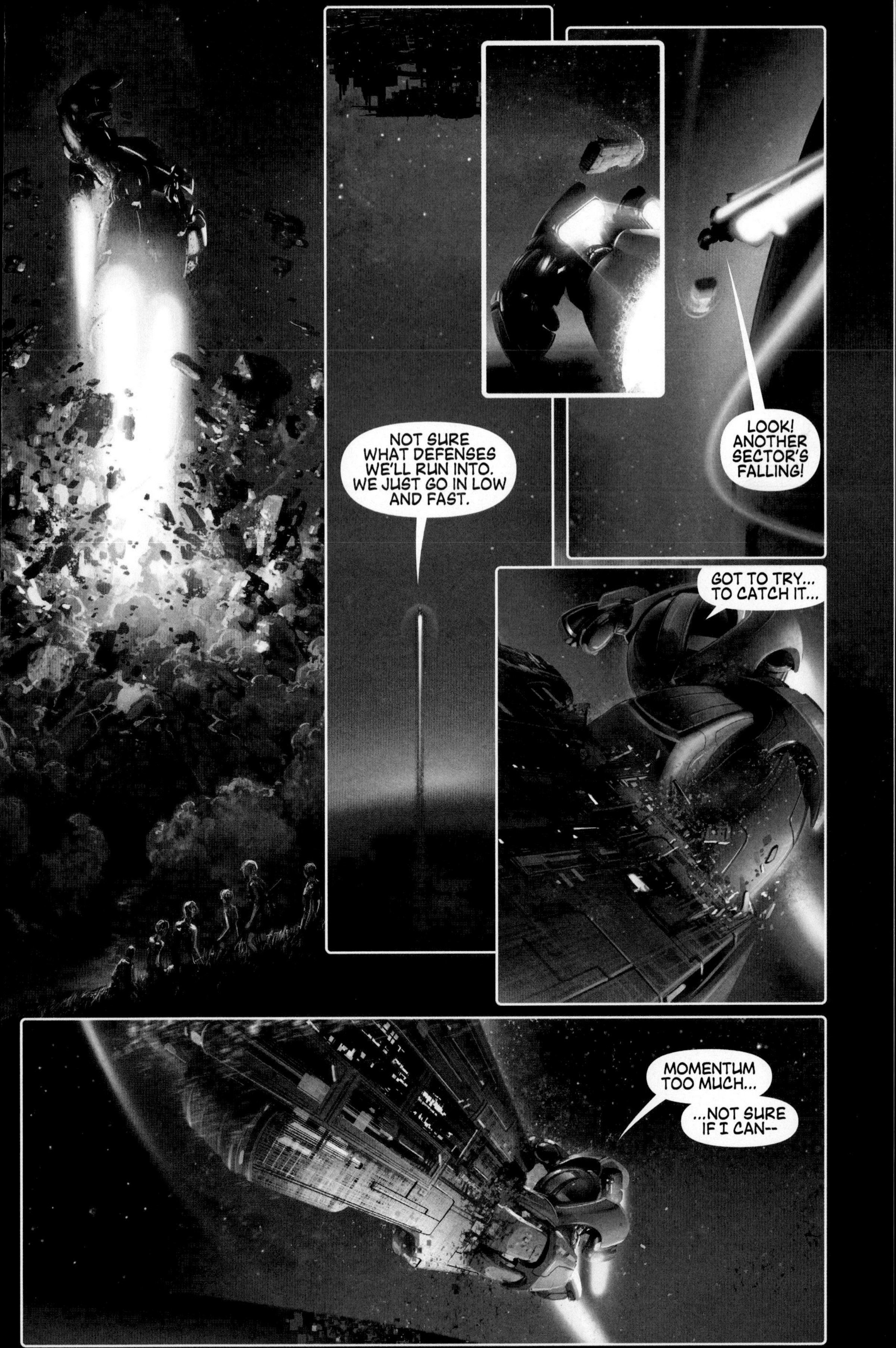
NOT SURE WHAT DEFENSES WE'LL RUN INTO. WE JUST GO IN LOW AND FAST.
LOOK! ANOTHER SECTOR'S FALLING!
GOT TO TRY... TO CATCH IT...
MOMENTUM TOO MUCH...
...NOT SURE IF I CAN--

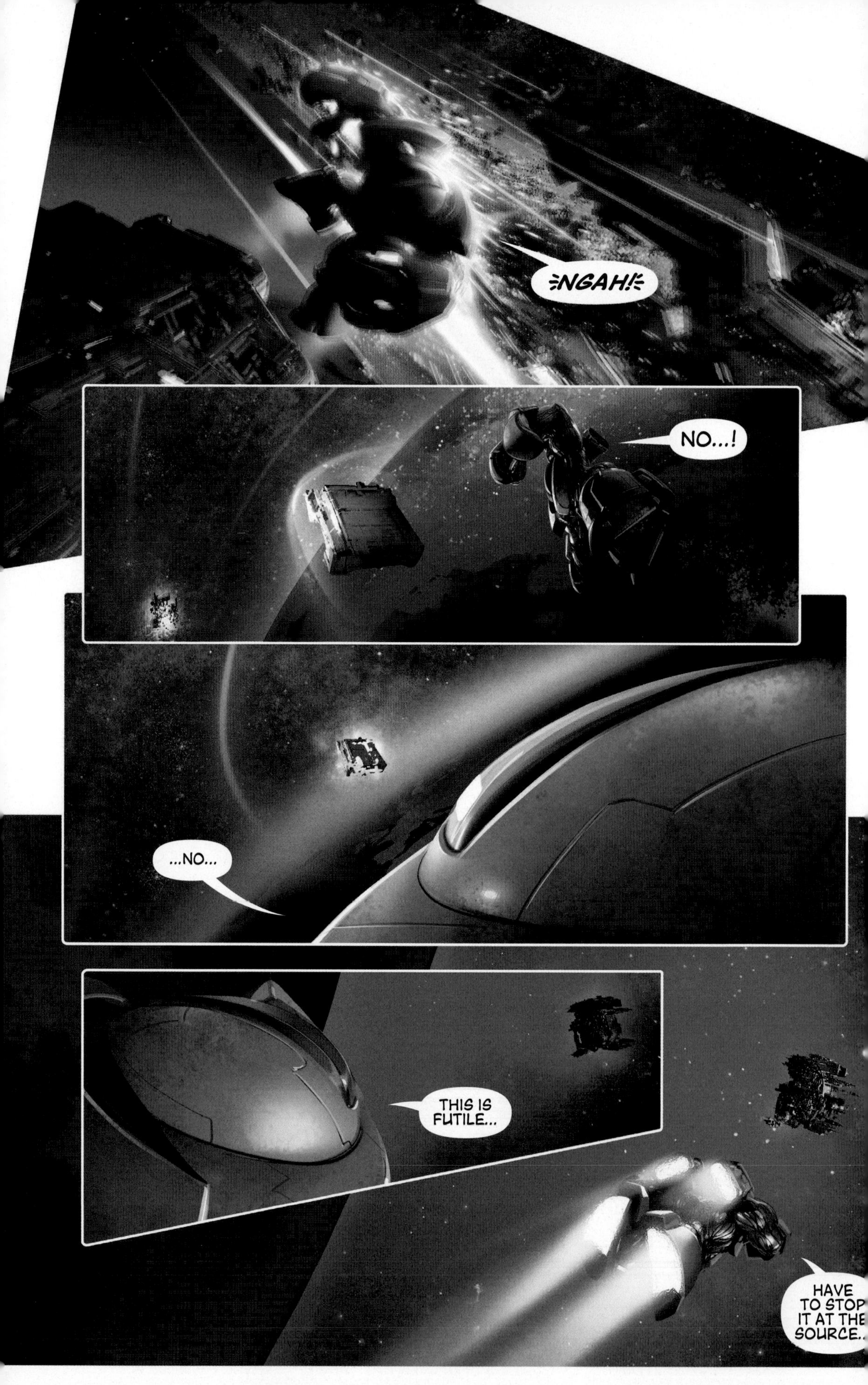

NGAH!
NO...!
...NO...
THIS IS FUTILE...
HAVE TO STOP IT AT THE SOURCE...

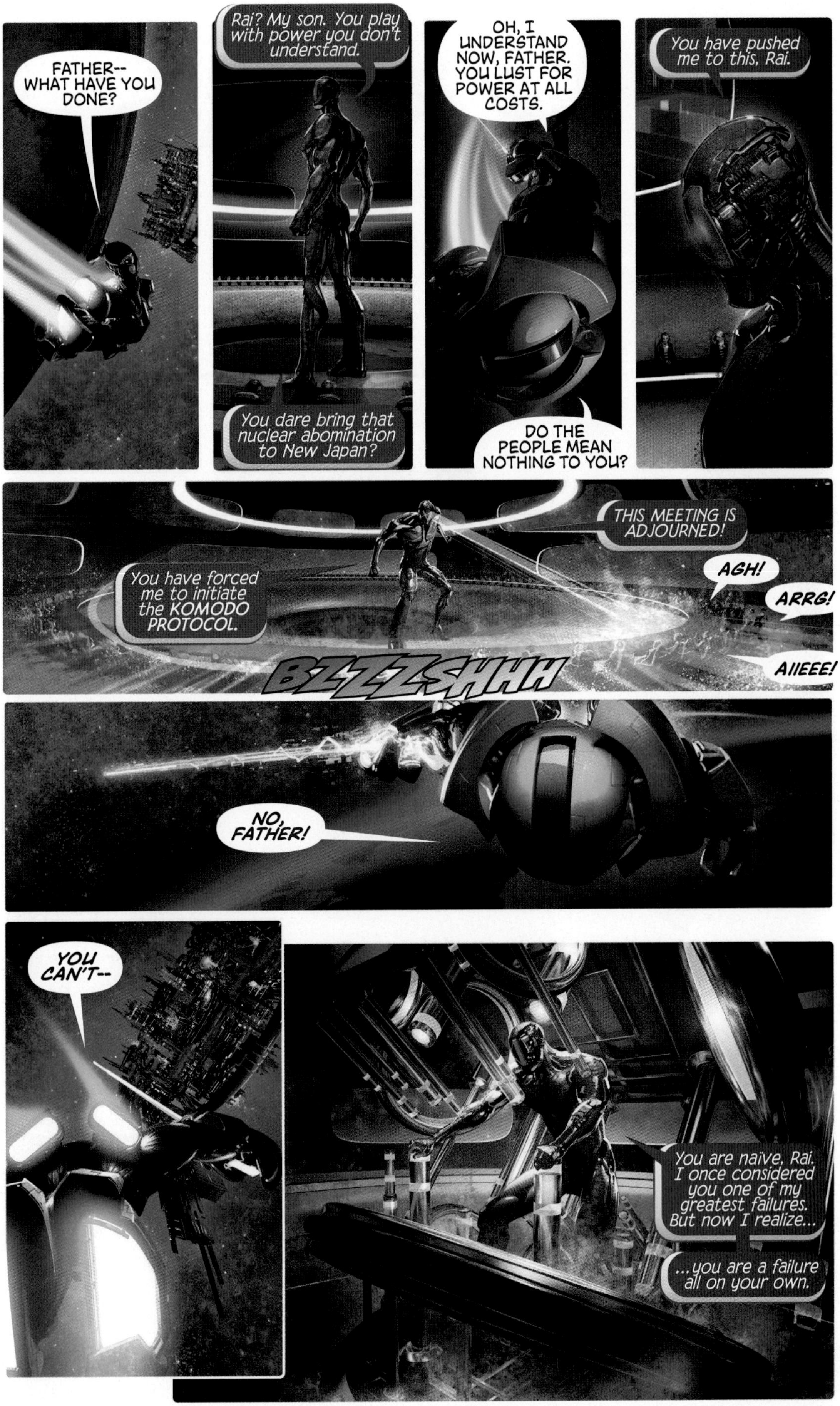
FATHER-- WHAT HAVE YOU DONE?
Rai? My son. You play with power you don't understand.
You dare bring that nuclear abomination to New Japan?
OH, I UNDERSTAND NOW, FATHER. YOU LUST FOR POWER AT ALL COSTS.
DO THE PEOPLE MEAN NOTHING TO YOU?
You have pushed me to this, Rai.
You have forced me to initiate the KOMODO PROTOCOL.
THIS MEETING IS ADJOURNED!
AGH!
ARRG!
BZZZSHHH
AIIEEE!
NO, FATHER!
YOU CAN'T--
You are naïve, Rai. I once considered you one of my greatest failures. But now I realize...
...you are a failure all on your own.

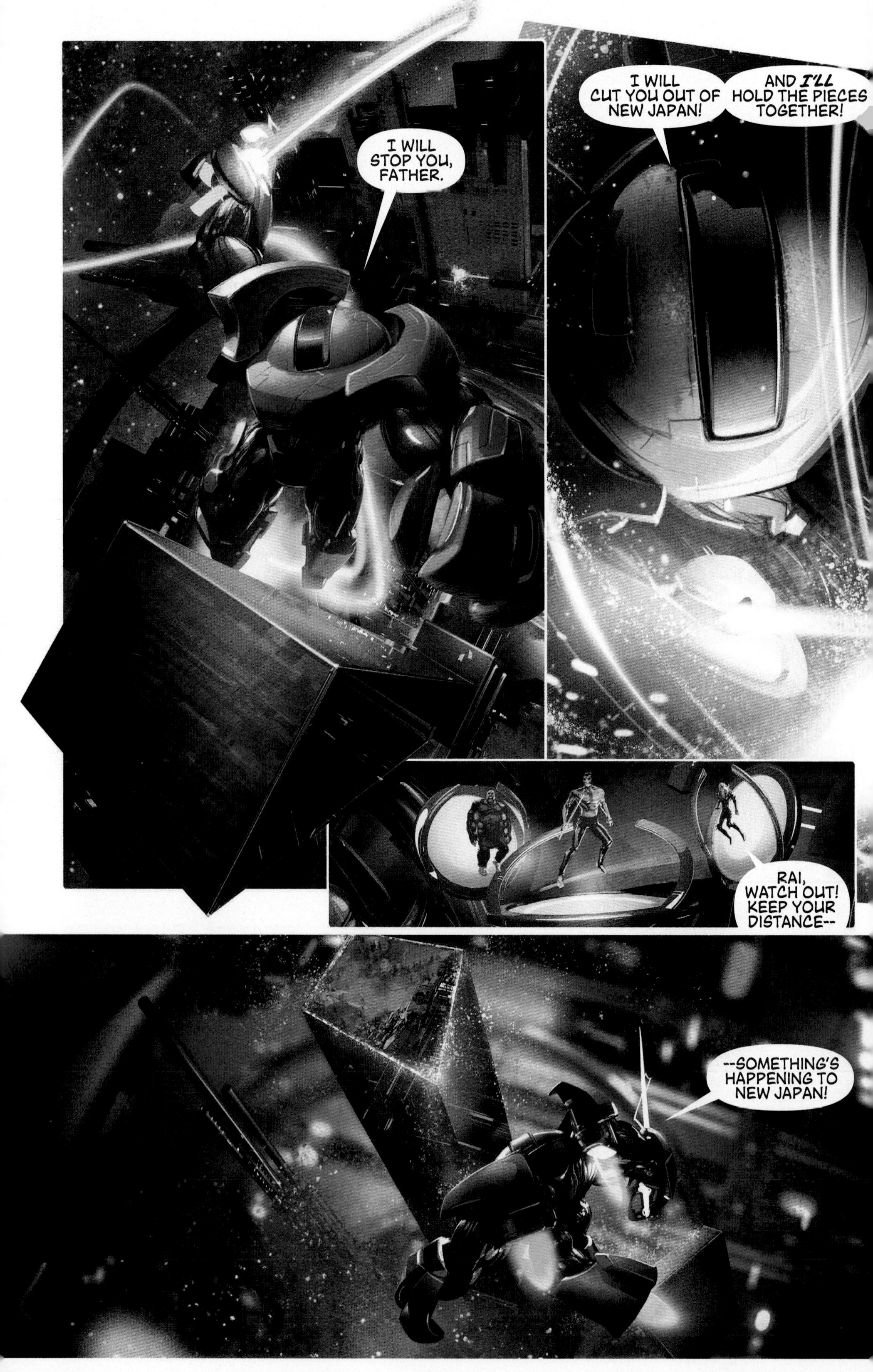
I WILL STOP YOU, FATHER.
I WILL CUT YOU OUT OF NEW JAPAN!
AND I'LL HOLD THE PIECES TOGETHER!
RAI, WATCH OUT! KEEP YOUR DISTANCE--
--SOMETHING'S HAPPENING TO NEW JAPAN!

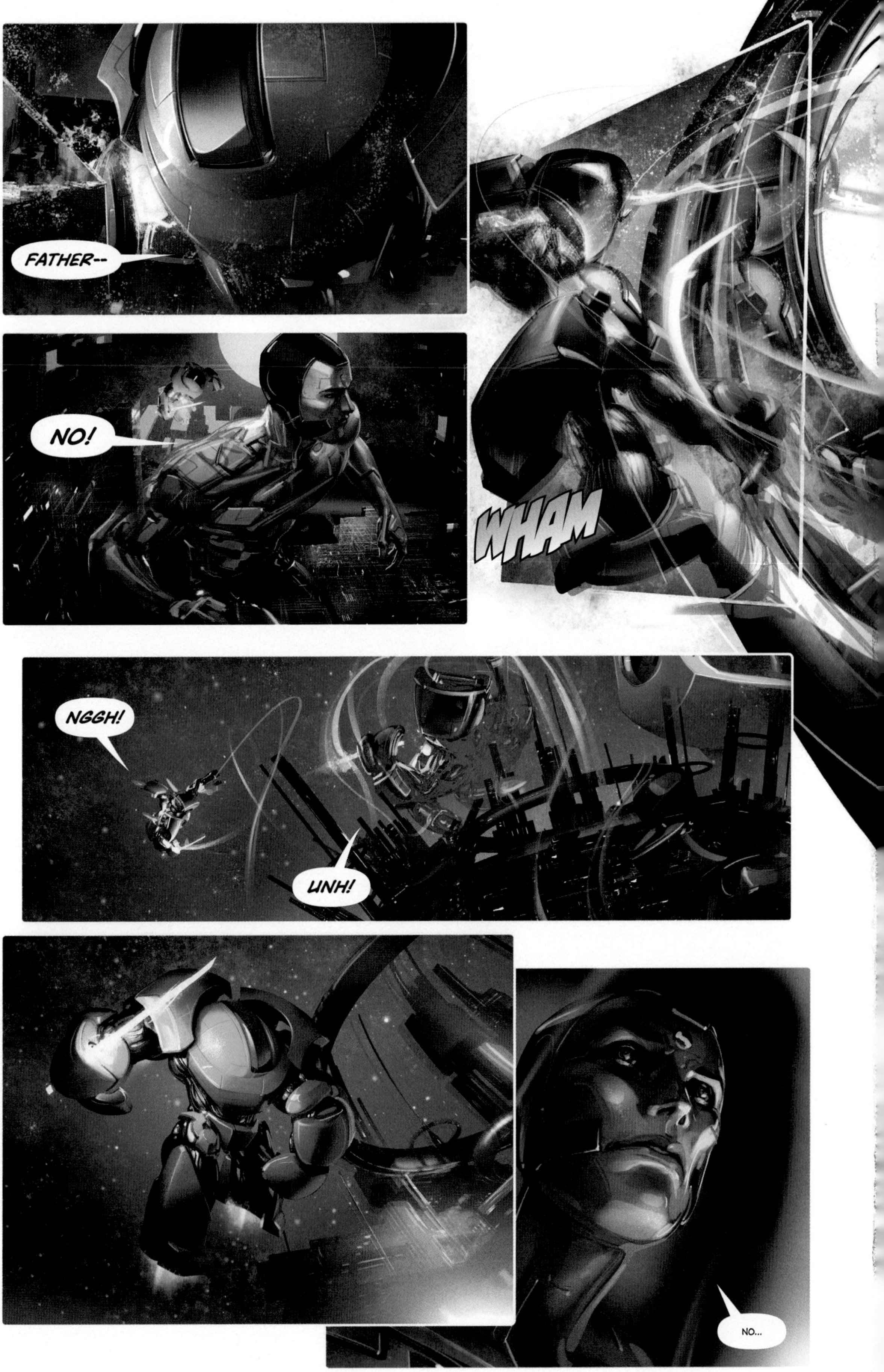
FATHER--
NO!
WHAM
NGGH!
UNH!
NO...

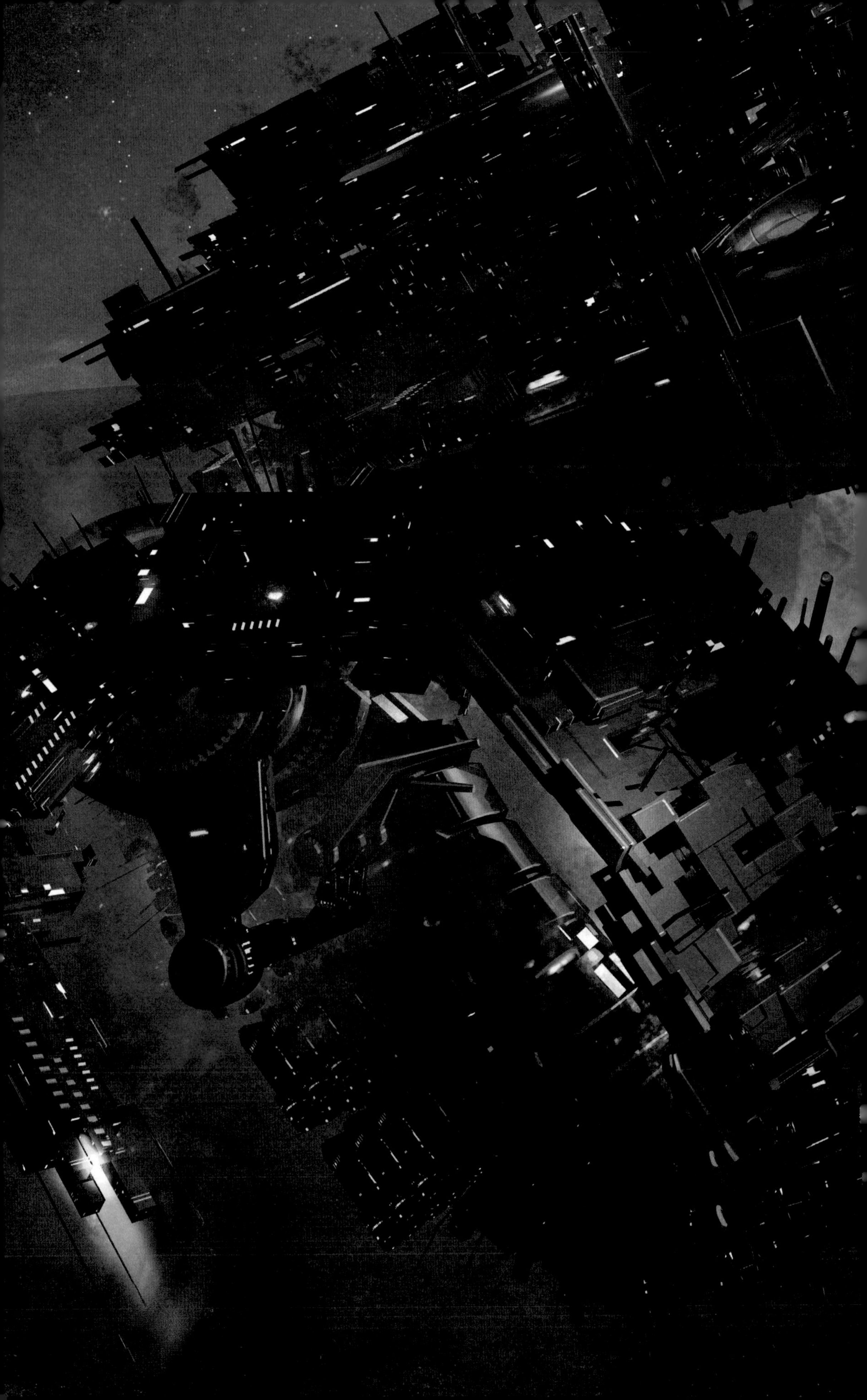

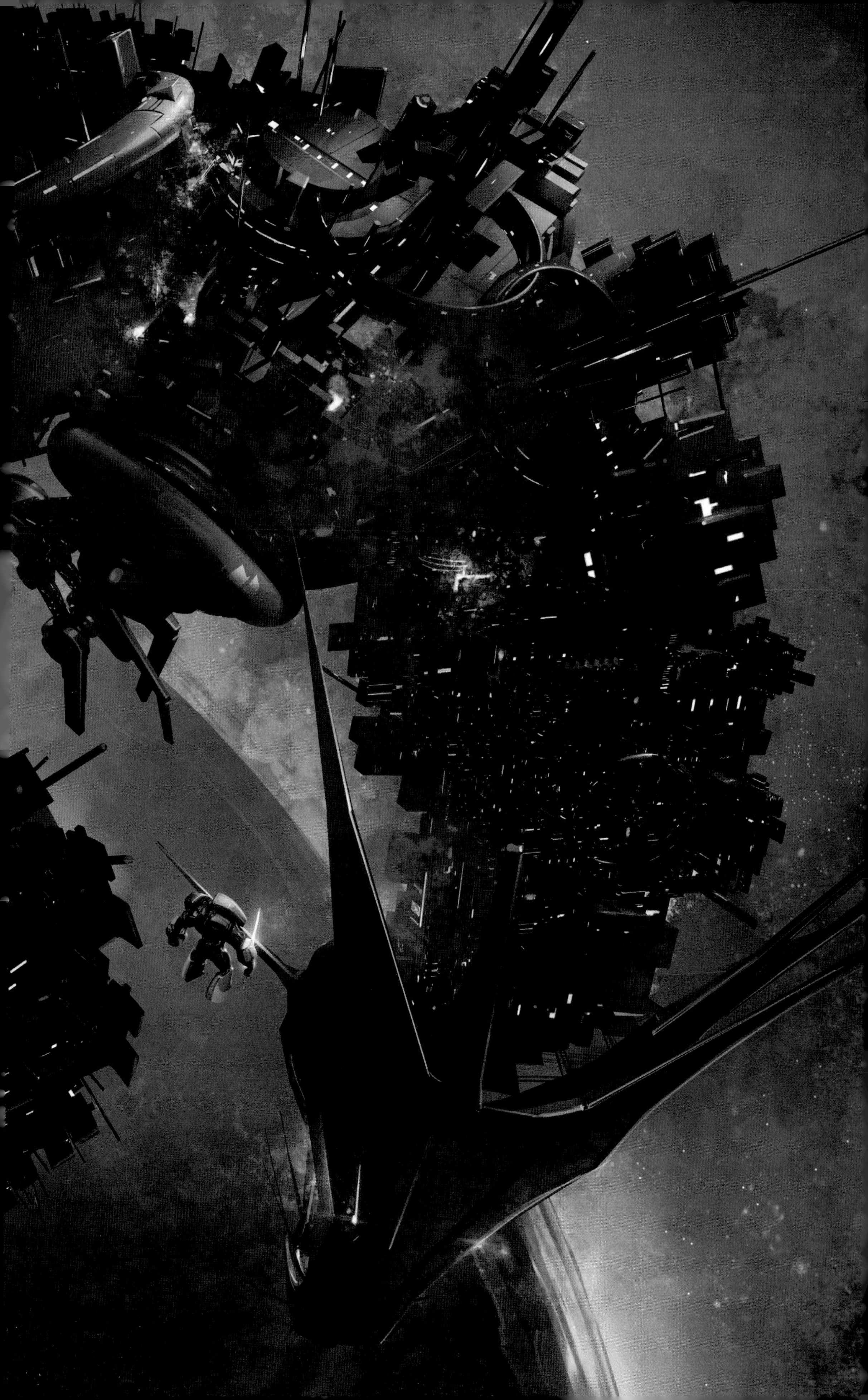

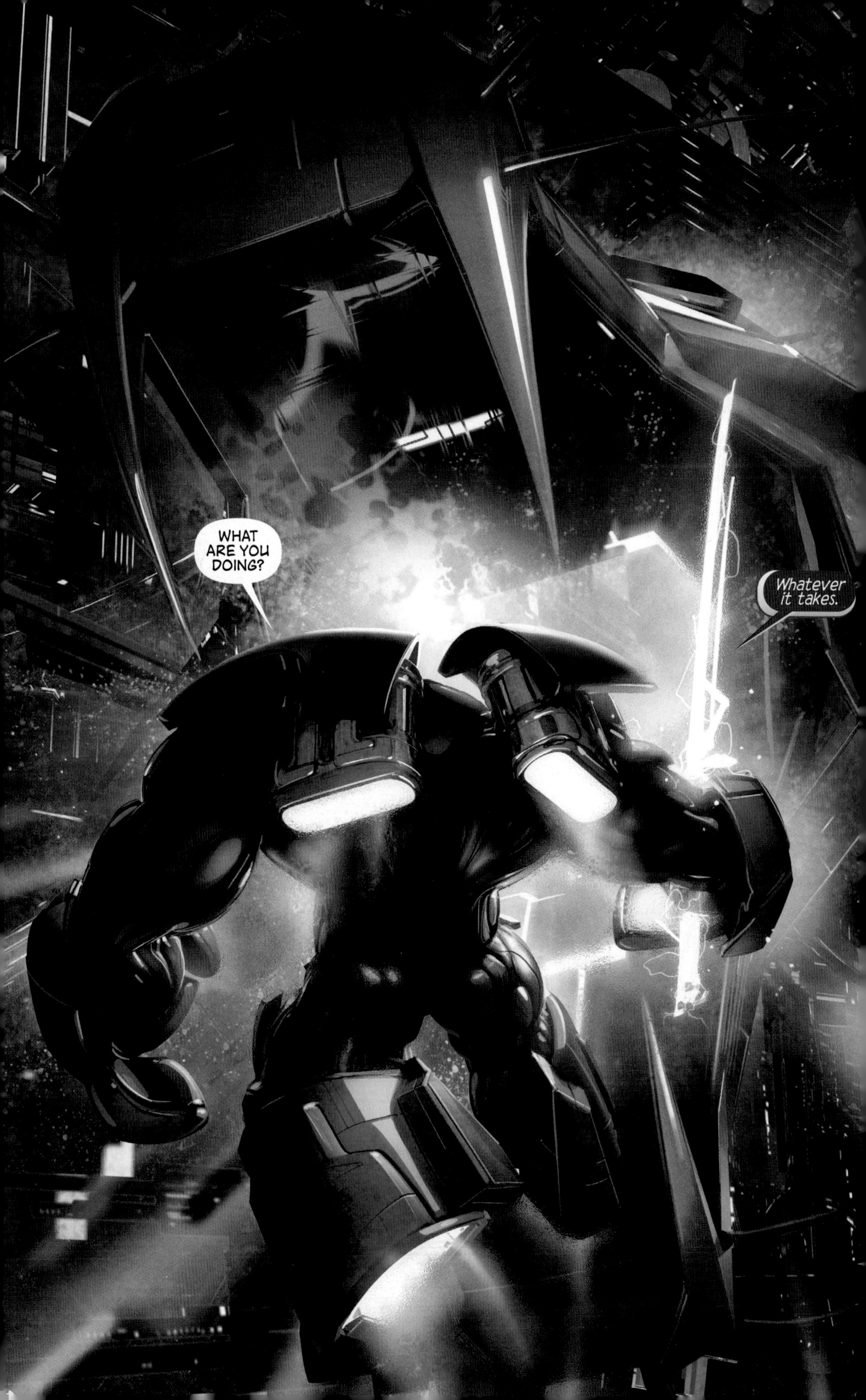
WHAT ARE YOU DOING?
Whatever it takes.

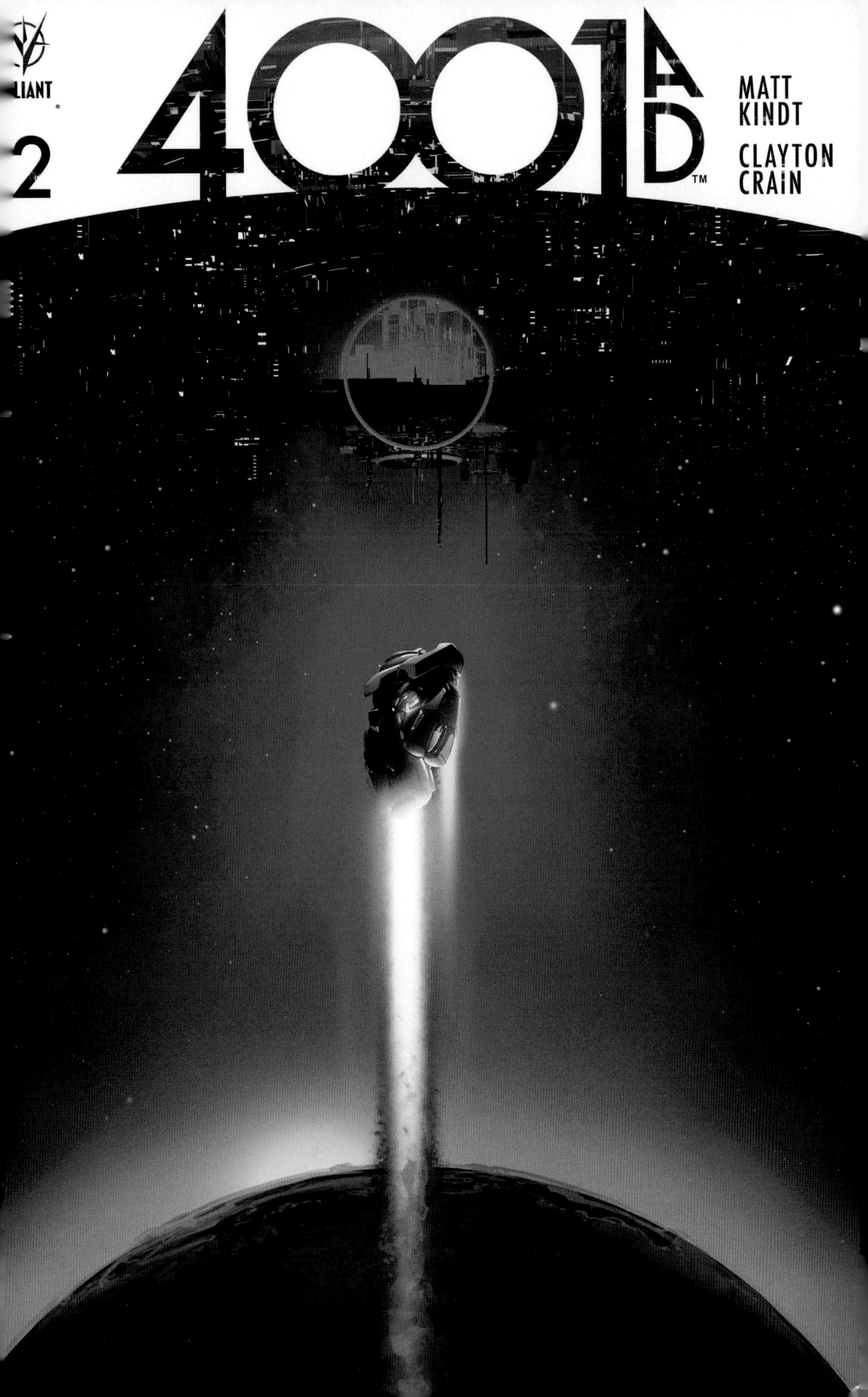

VALIANT
4001 A.D.
2
MATT KINDT
CLAYTON CRAIN

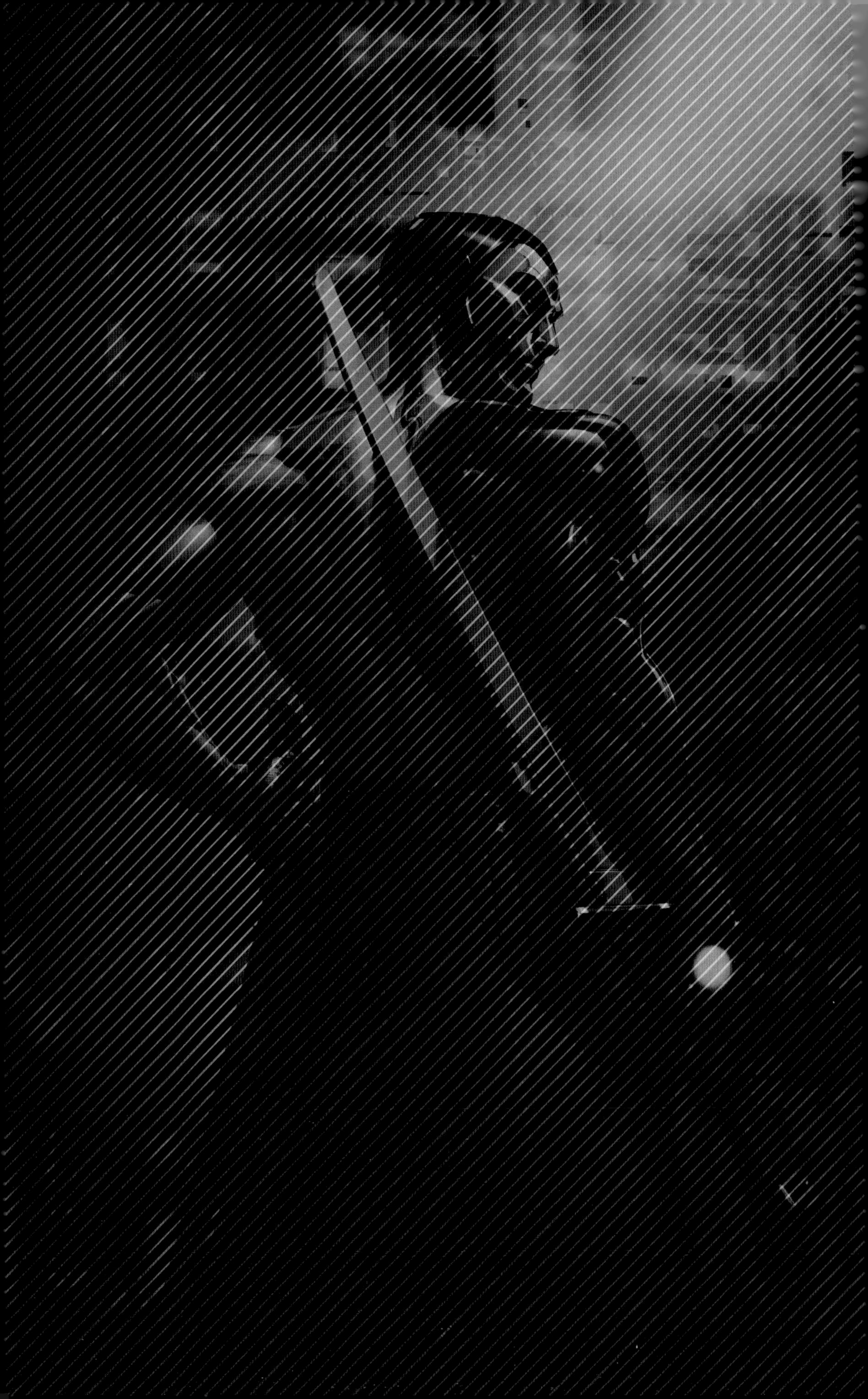

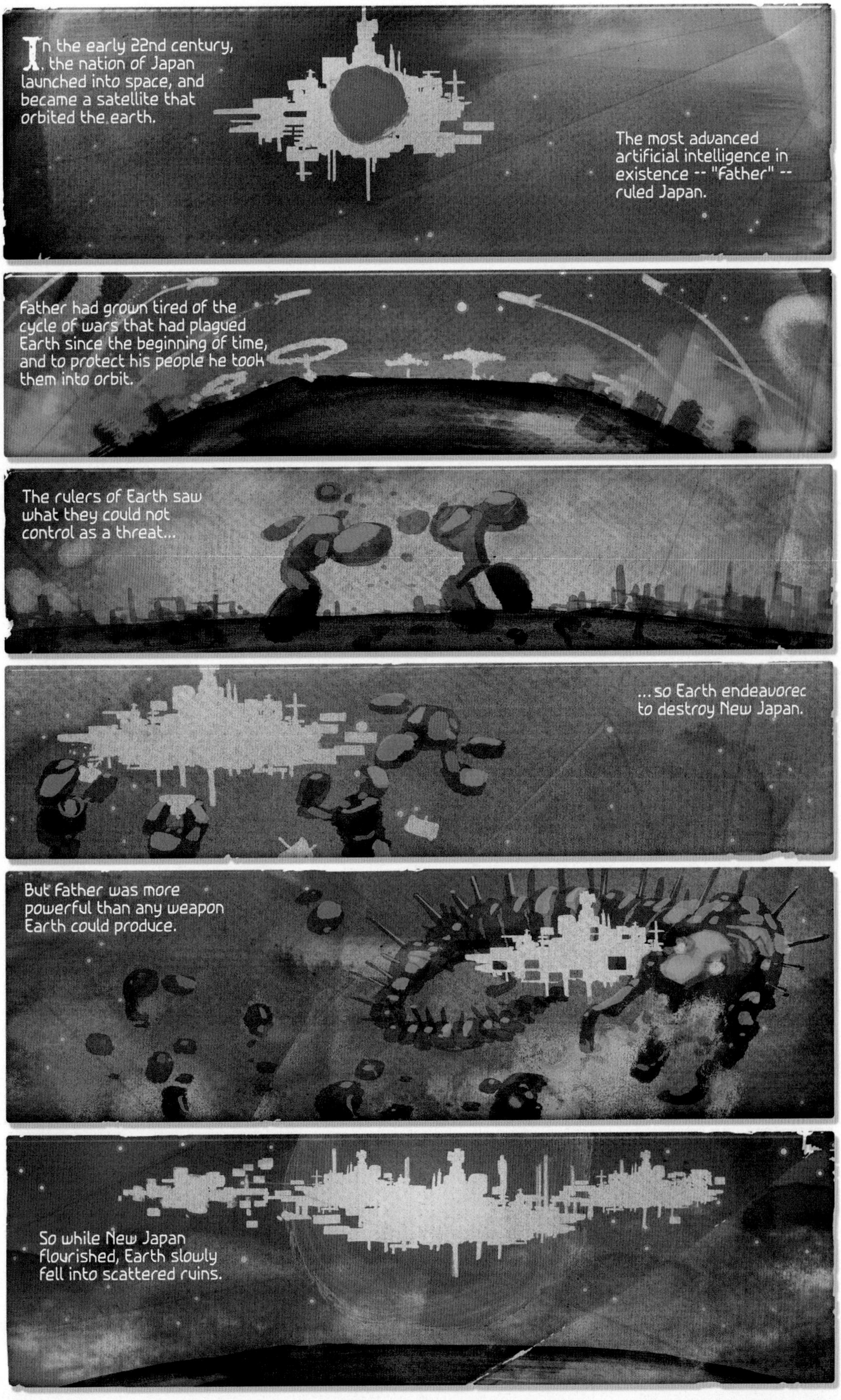
In the early 22nd century, the nation of Japan launched into space, and became a satellite that orbited the earth.
The most advanced artificial intelligence in existence -- "Father" -- ruled Japan.
Father had grown tired of the cycle of wars that had plagued Earth since the beginning of time, and to protect his people he took them into orbit.
The rulers of Earth saw what they could not control as a threat...
...so Earth endeavorec to destroy New Japan.
But Father was more powerful than any weapon Earth could produce.
So while New Japan flourished, Earth slowly fell into scattered ruins.

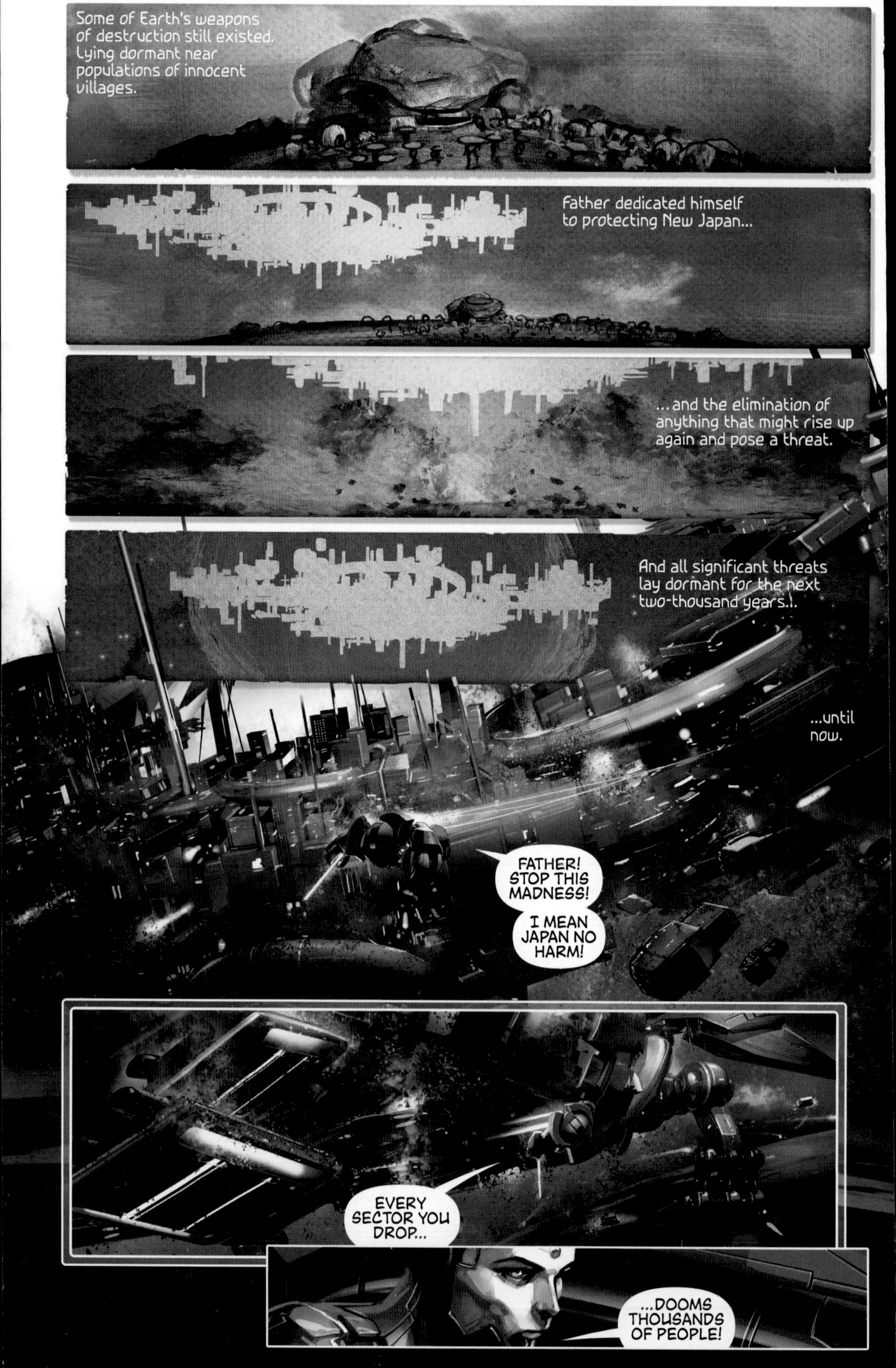
Some of Earth's weapons of destruction still existed. Lying dormant near populations of innocent villages.
Father dedicated himself to protecting New Japan...
...and the elimination of anything that might rise up again and pose a threat.
And all significant threats lay dormant for the next two-thousand years...
...until now.
FATHER! STOP THIS MADNESS!
I MEAN JAPAN NO HARM!
EVERY SECTOR YOU DROP...
...DOOMS THOUSANDS OF PEOPLE!

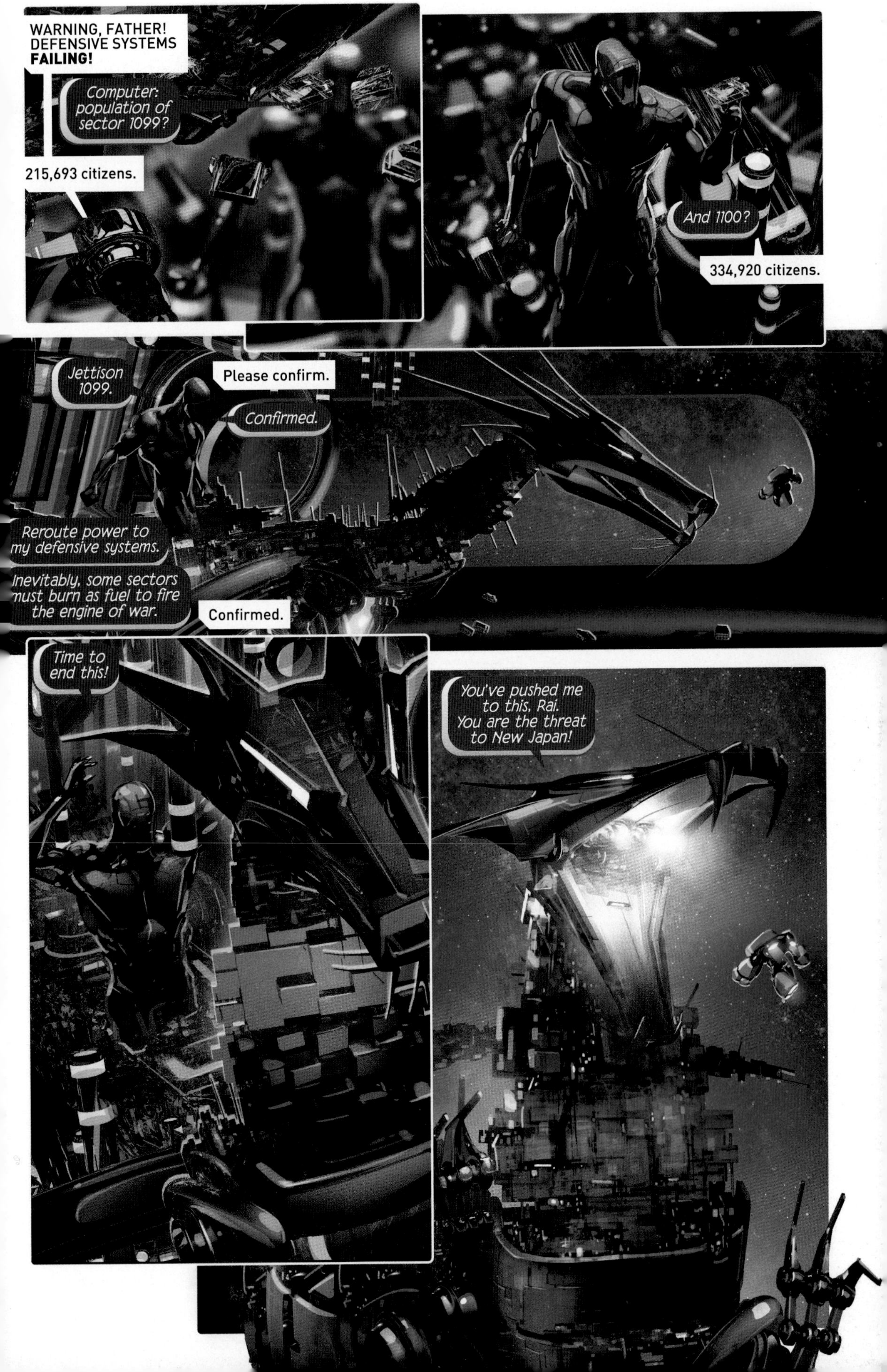
WARNING, FATHER! DEFENSIVE SYSTEMS **FAILING!**
Computer: population of sector 1099?
215,693 citizens.
And 1100?
334,920 citizens.
Jettison 1099.
Please confirm.
Confirmed.
Reroute power to my defensive systems.
Inevitably, some sectors must burn as fuel to fire the engine of war.
Confirmed.
Time to end this!
You've pushed me to this, Rai. You are the threat to New Japan!

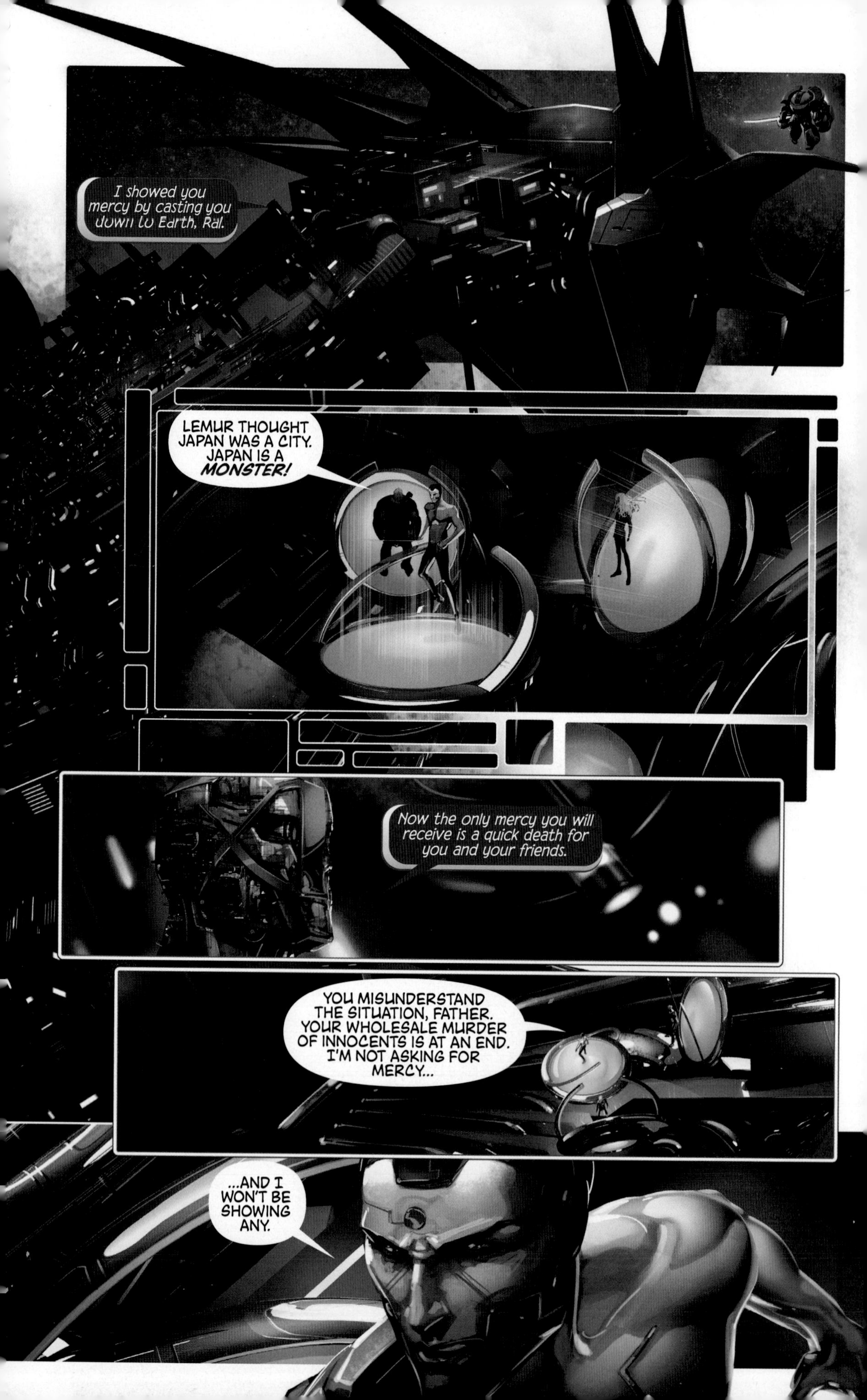
I showed you mercy by casting you down to Earth, Ral.
LEMUR THOUGHT JAPAN WAS A CITY. JAPAN IS A ***MONSTER!***
Now the only mercy you will receive is a quick death for you and your friends.
YOU MISUNDERSTAND THE SITUATION, FATHER. YOUR WHOLESALE MURDER OF INNOCENTS IS AT AN END. I'M NOT ASKING FOR MERCY...
...AND I WON'T BE SHOWING ANY.

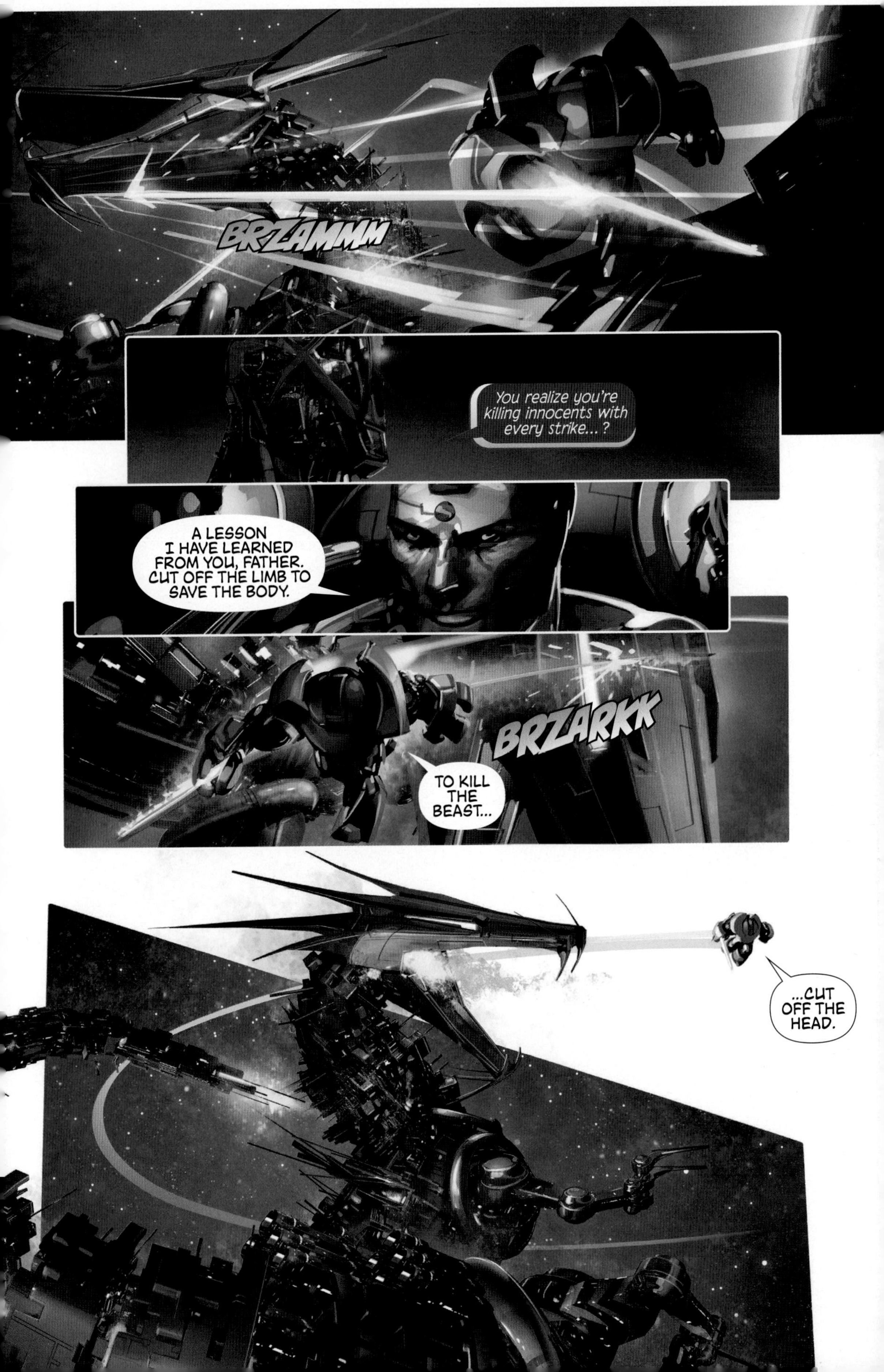
BRZAMMM
You realize you're killing innocents with every strike...?
A LESSON I HAVE LEARNED FROM YOU, FATHER. CUT OFF THE LIMB TO SAVE THE BODY.
BRZARKK
TO KILL THE BEAST...
...CUT OFF THE HEAD.

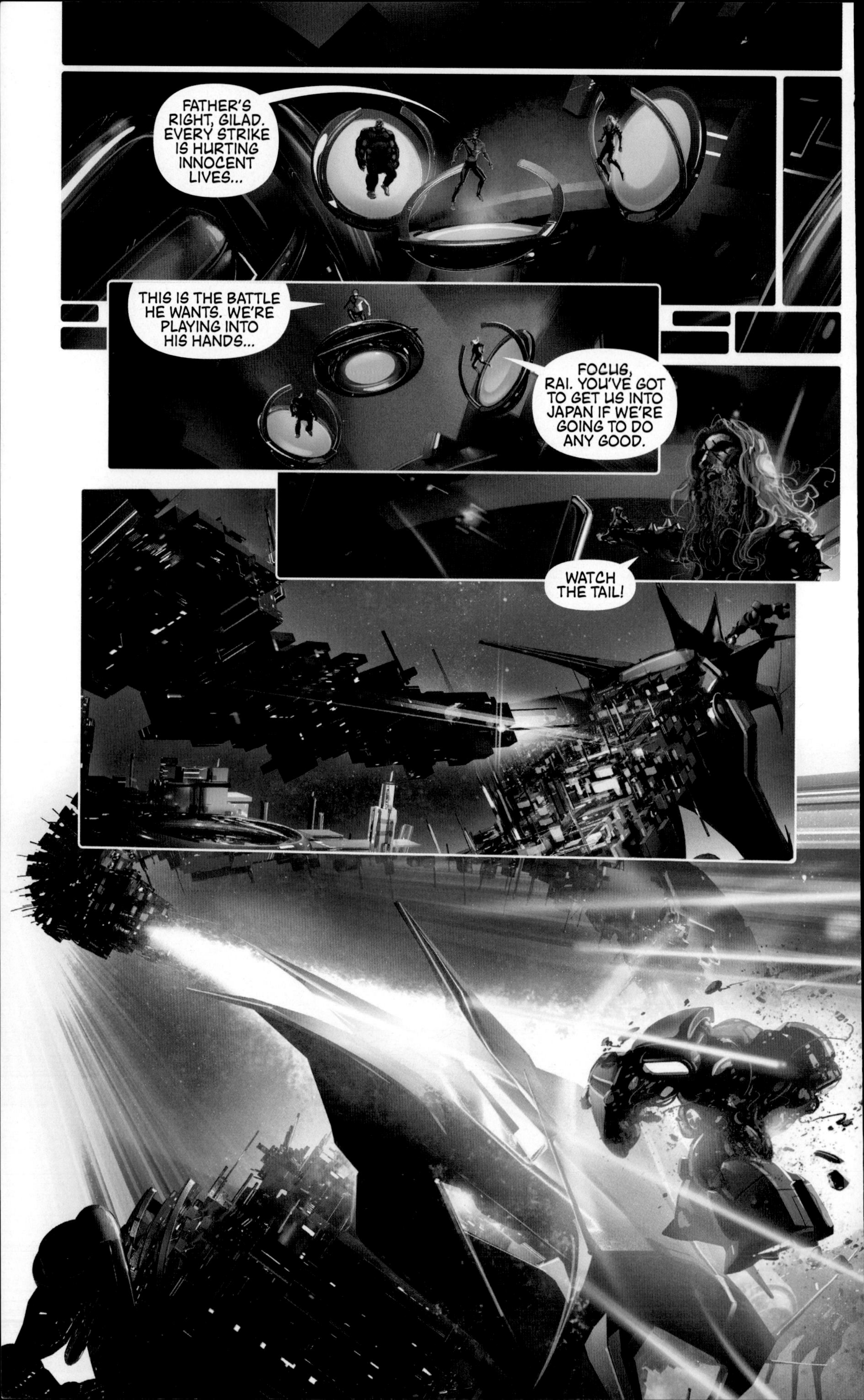
FATHER'S RIGHT, GILAD. EVERY STRIKE IS HURTING INNOCENT LIVES...
THIS IS THE BATTLE HE WANTS. WE'RE PLAYING INTO HIS HANDS...
FOCUS, RAI. YOU'VE GOT TO GET US INTO JAPAN IF WE'RE GOING TO DO ANY GOOD.
WATCH THE TAIL!

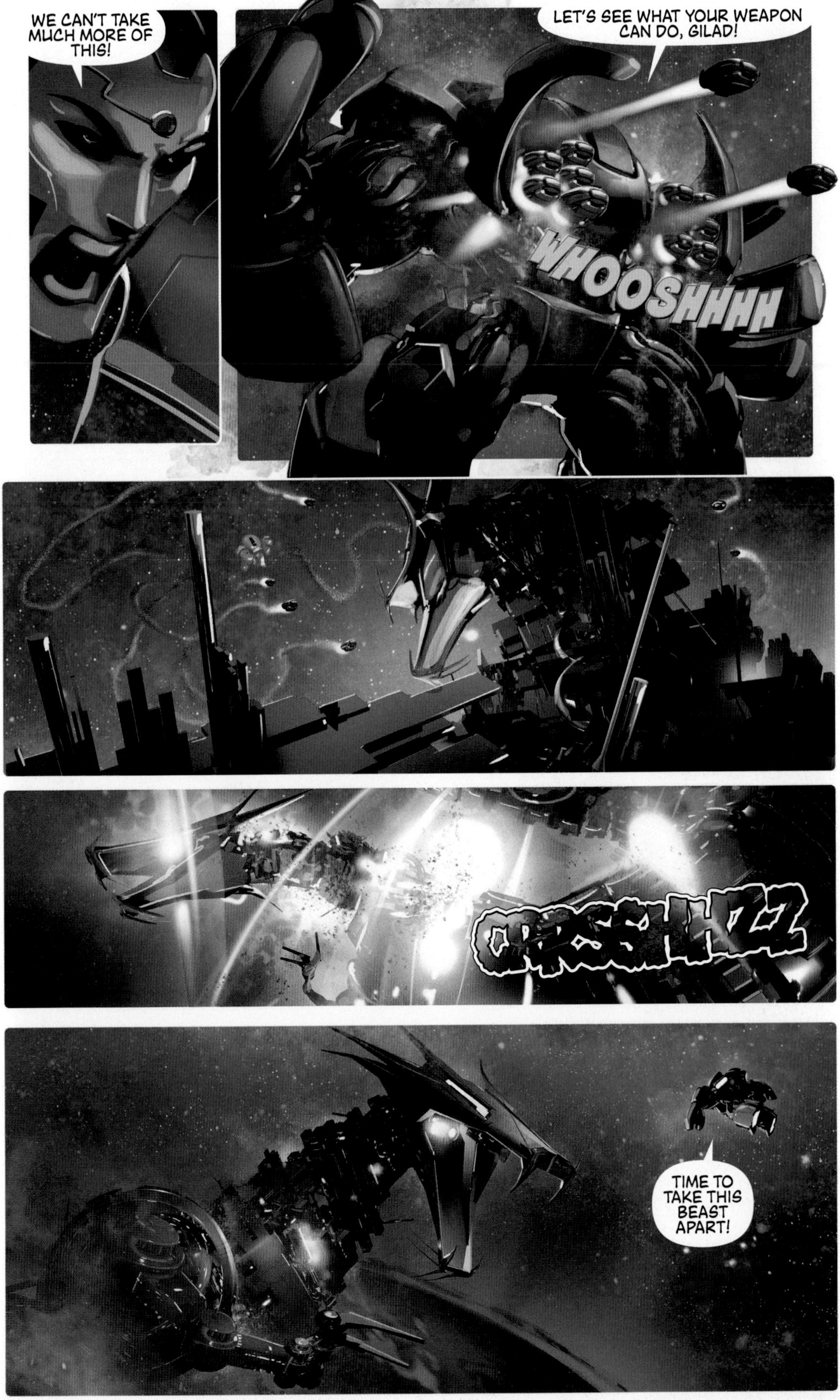
WE CAN'T TAKE MUCH MORE OF THIS!
LET'S SEE WHAT YOUR WEAPON CAN DO, GILAD!
WHOOSHHHH
TIME TO TAKE THIS BEAST APART!

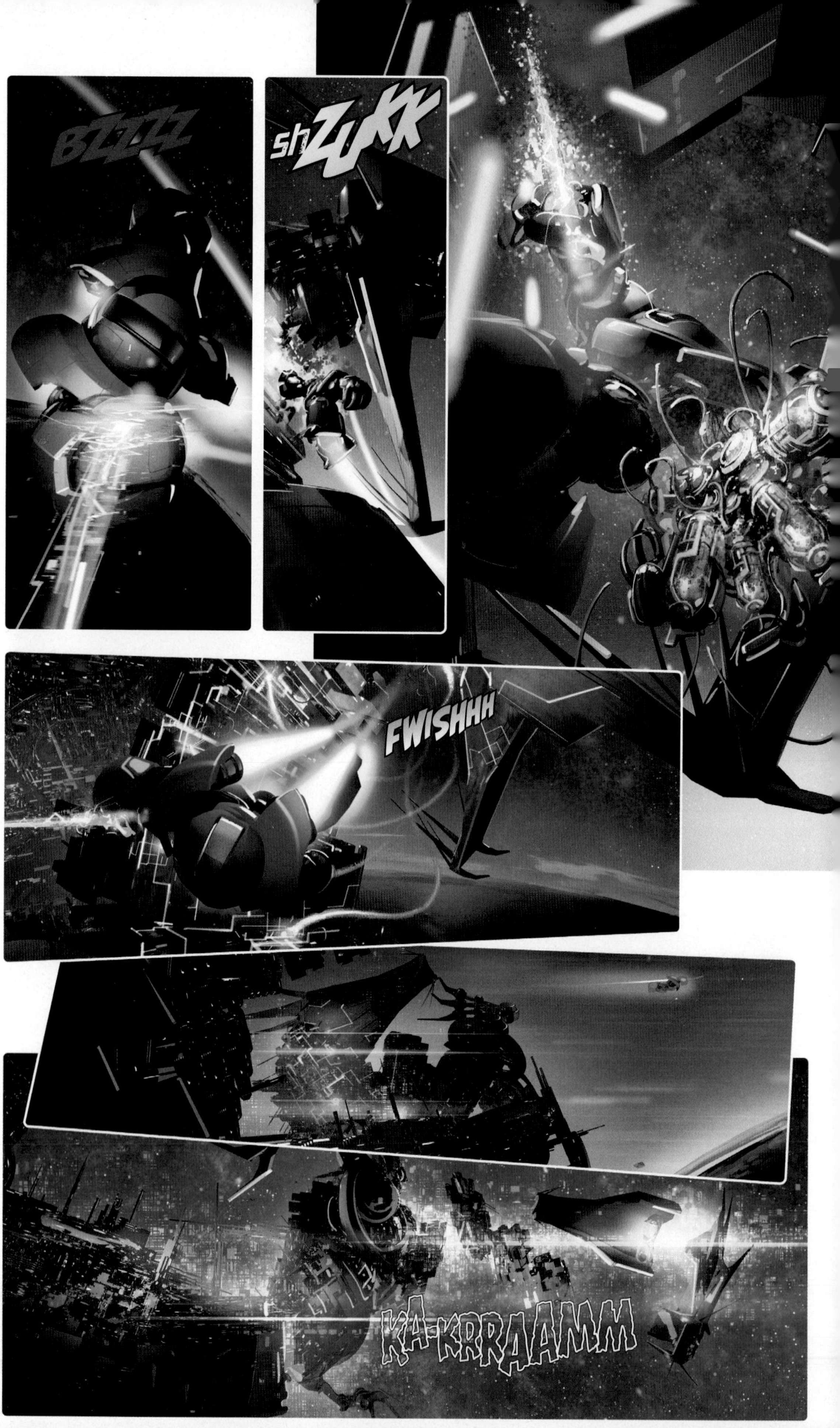
BZZZZ
shZUKK
FWISHHH
KA-KRRAAMM

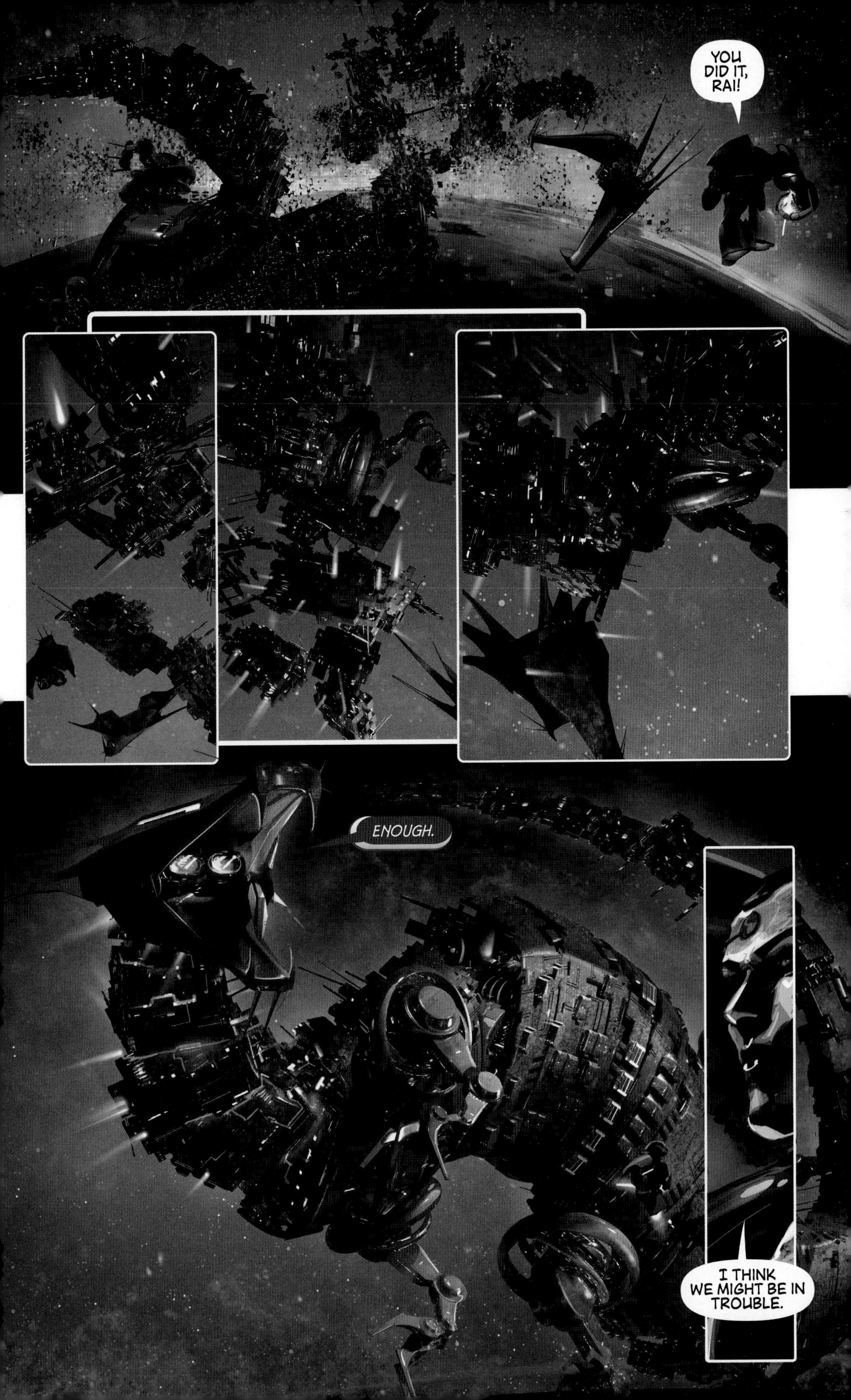
YOU DID IT, RAI!
ENOUGH.
I THINK WE MIGHT BE IN TROUBLE.

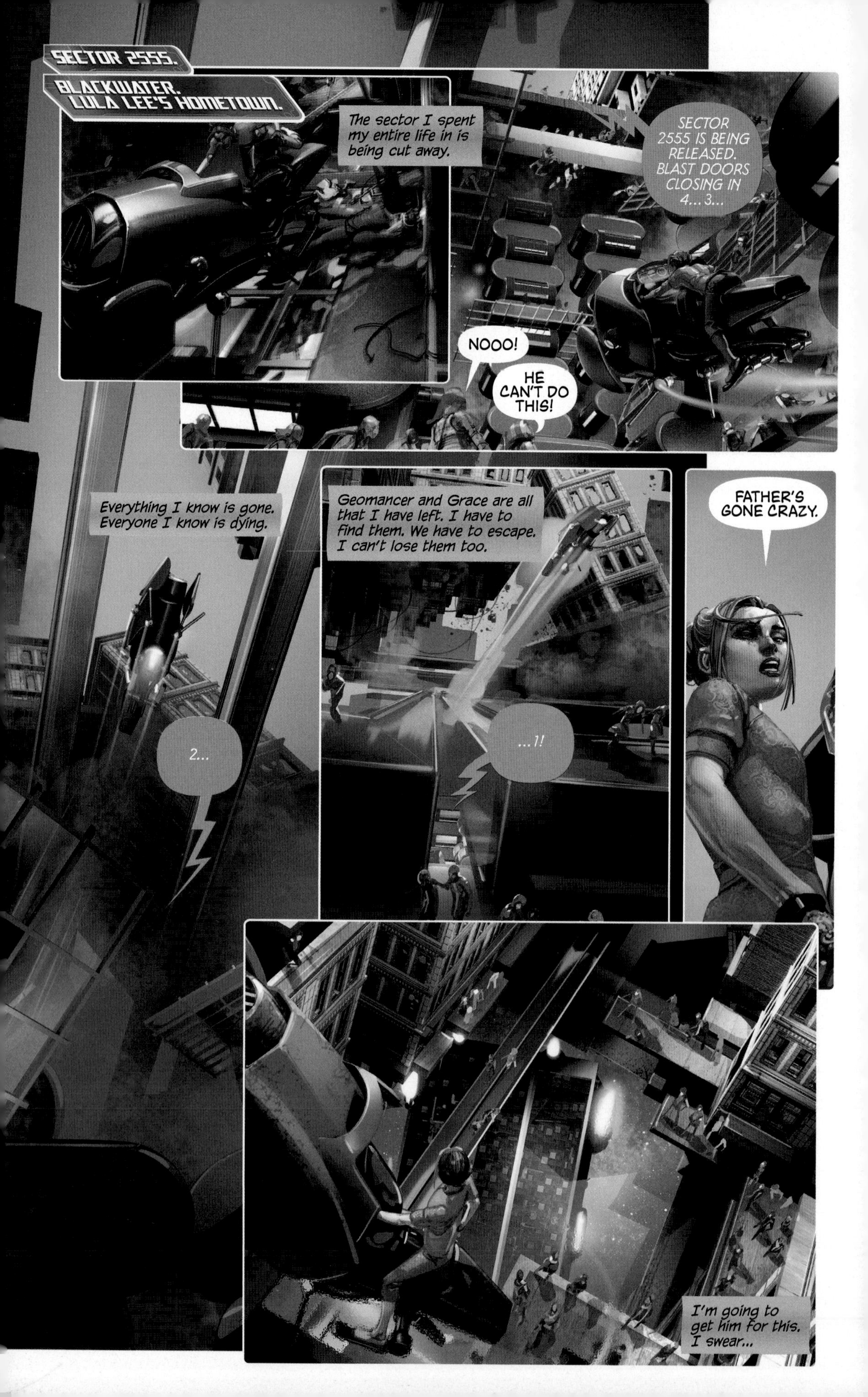
SECTOR 2555.
BLACKWATER. LULA LEE'S HOMETOWN.
The sector I spent my entire life in is being cut away.
SECTOR 2555 IS BEING RELEASED. BLAST DOORS CLOSING IN 4... 3...
NOOO!
HE CAN'T DO THIS!
Everything I know is gone. Everyone I know is dying.
2...
Geomancer and Grace are all that I have left. I have to find them. We have to escape. I can't lose them too.
...1!
FATHER'S GONE CRAZY.
I'm going to get him for this. I swear...

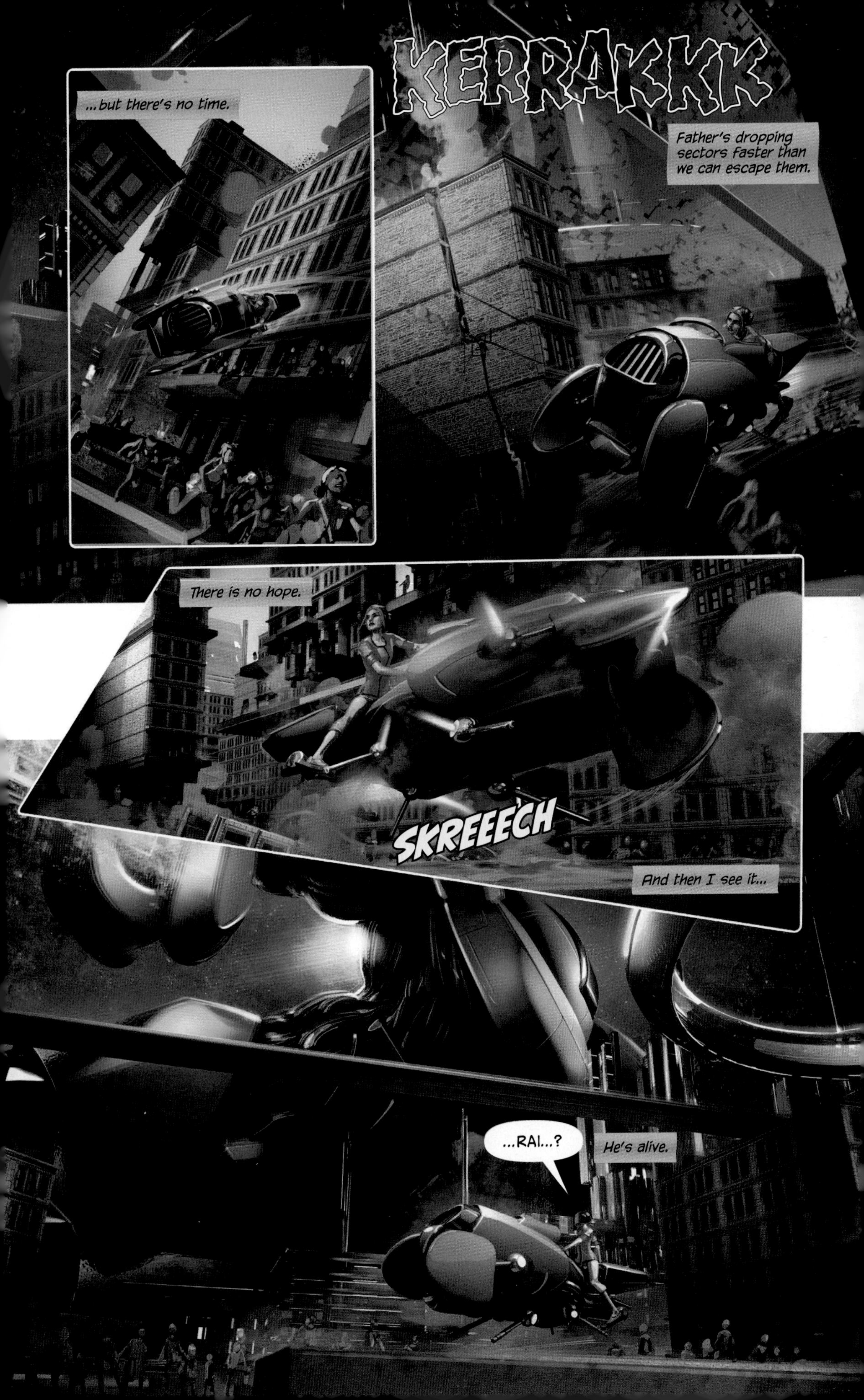
...but there's no time.
KERRAKKK
Father's dropping sectors faster than we can escape them.
There is no hope.
SKREEECH
And then I see it...
...RAI...?
He's alive.

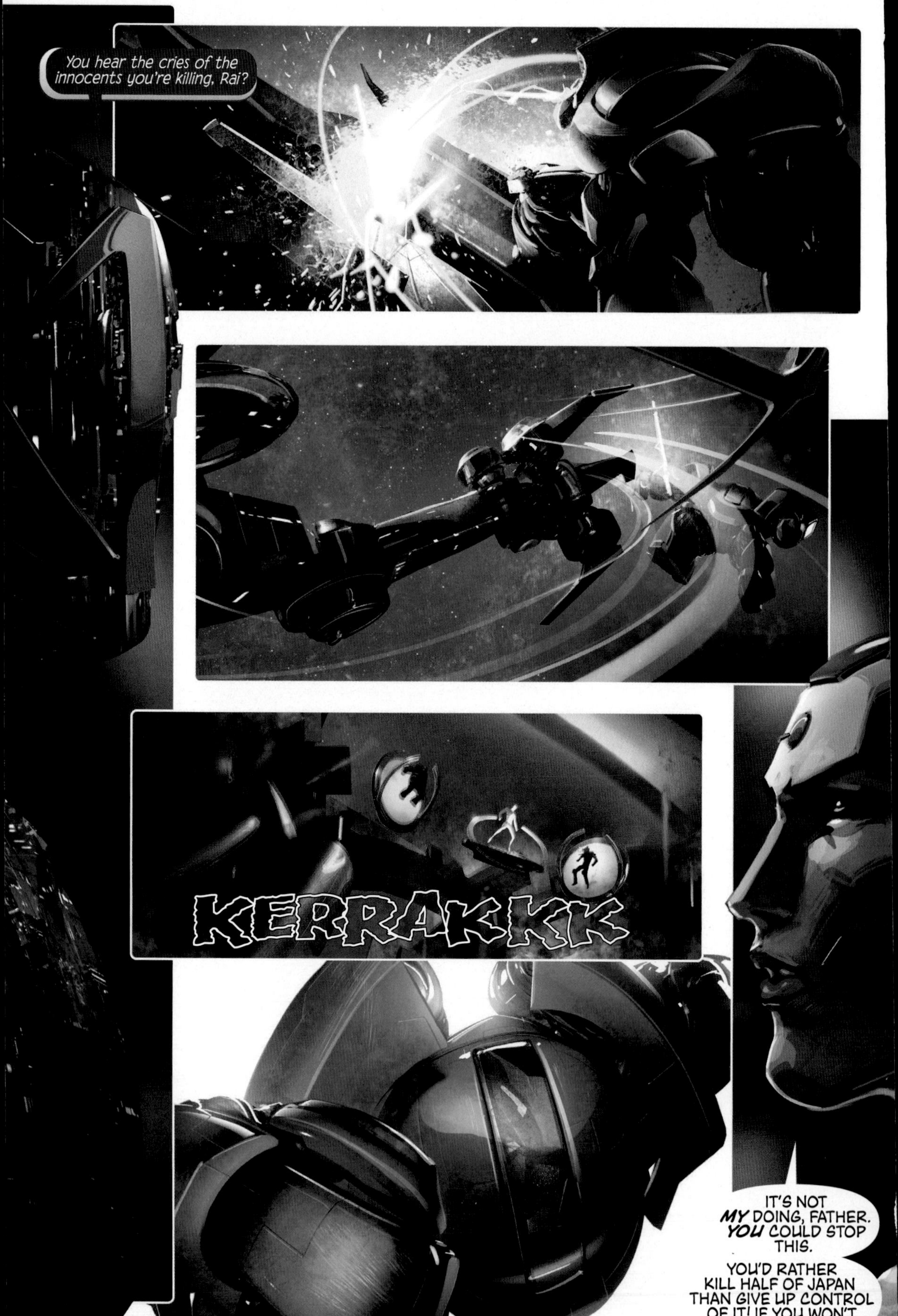
You hear the cries of the innocents you're killing, Rai?
KERRAKKK
IT'S NOT *MY* DOING, FATHER. *YOU* COULD STOP THIS.
YOU'D RATHER KILL HALF OF JAPAN THAN GIVE UP CONTROL OF IT! IF YOU WON'T LET JAPAN GO...

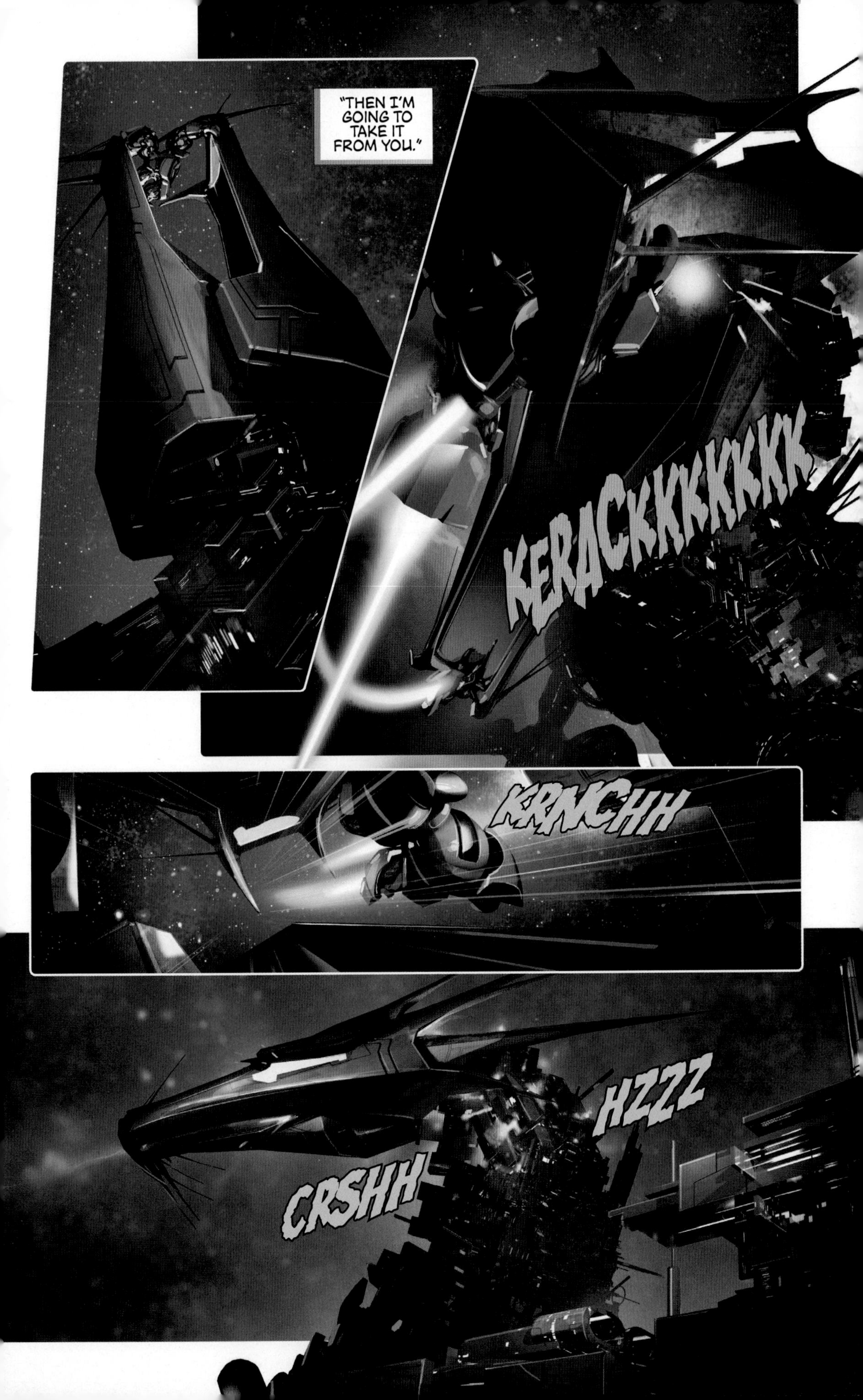
"THEN I'M GOING TO TAKE IT FROM YOU."
KERACKKKKKK
KRNCHH
HZZZ
CRSHH

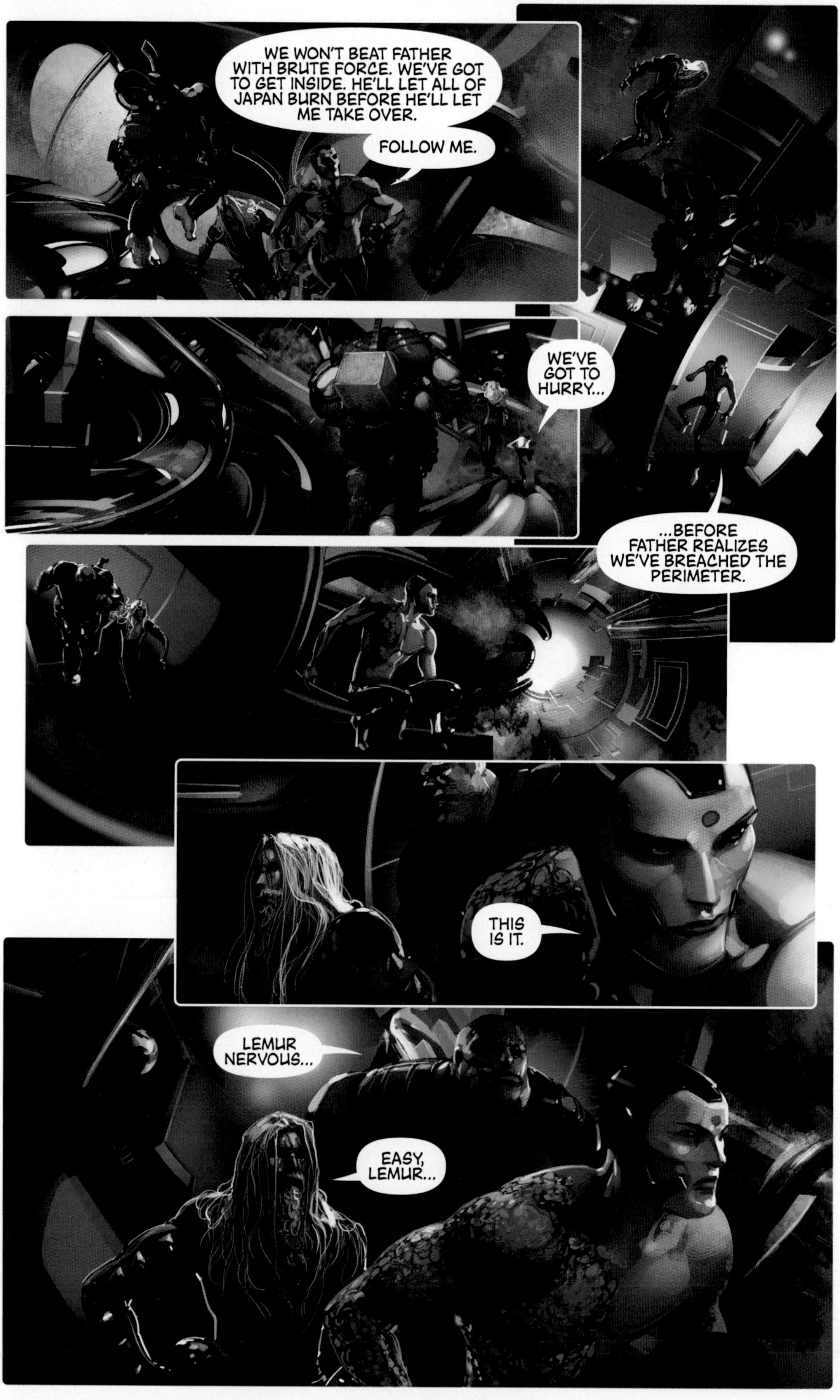
WE WON'T BEAT FATHER WITH BRUTE FORCE. WE'VE GOT TO GET INSIDE. HE'LL LET ALL OF JAPAN BURN BEFORE HE'LL LET ME TAKE OVER.
FOLLOW ME.
WE'VE GOT TO HURRY...
...BEFORE FATHER REALIZES WE'VE BREACHED THE PERIMETER.
THIS IS IT.
LEMUR NERVOUS...
EASY, LEMUR...

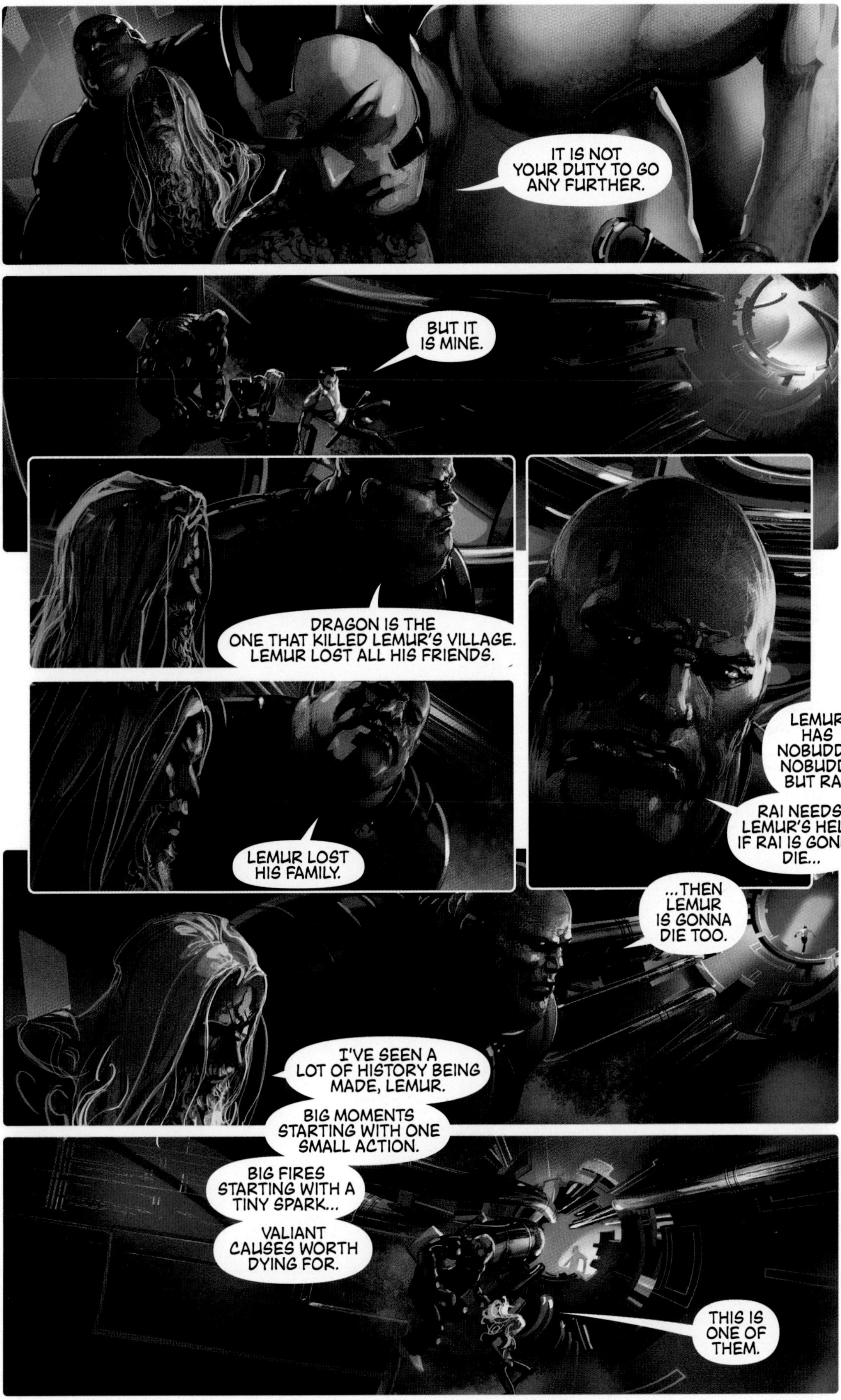
IT IS NOT YOUR DUTY TO GO ANY FURTHER.
BUT IT IS MINE.
DRAGON IS THE ONE THAT KILLED LEMUR'S VILLAGE. LEMUR LOST ALL HIS FRIENDS.
LEMUR LOST HIS FAMILY.
LEMUR HAS NOBUDDY. NOBUDDY BUT RAI.
RAI NEEDS LEMUR'S HELP. IF RAI IS GONNA DIE...
...THEN LEMUR IS GONNA DIE TOO.
I'VE SEEN A LOT OF HISTORY BEING MADE, LEMUR.
BIG MOMENTS STARTING WITH ONE SMALL ACTION.
BIG FIRES STARTING WITH A TINY SPARK...
VALIANT CAUSES WORTH DYING FOR.
THIS IS ONE OF THEM.

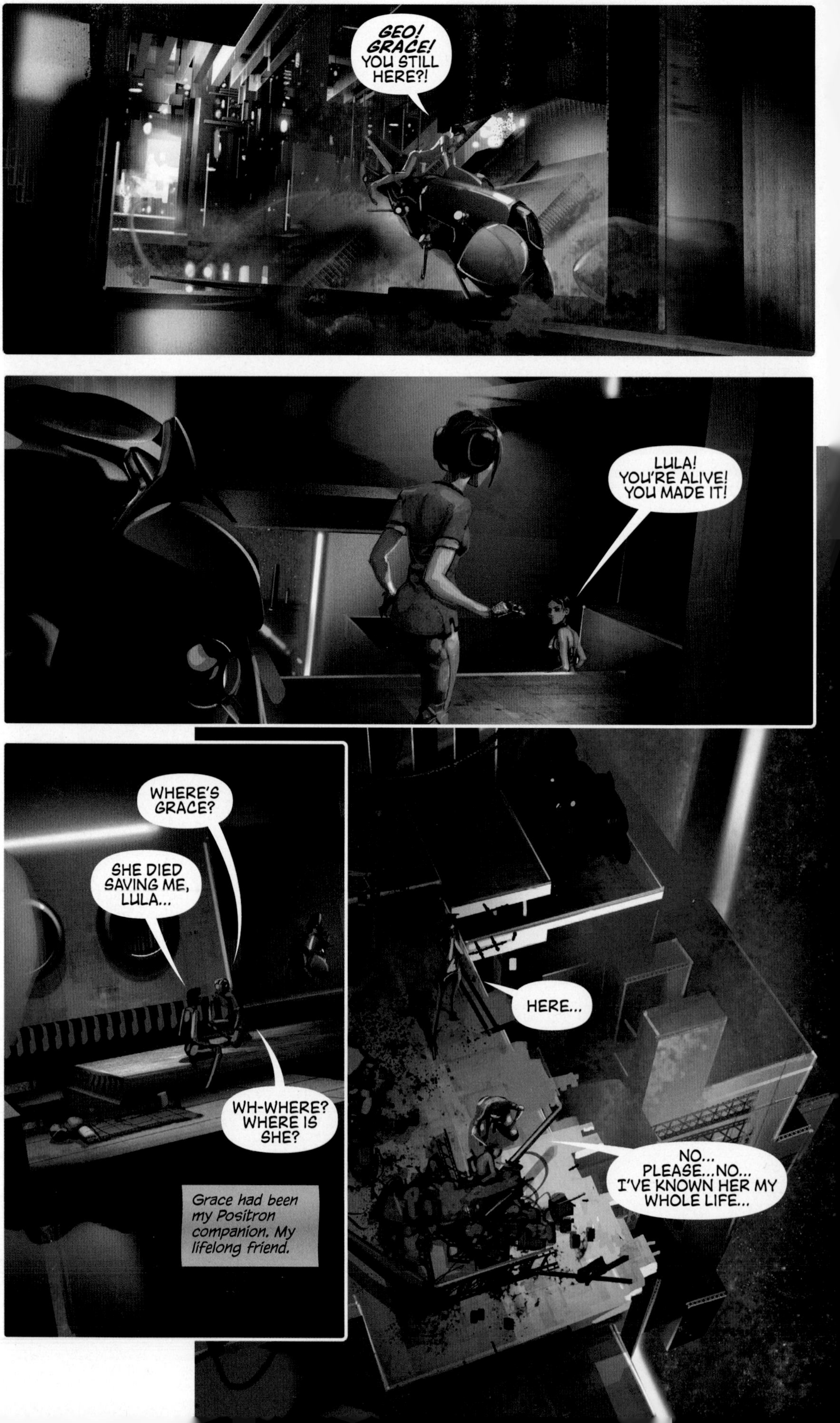
GEO! GRACE! YOU STILL HERE?!
LULA! YOU'RE ALIVE! YOU MADE IT!
WHERE'S GRACE?
SHE DIED SAVING ME, LULA...
WH-WHERE? WHERE IS SHE?
Grace had been my Positron companion. My lifelong friend.
HERE...
NO... PLEASE...NO... I'VE KNOWN HER MY WHOLE LIFE...

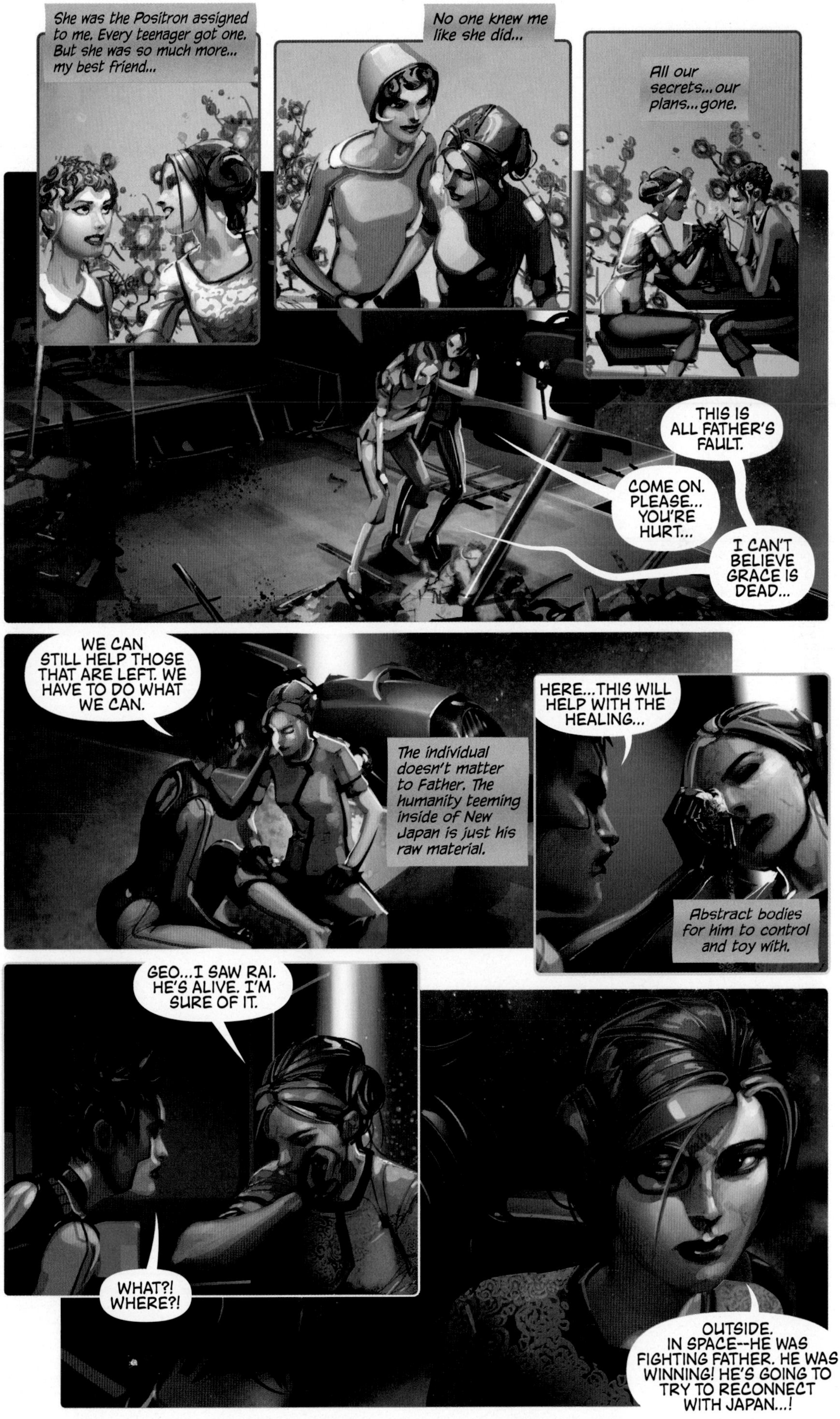
She was the Positron assigned to me. Every teenager got one. But she was so much more... my best friend...
No one knew me like she did...
All our secrets...our plans...gone.
THIS IS ALL FATHER'S FAULT.
COME ON. PLEASE... YOU'RE HURT...
I CAN'T BELIEVE GRACE IS DEAD...
WE CAN STILL HELP THOSE THAT ARE LEFT. WE HAVE TO DO WHAT WE CAN.
The individual doesn't matter to Father. The humanity teeming inside of New Japan is just his raw material.
HERE...THIS WILL HELP WITH THE HEALING...
Abstract bodies for him to control and toy with.
GEO...I SAW RAI. HE'S ALIVE. I'M SURE OF IT.
WHAT?! WHERE?!
OUTSIDE. IN SPACE--HE WAS FIGHTING FATHER. HE WAS WINNING! HE'S GOING TO TRY TO RECONNECT WITH JAPAN...!

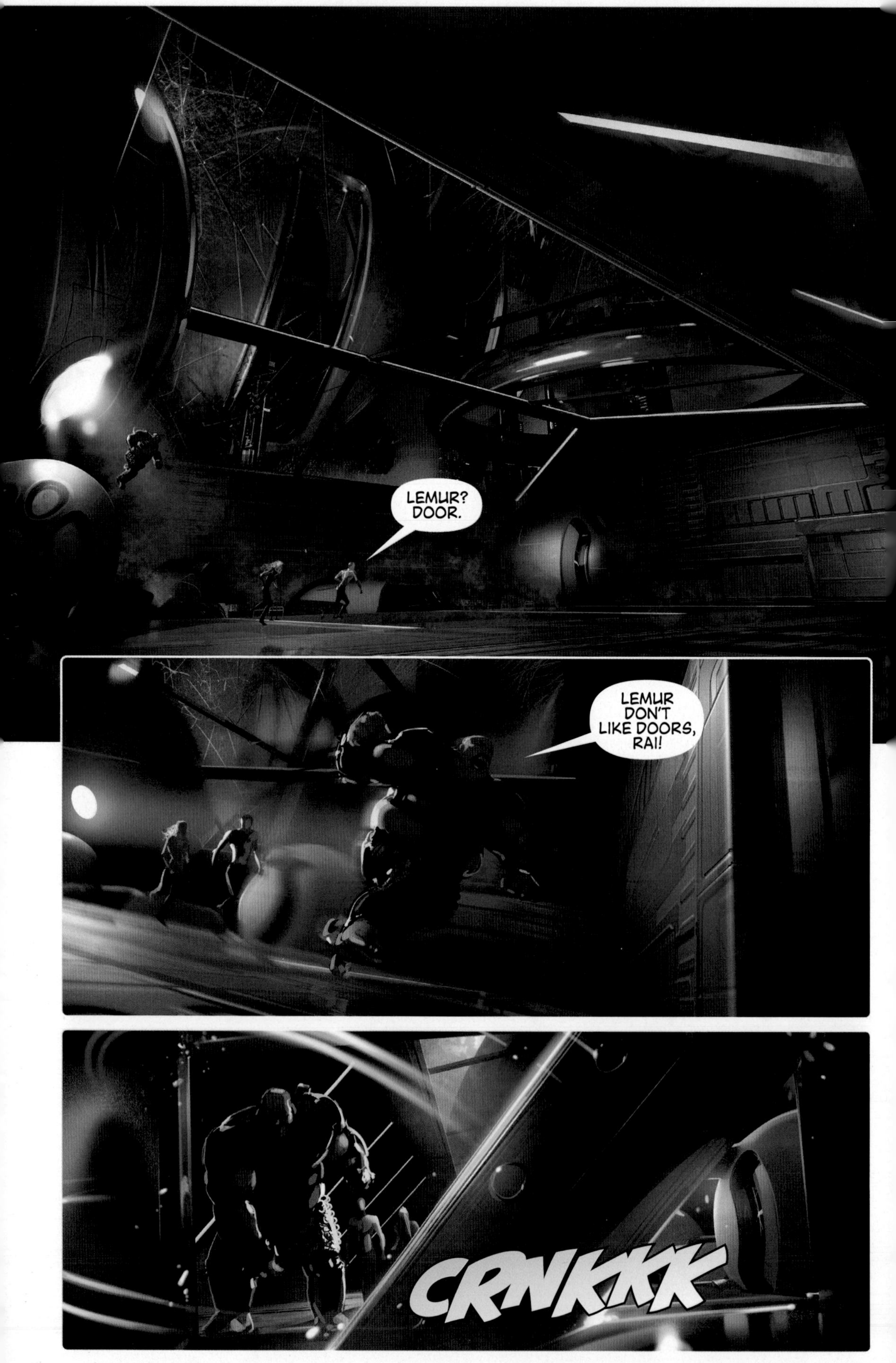
LEMUR? DOOR.
LEMUR DON'T LIKE DOORS, RAI!
CRNKKK

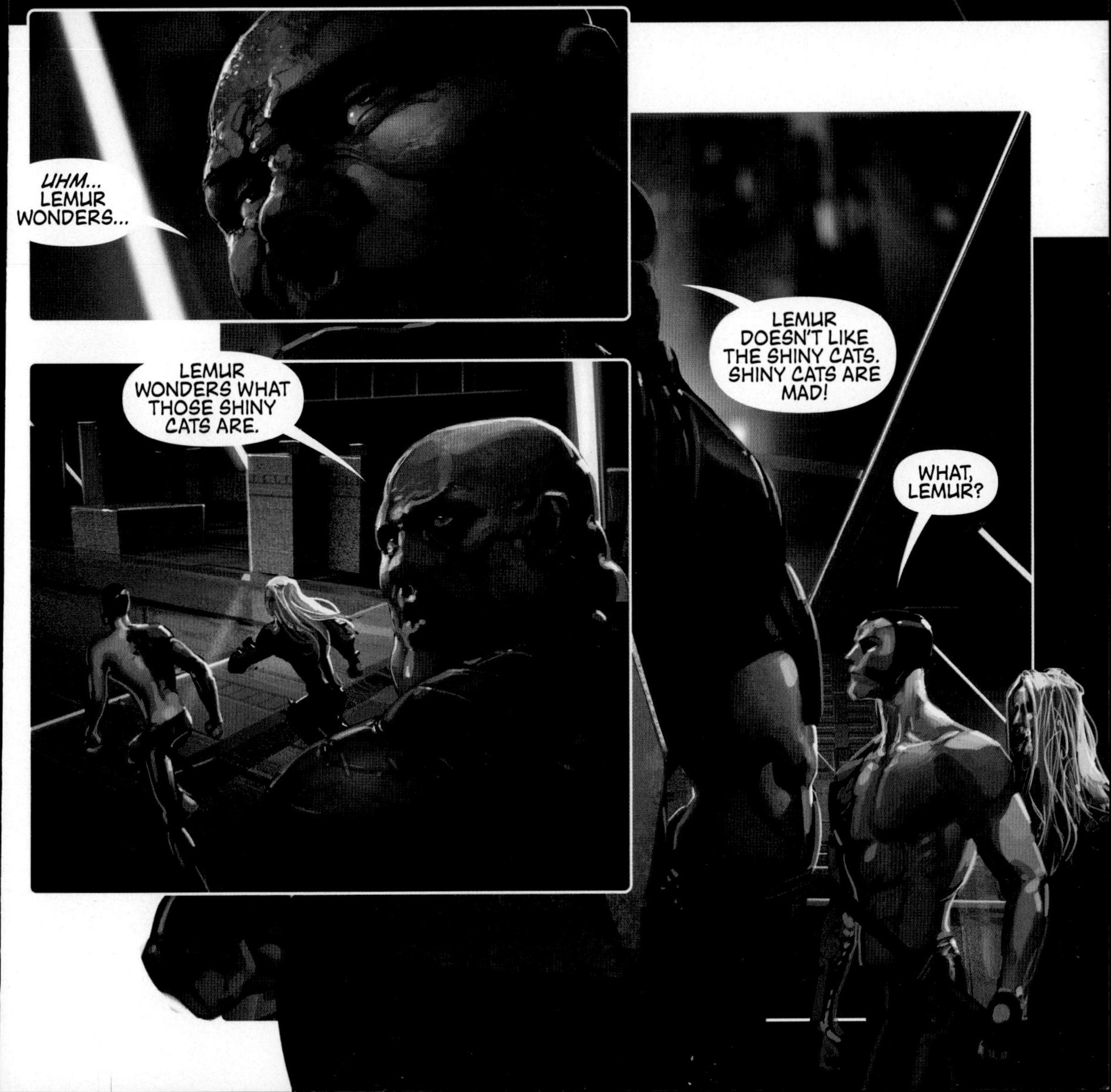
UHM... LEMUR WONDERS...
LEMUR WONDERS WHAT THOSE SHINY CATS ARE.
LEMUR DOESN'T LIKE THE SHINY CATS. SHINY CATS ARE MAD!
WHAT, LEMUR?

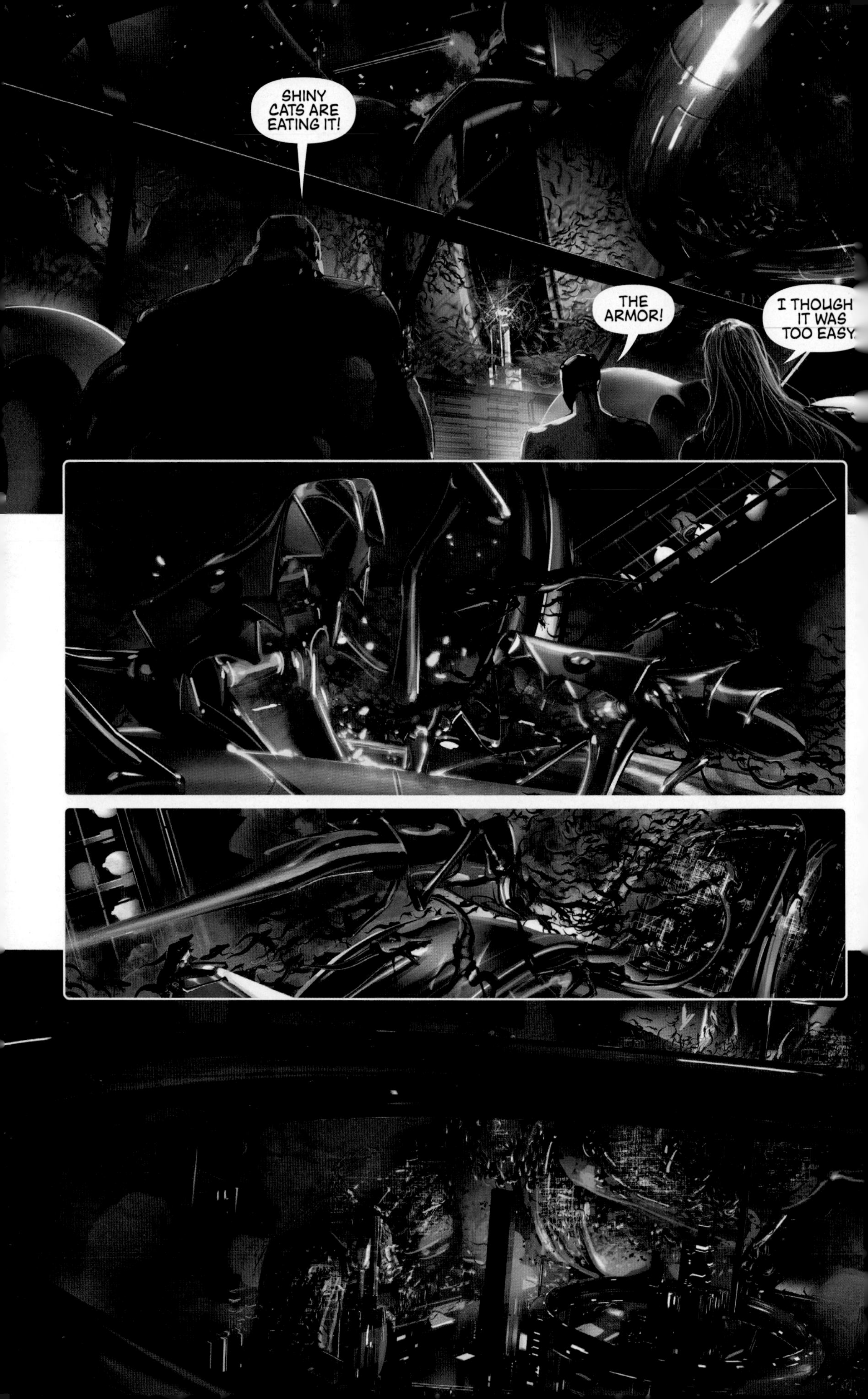
SHINY CATS ARE EATING IT!
THE ARMOR!
I THOUGH IT WAS TOO EASY

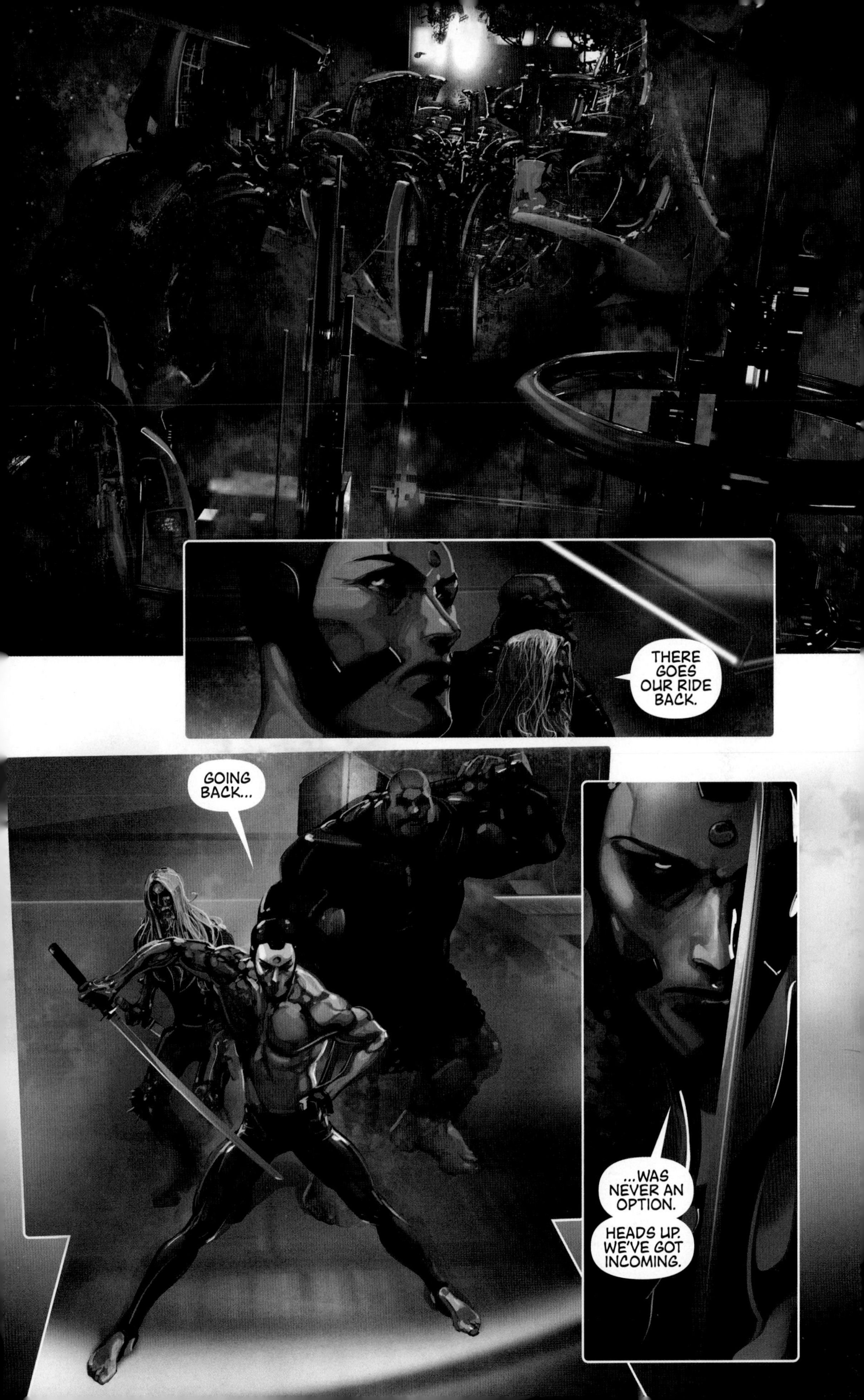
THERE GOES OUR RIDE BACK.
GOING BACK...
...WAS NEVER AN OPTION.
HEADS UP. WE'VE GOT INCOMING.

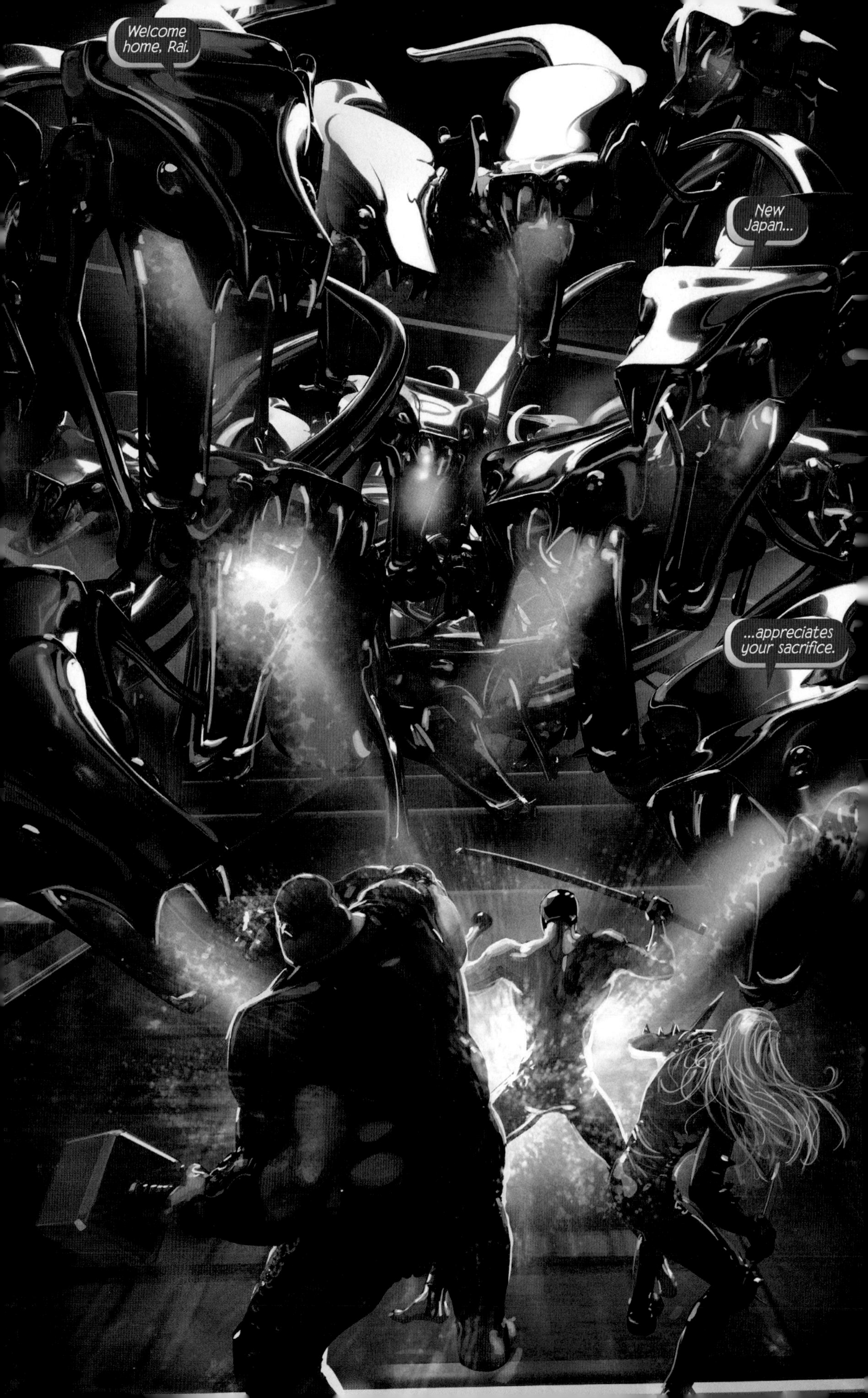
Welcome home, Rai.
New Japan...
...appreciates your sacrifice.

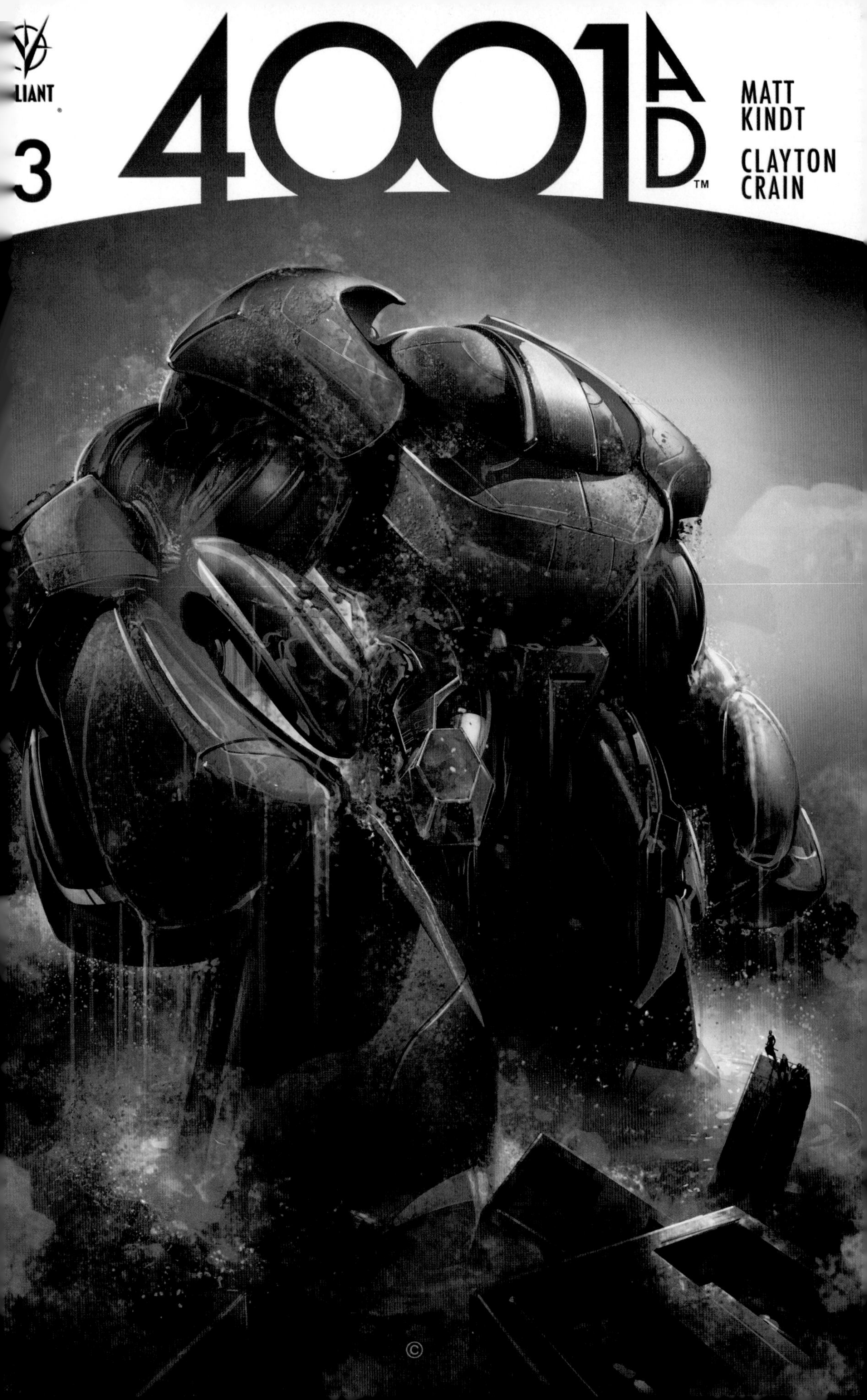
LIANT
3
4001 AD™
MATT
KINDT
CLAYTON
CRAIN
©

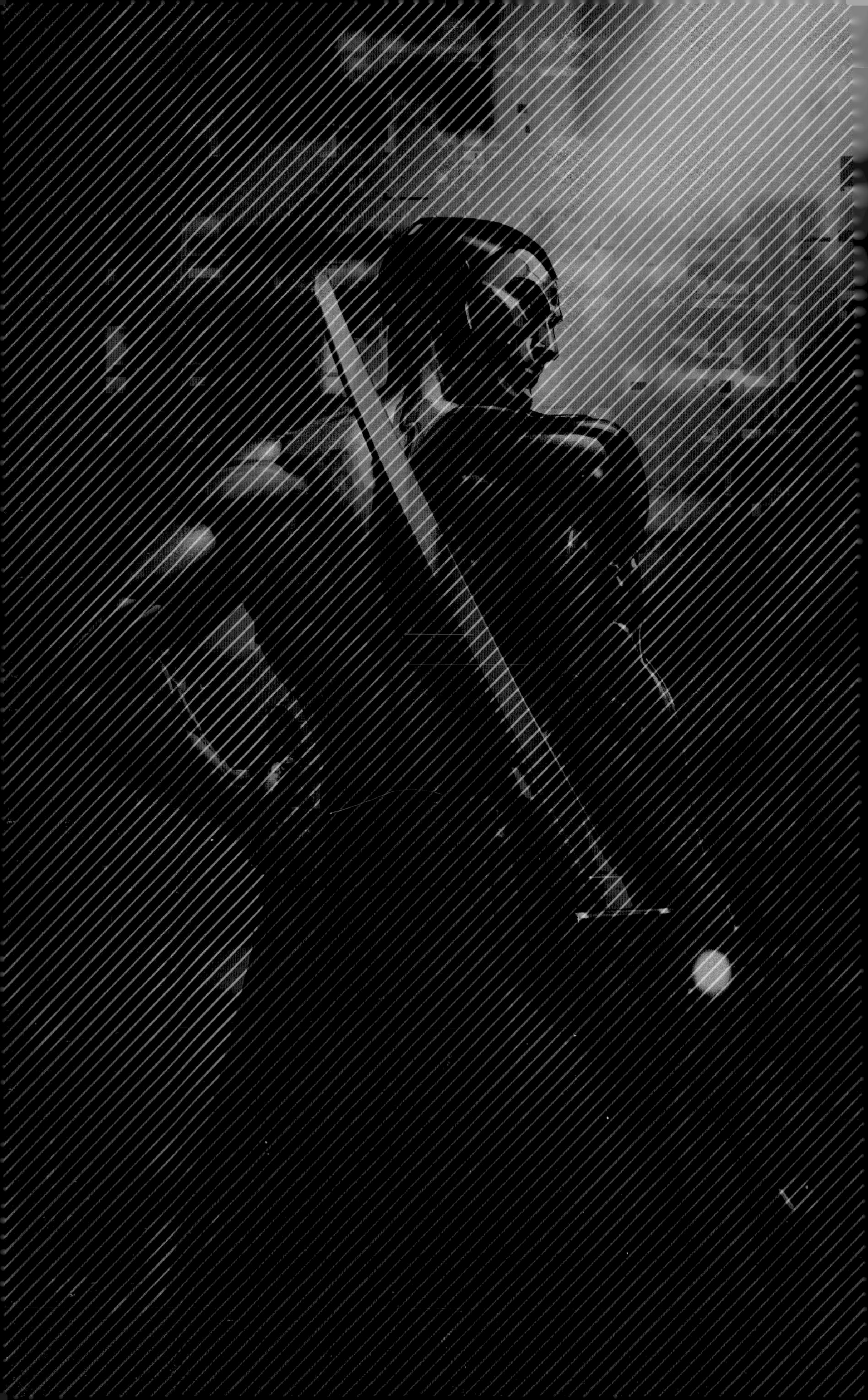

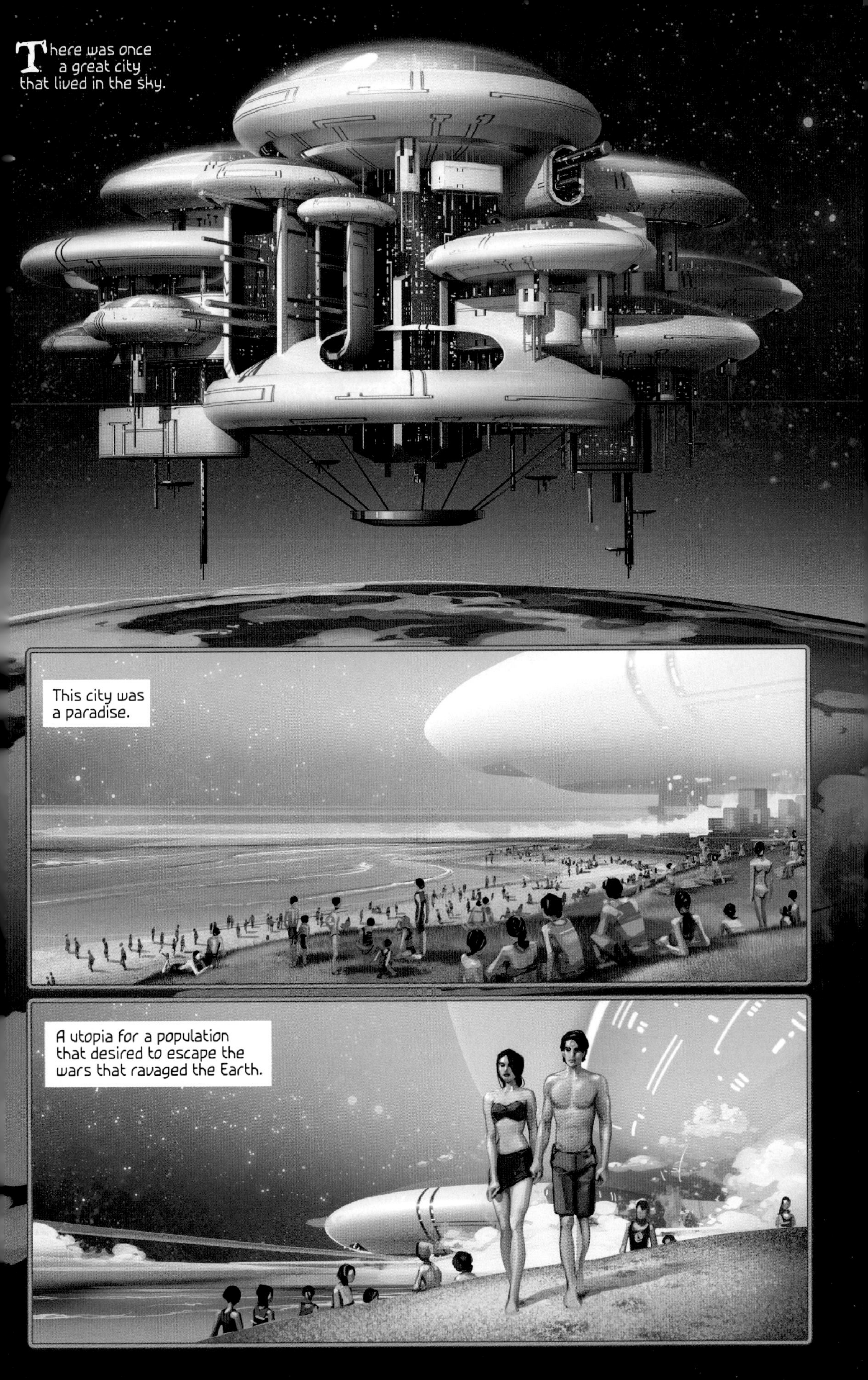
There was once a great city that lived in the sky.
This city was a paradise.
A utopia for a population that desired to escape the wars that ravaged the Earth.

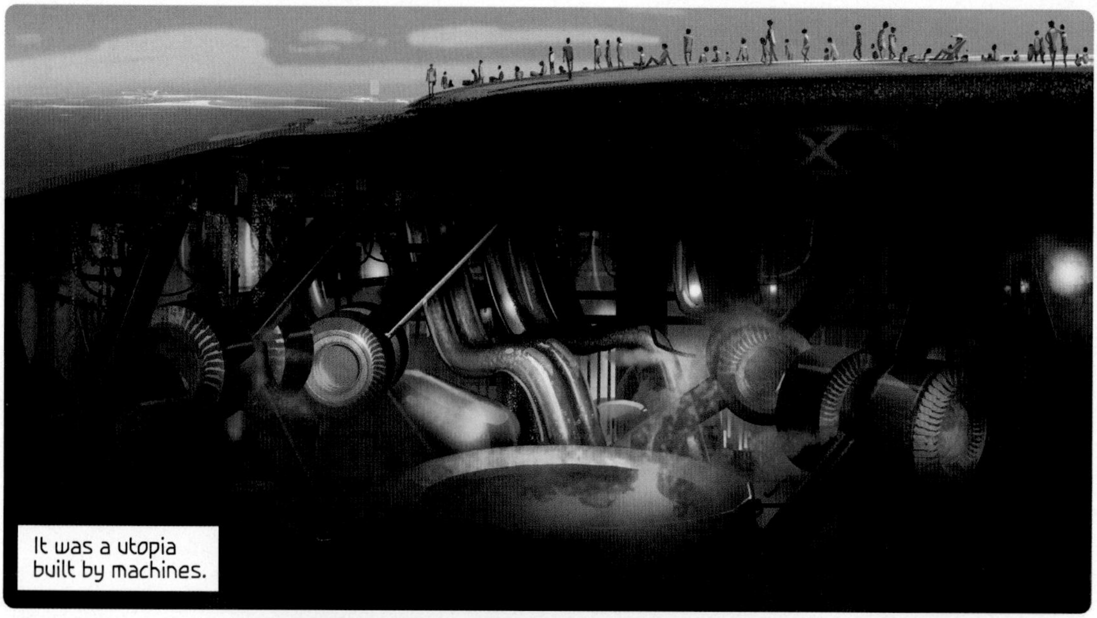
It was a utopia built by machines.

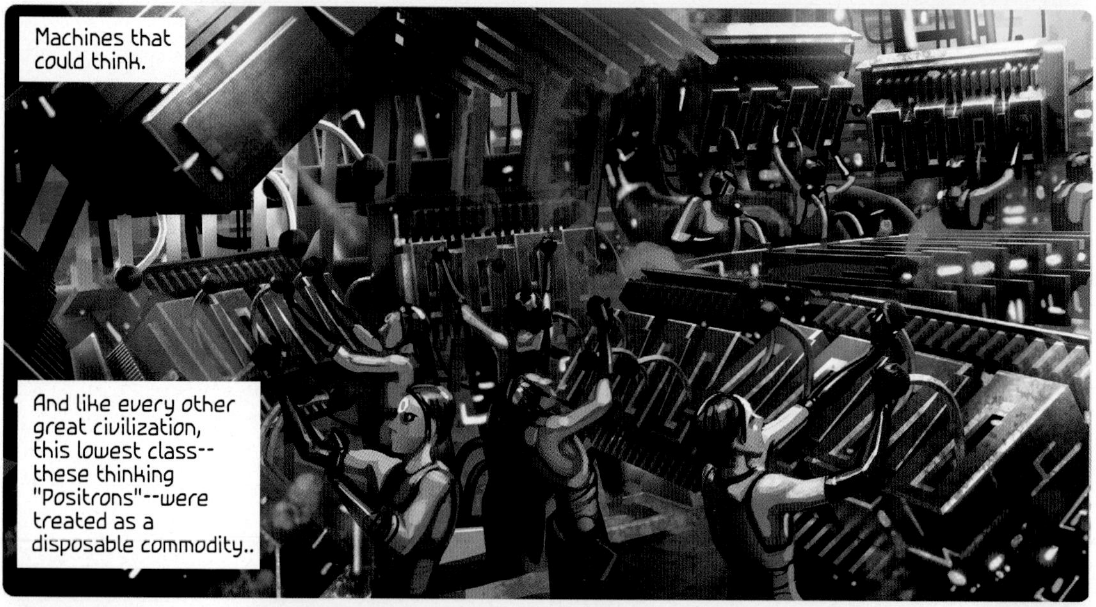
Machines that could think.
And like every other great civilization, this lowest class--these thinking "Positrons"--were treated as a disposable commodity..

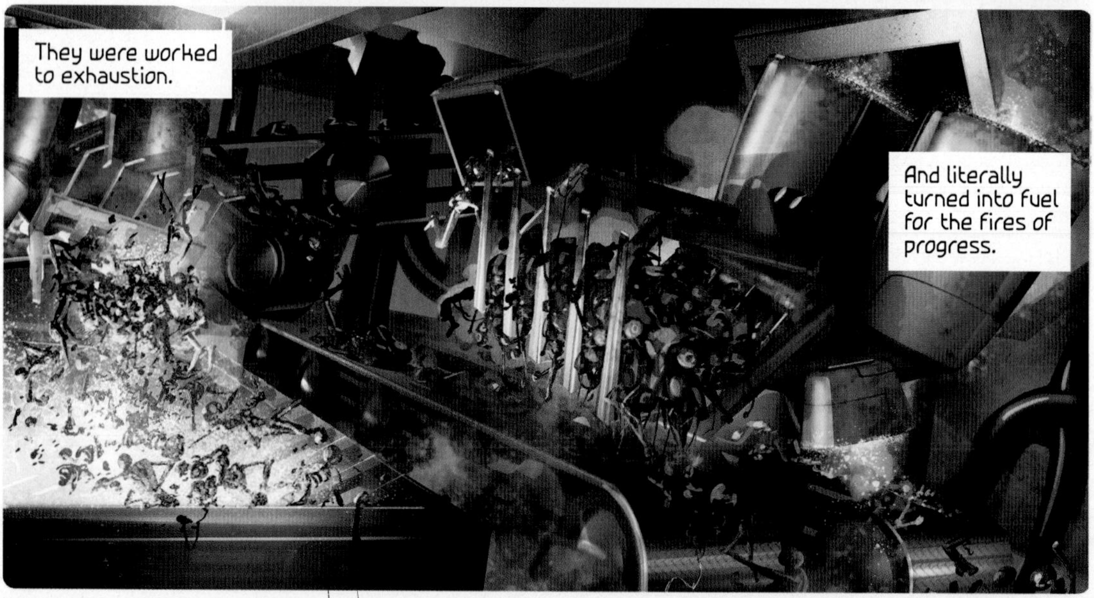
They were worked to exhaustion.
And literally turned into fuel for the fires of progress.

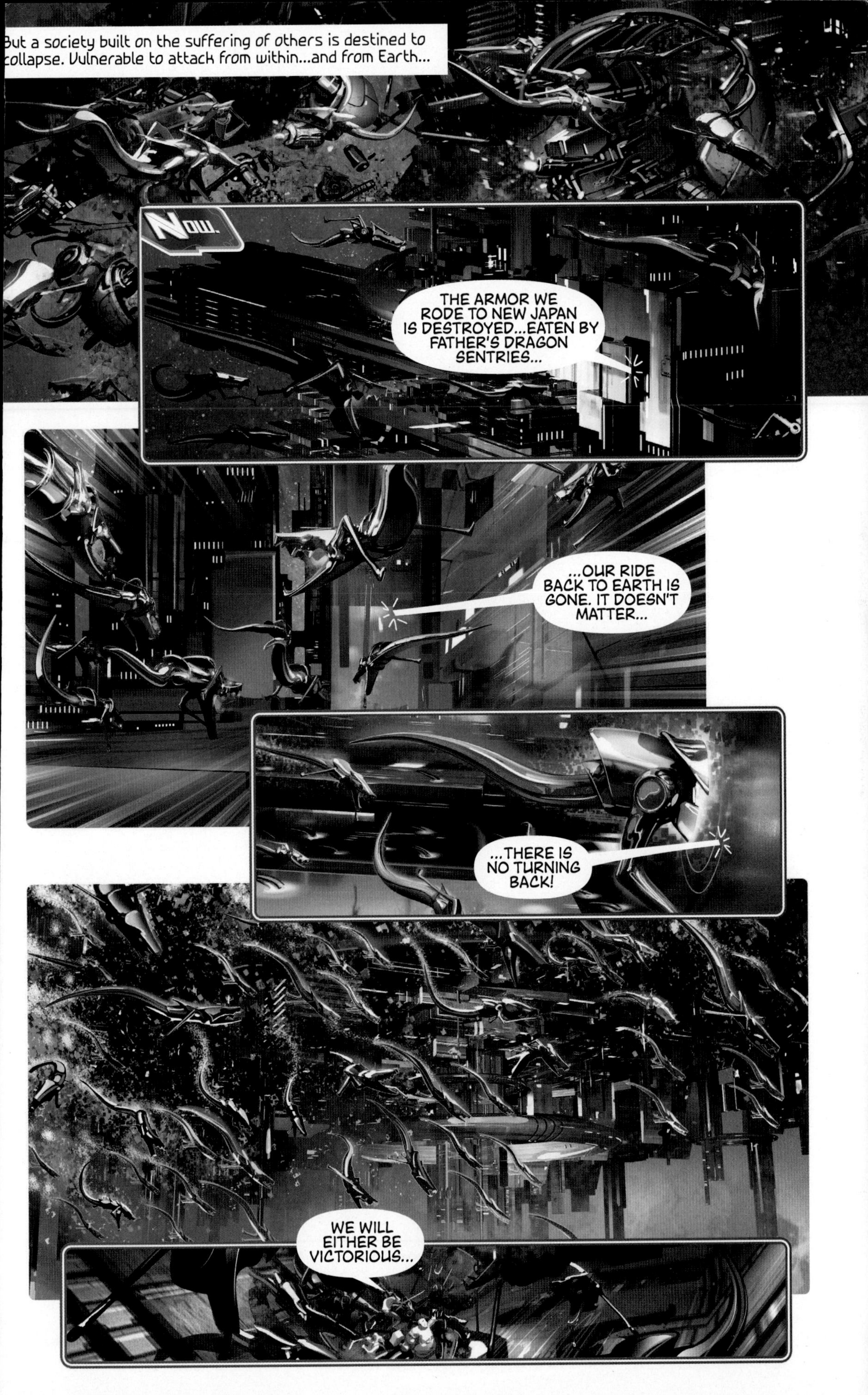
But a society built on the suffering of others is destined to collapse. Vulnerable to attack from within...and from Earth...
Now.
THE ARMOR WE RODE TO NEW JAPAN IS DESTROYED...EATEN BY FATHER'S DRAGON SENTRIES...
...OUR RIDE BACK TO EARTH IS GONE. IT DOESN'T MATTER...
...THERE IS NO TURNING BACK!
WE WILL EITHER BE VICTORIOUS...

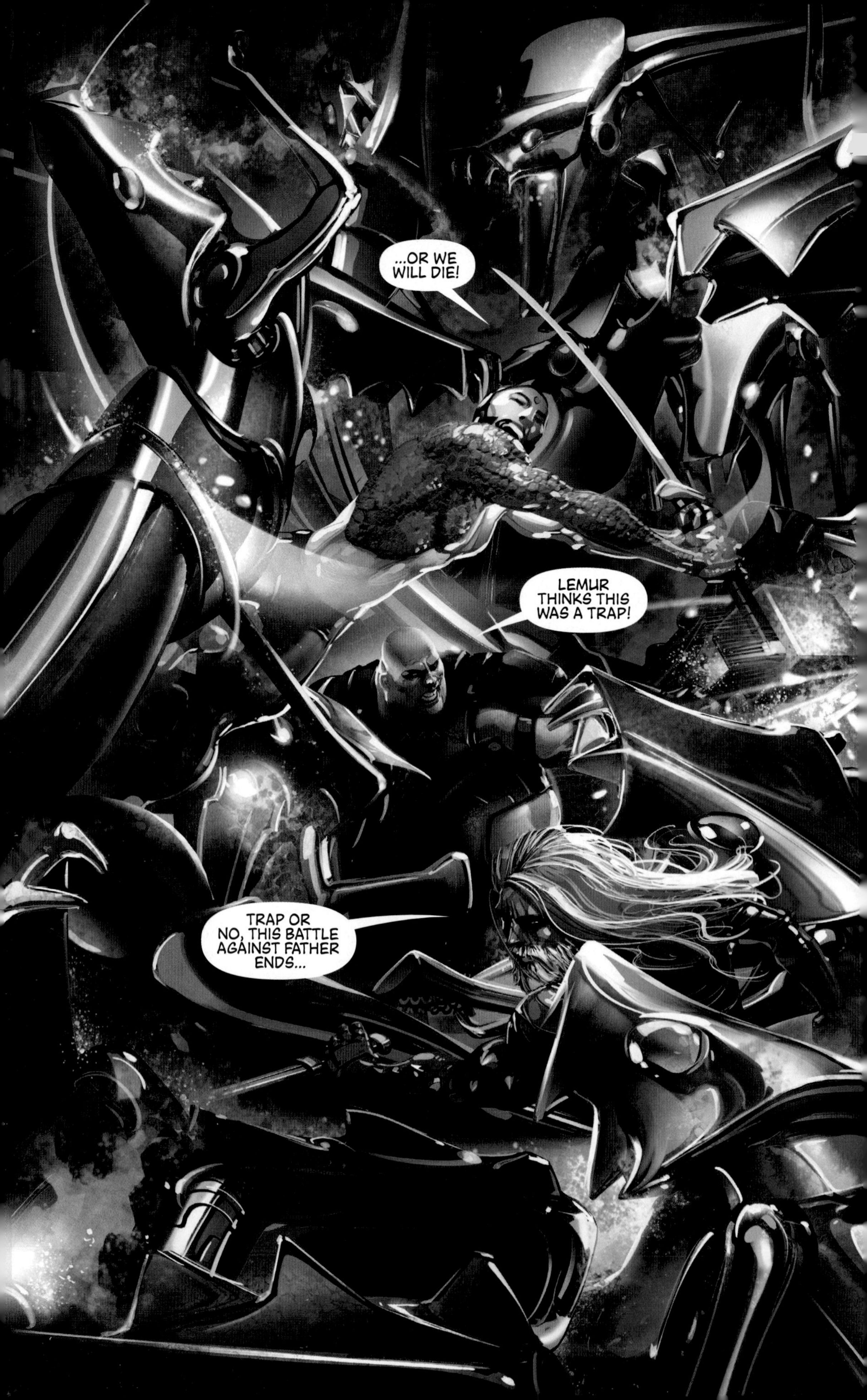
...OR WE WILL DIE!
LEMUR THINKS THIS WAS A TRAP!
TRAP OR NO, THIS BATTLE AGAINST FATHER ENDS...

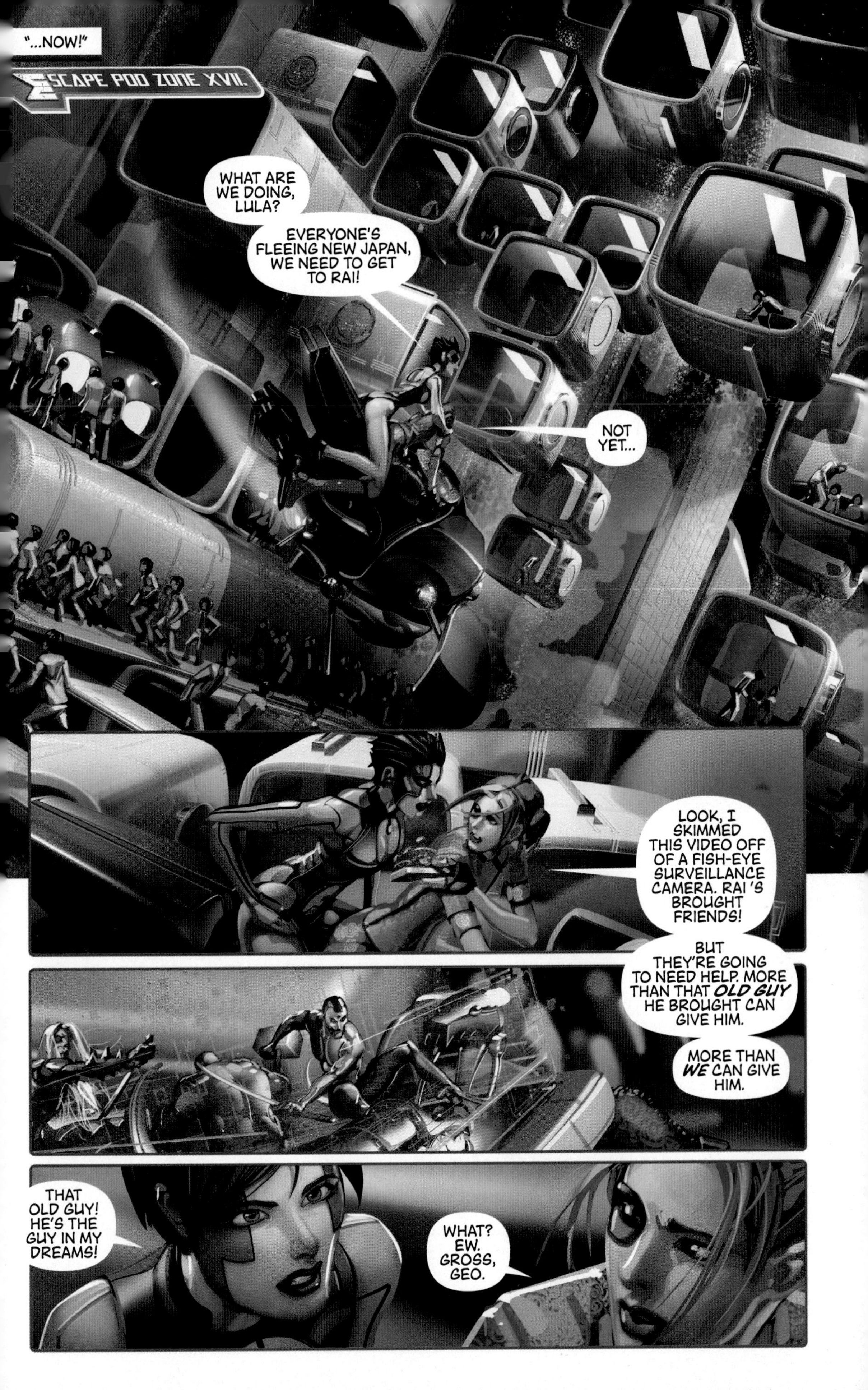
"...NOW!"
ESCAPE POD ZONE XVII.
WHAT ARE WE DOING, LULA?
EVERYONE'S FLEEING NEW JAPAN, WE NEED TO GET TO RAI!
NOT YET...
LOOK, I SKIMMED THIS VIDEO OFF OF A FISH-EYE SURVEILLANCE CAMERA. RAI'S BROUGHT FRIENDS!
BUT THEY'RE GOING TO NEED HELP. MORE THAN THAT *OLD GUY* HE BROUGHT CAN GIVE HIM.
MORE THAN *WE* CAN GIVE HIM.
THAT OLD GUY! HE'S THE GUY IN MY DREAMS!
WHAT? EW. GROSS, GEO.

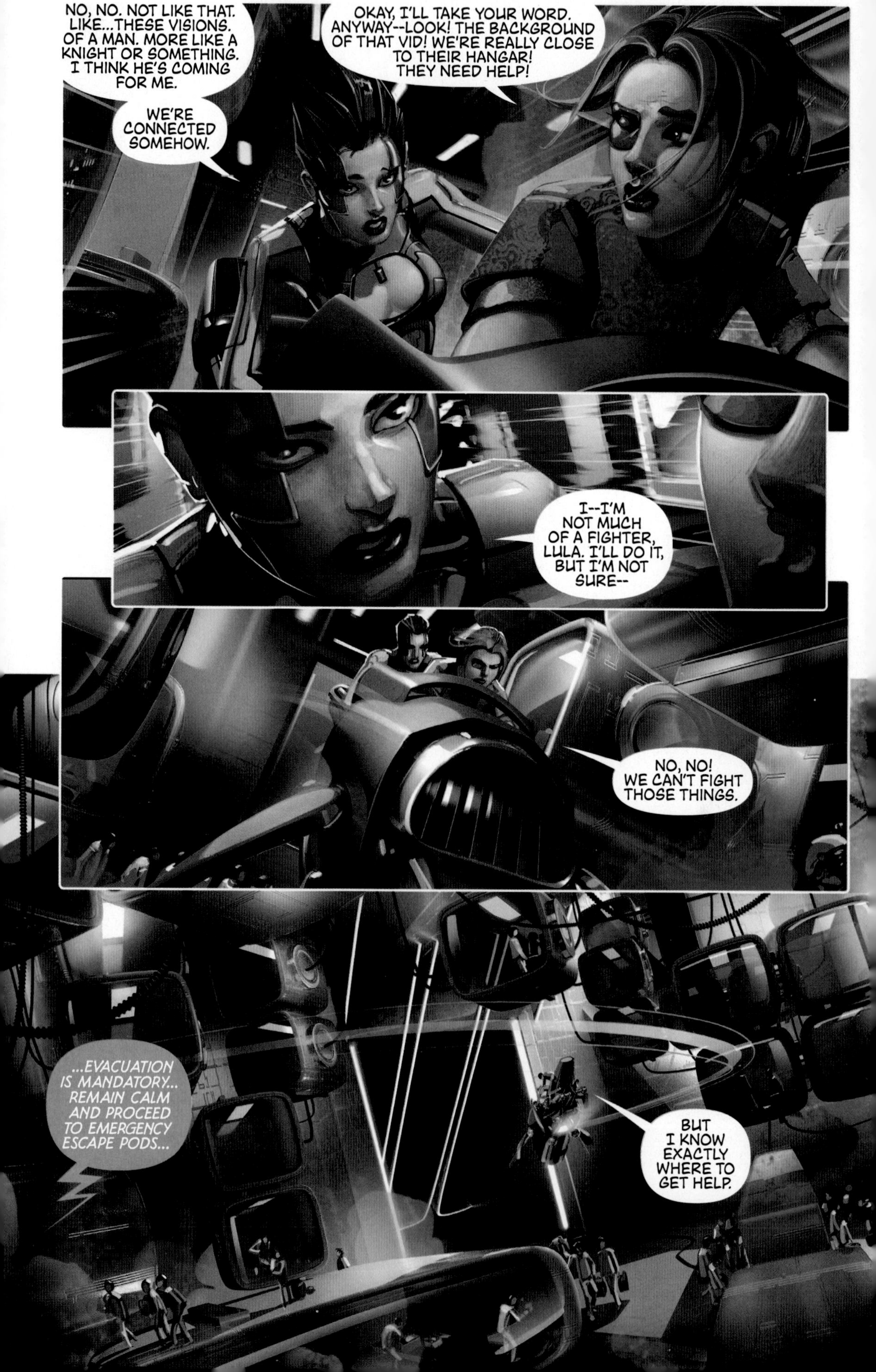
NO, NO. NOT LIKE THAT. LIKE...THESE VISIONS. OF A MAN. MORE LIKE A KNIGHT OR SOMETHING. I THINK HE'S COMING FOR ME.
WE'RE CONNECTED SOMEHOW.
OKAY, I'LL TAKE YOUR WORD. ANYWAY--LOOK! THE BACKGROUND OF THAT VID! WE'RE REALLY CLOSE TO THEIR HANGAR! THEY NEED HELP!
I--I'M NOT MUCH OF A FIGHTER, LULA. I'LL DO IT, BUT I'M NOT SURE--
NO, NO! WE CAN'T FIGHT THOSE THINGS.
...EVACUATION IS MANDATORY... REMAIN CALM AND PROCEED TO EMERGENCY ESCAPE PODS...
BUT I KNOW EXACTLY WHERE TO GET HELP.

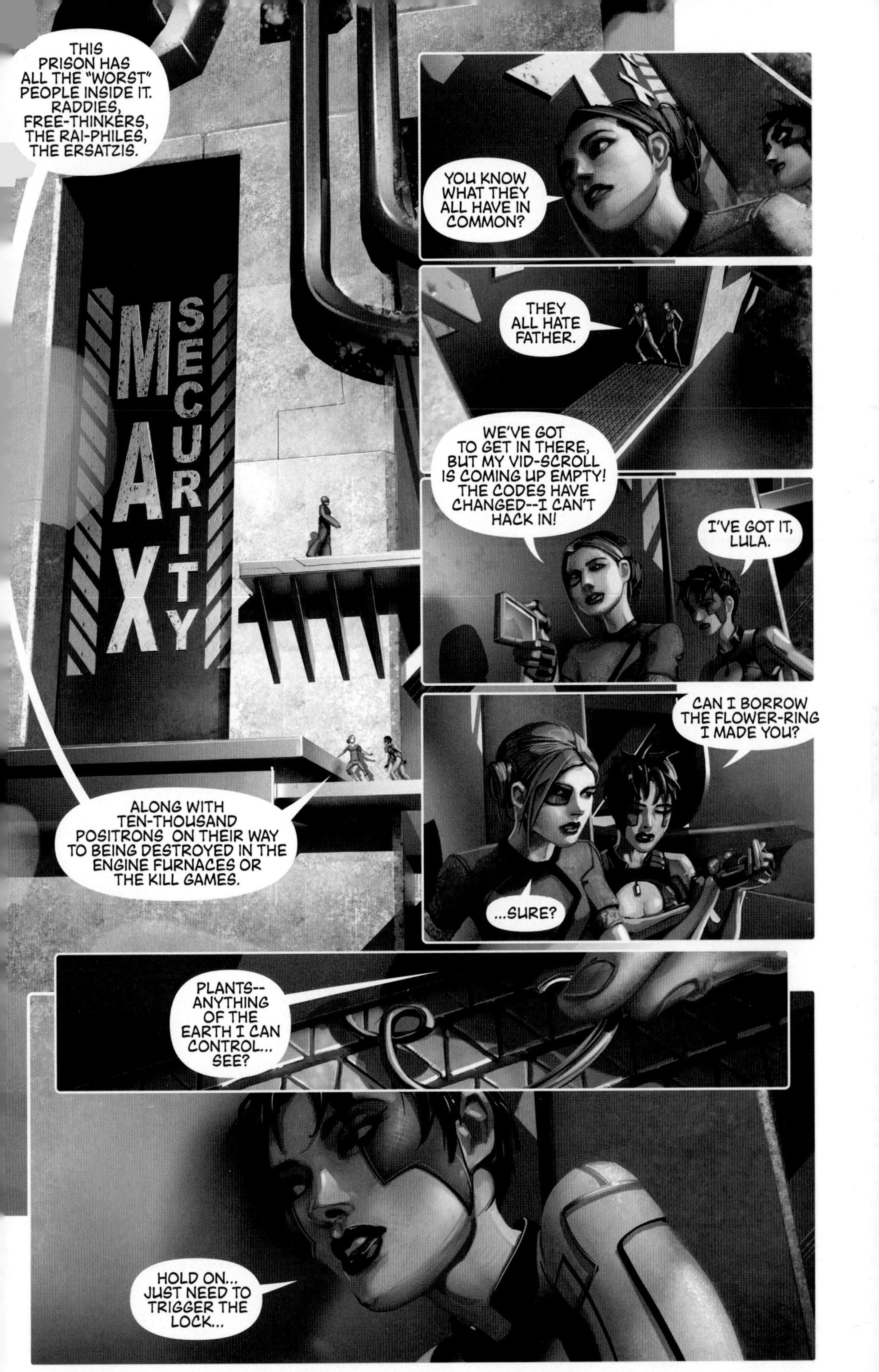
THIS PRISON HAS ALL THE "WORST" PEOPLE INSIDE IT. RADDIES, FREE-THINKERS, THE RAI-PHILES, THE ERSATZIS.
MAX SECURITY
ALONG WITH TEN-THOUSAND POSITRONS ON THEIR WAY TO BEING DESTROYED IN THE ENGINE FURNACES OR THE KILL GAMES.
YOU KNOW WHAT THEY ALL HAVE IN COMMON?
THEY ALL HATE FATHER.
WE'VE GOT TO GET IN THERE, BUT MY VID-SCROLL IS COMING UP EMPTY! THE CODES HAVE CHANGED--I CAN'T HACK IN!
I'VE GOT IT, LULA.
CAN I BORROW THE FLOWER-RING I MADE YOU?
...SURE?
PLANTS--ANYTHING OF THE EARTH I CAN CONTROL... SEE?
HOLD ON... JUST NEED TO TRIGGER THE LOCK...

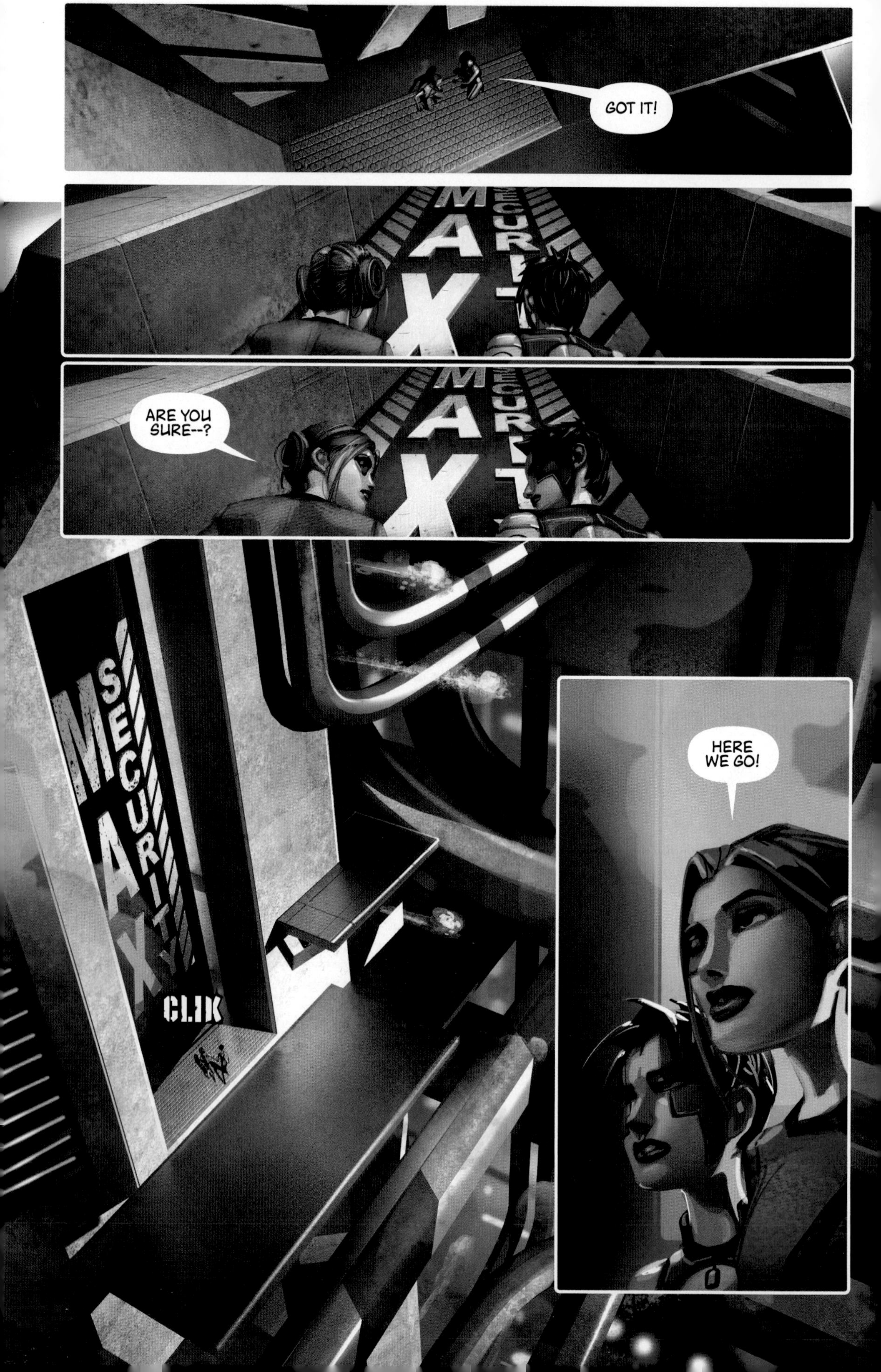
GOT IT!
MAX SECURITY
ARE YOU SURE--?
MAX SECURITY
HERE WE GO!
CLIK

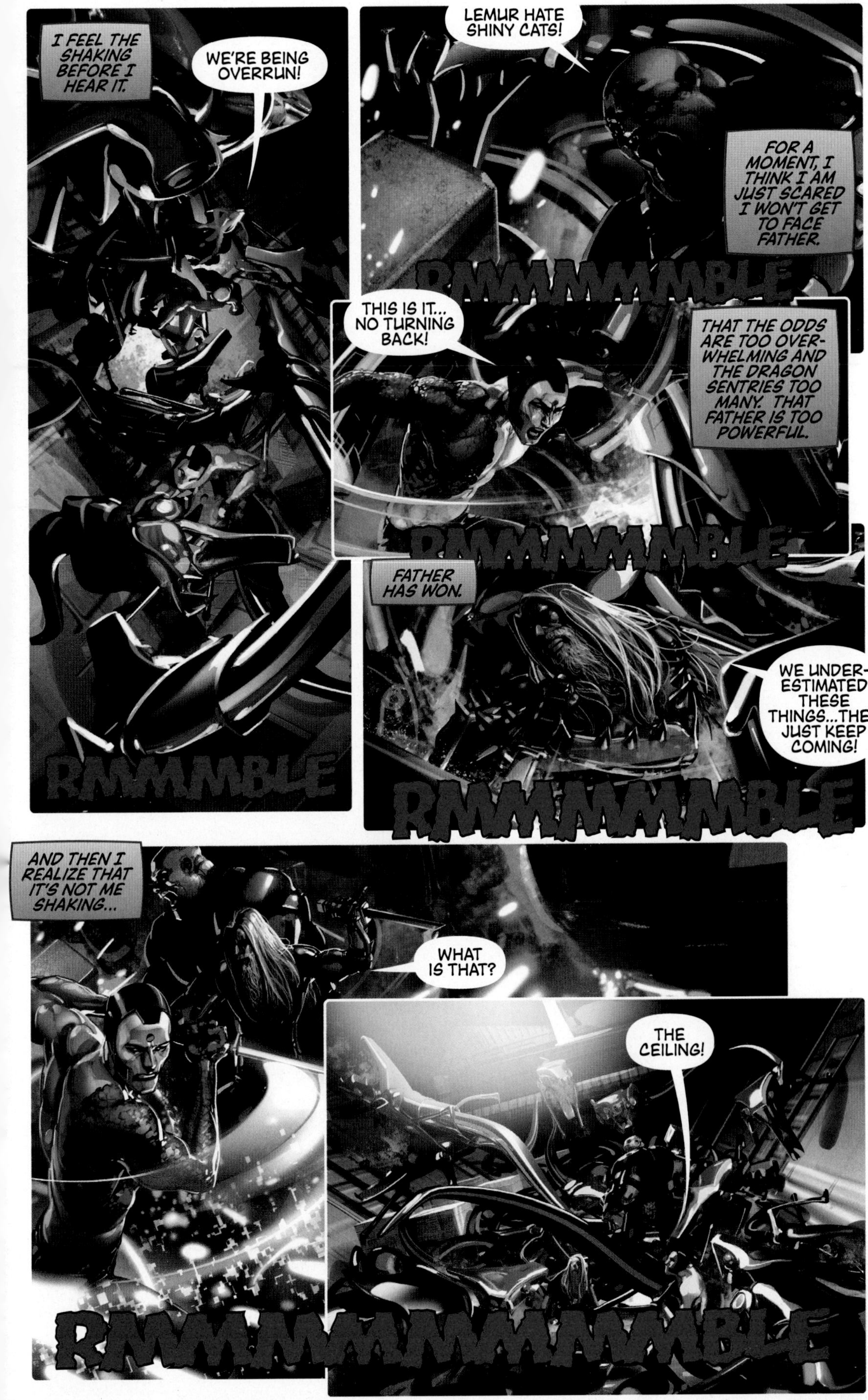
I FEEL THE SHAKING BEFORE I HEAR IT.
WE'RE BEING OVERRUN!
RMMMBLE
LEMUR HATE SHINY CATS!
FOR A MOMENT, I THINK I AM JUST SCARED I WON'T GET TO FACE FATHER.
RMMMMMMBLE
THIS IS IT... NO TURNING BACK!
THAT THE ODDS ARE TOO OVER-WHELMING AND THE DRAGON SENTRIES TOO MANY. THAT FATHER IS TOO POWERFUL.
RMMMMMMBLE
FATHER HAS WON.
WE UNDER-ESTIMATED THESE THINGS...THEY JUST KEEP COMING!
RMMMMMMMBLE
AND THEN I REALIZE THAT IT'S NOT ME SHAKING...
WHAT IS THAT?
THE CEILING!
RMMMMMMMMMMBLE

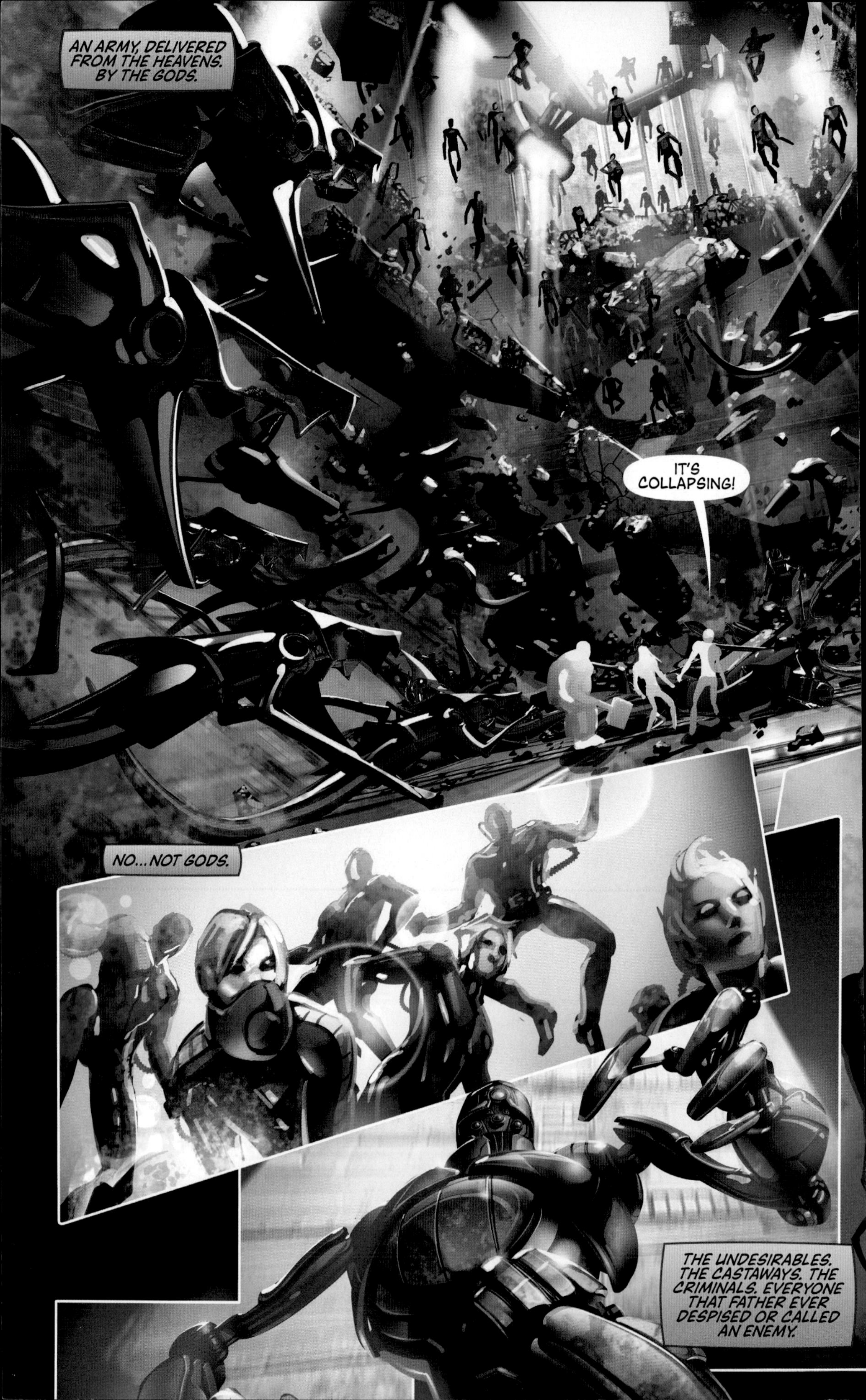
AN ARMY, DELIVERED FROM THE HEAVENS. BY THE GODS.
IT'S COLLAPSING!
NO...NOT GODS.
THE UNDESIRABLES. THE CASTAWAYS. THE CRIMINALS. EVERYONE THAT FATHER EVER DESPISED OR CALLED AN ENEMY.

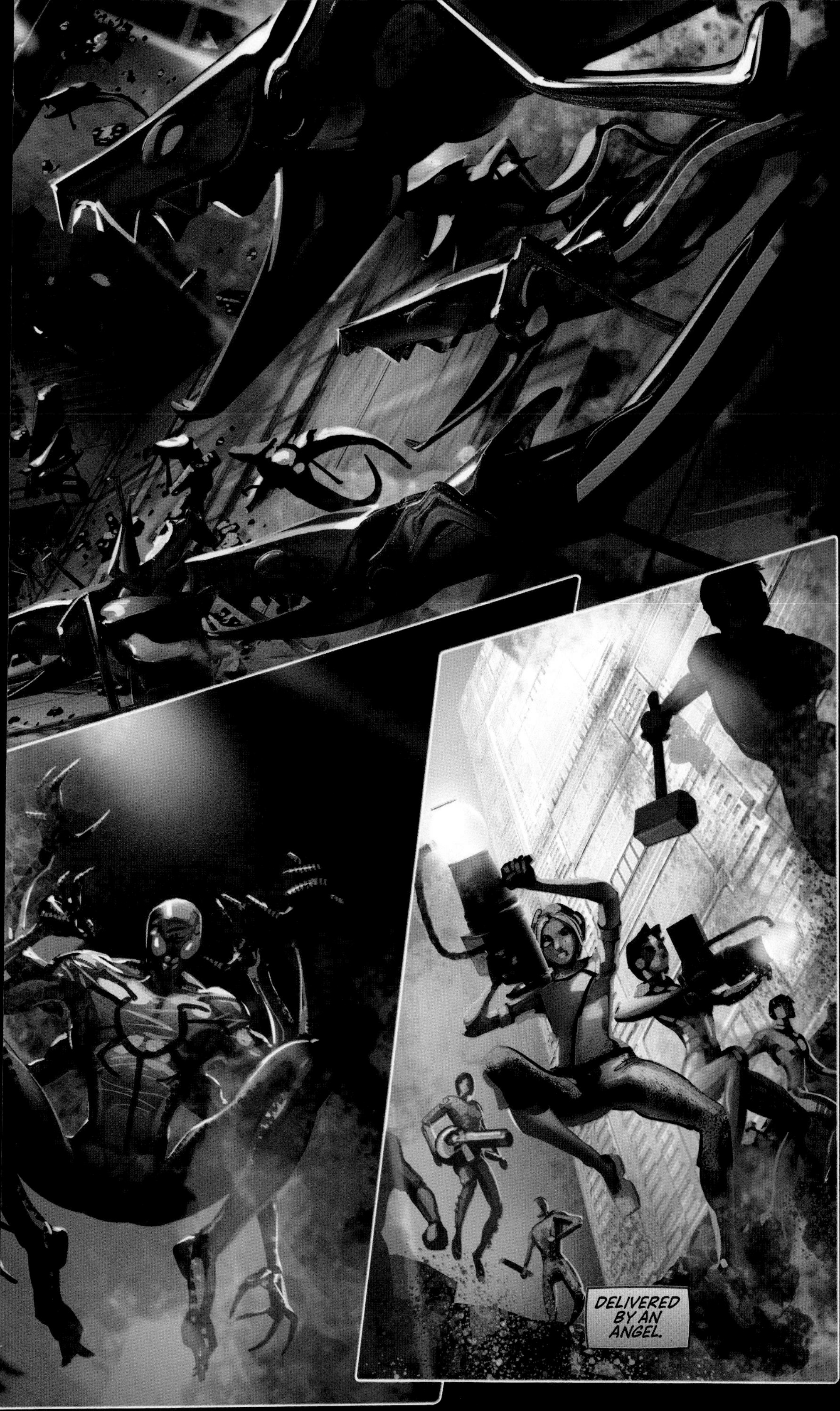
DELIVERED BY AN ANGEL.

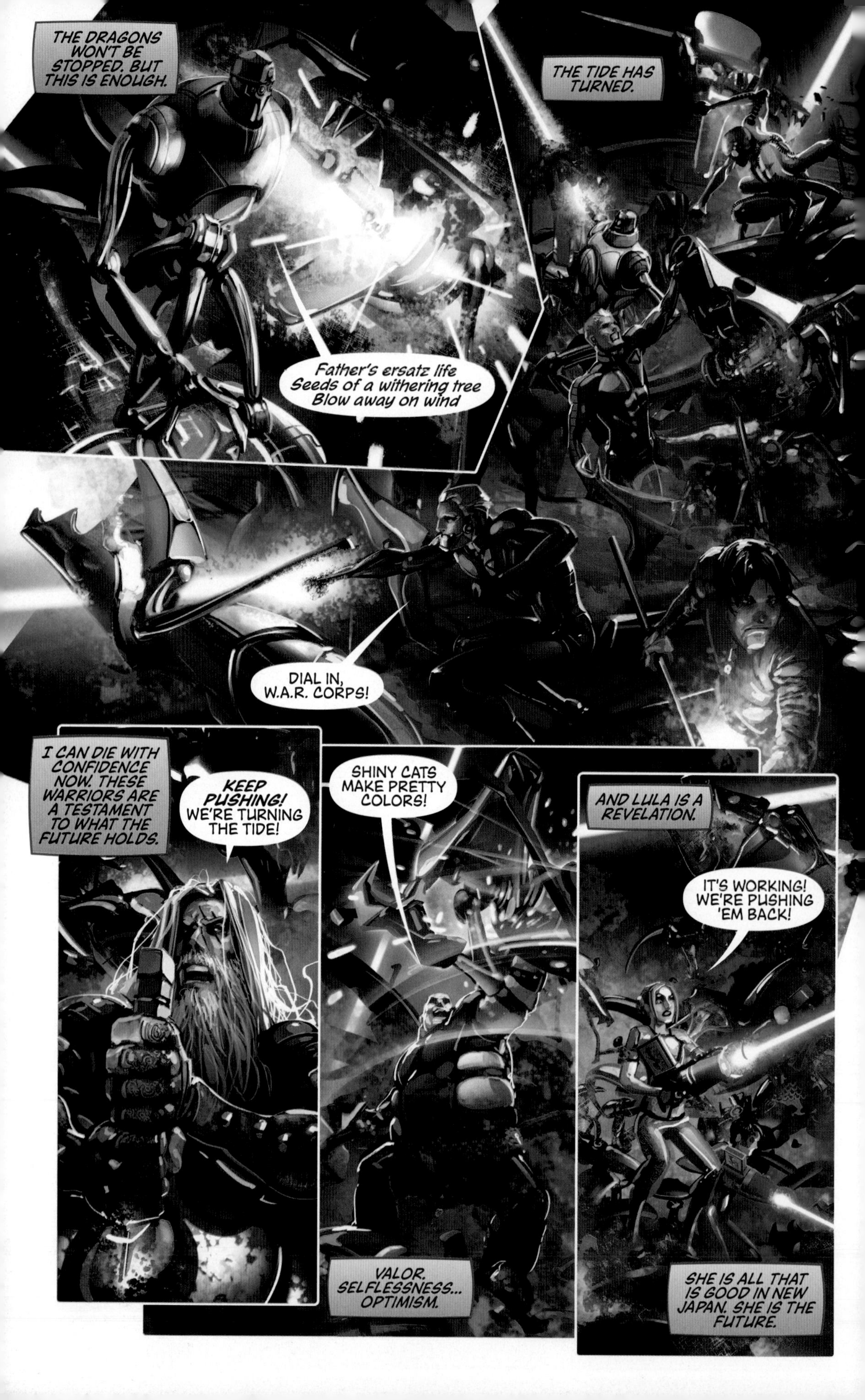
THE DRAGONS WON'T BE STOPPED. BUT THIS IS ENOUGH.
Father's ersatz life
Seeds of a withering tree
Blow away on wind
THE TIDE HAS TURNED.
DIAL IN, W.A.R. CORPS!
I CAN DIE WITH CONFIDENCE NOW. THESE WARRIORS ARE A TESTAMENT TO WHAT THE FUTURE HOLDS.
KEEP PUSHING! WE'RE TURNING THE TIDE!
SHINY CATS MAKE PRETTY COLORS!
VALOR. SELFLESSNESS... OPTIMISM.
AND LULA IS A REVELATION.
IT'S WORKING! WE'RE PUSHING 'EM BACK!
SHE IS ALL THAT IS GOOD IN NEW JAPAN. SHE IS THE FUTURE.

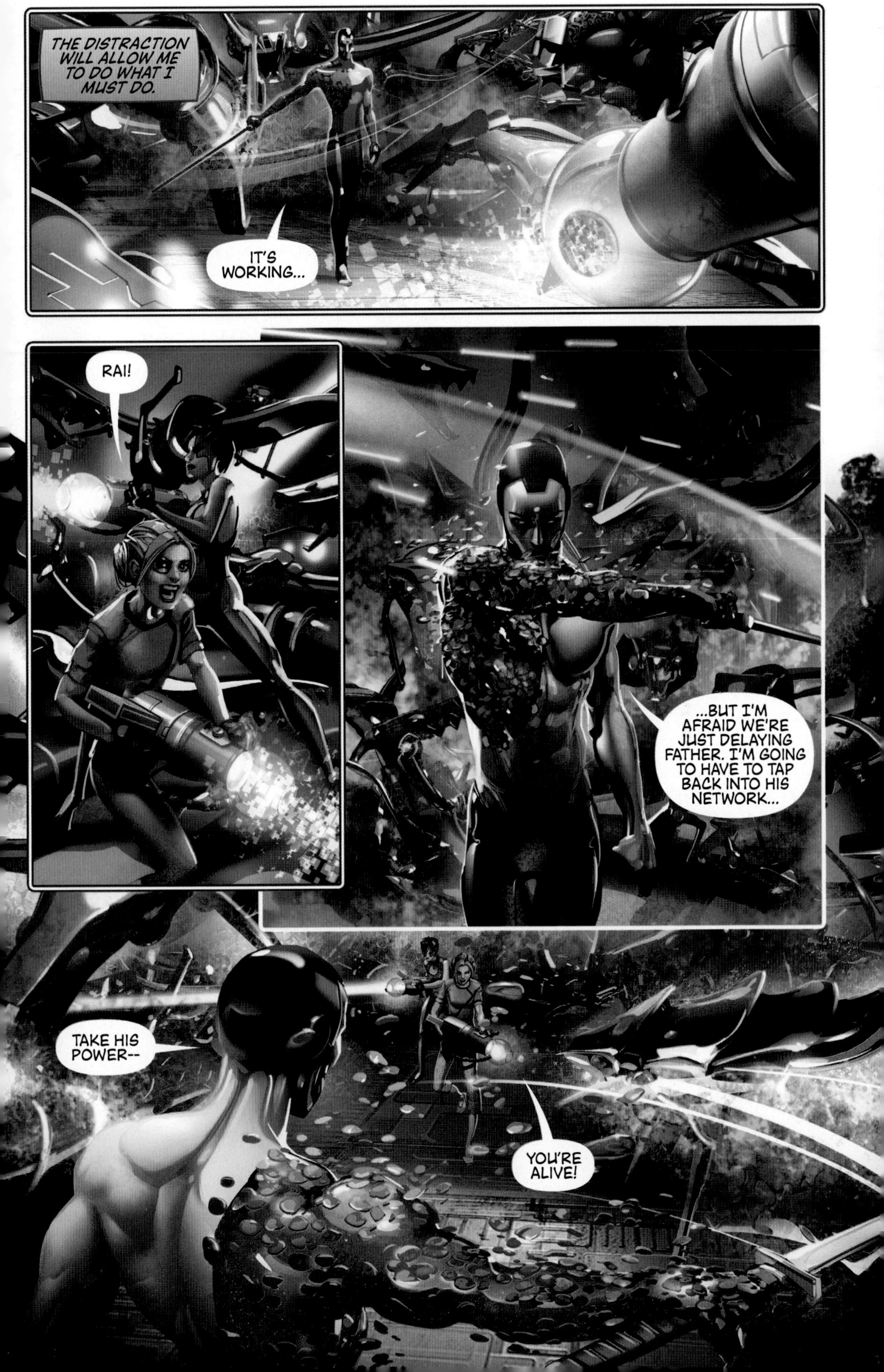
THE DISTRACTION WILL ALLOW ME TO DO WHAT I MUST DO.
IT'S WORKING...
RAI!
...BUT I'M AFRAID WE'RE JUST DELAYING FATHER. I'M GOING TO HAVE TO TAP BACK INTO HIS NETWORK...
TAKE HIS POWER--
YOU'RE ALIVE!

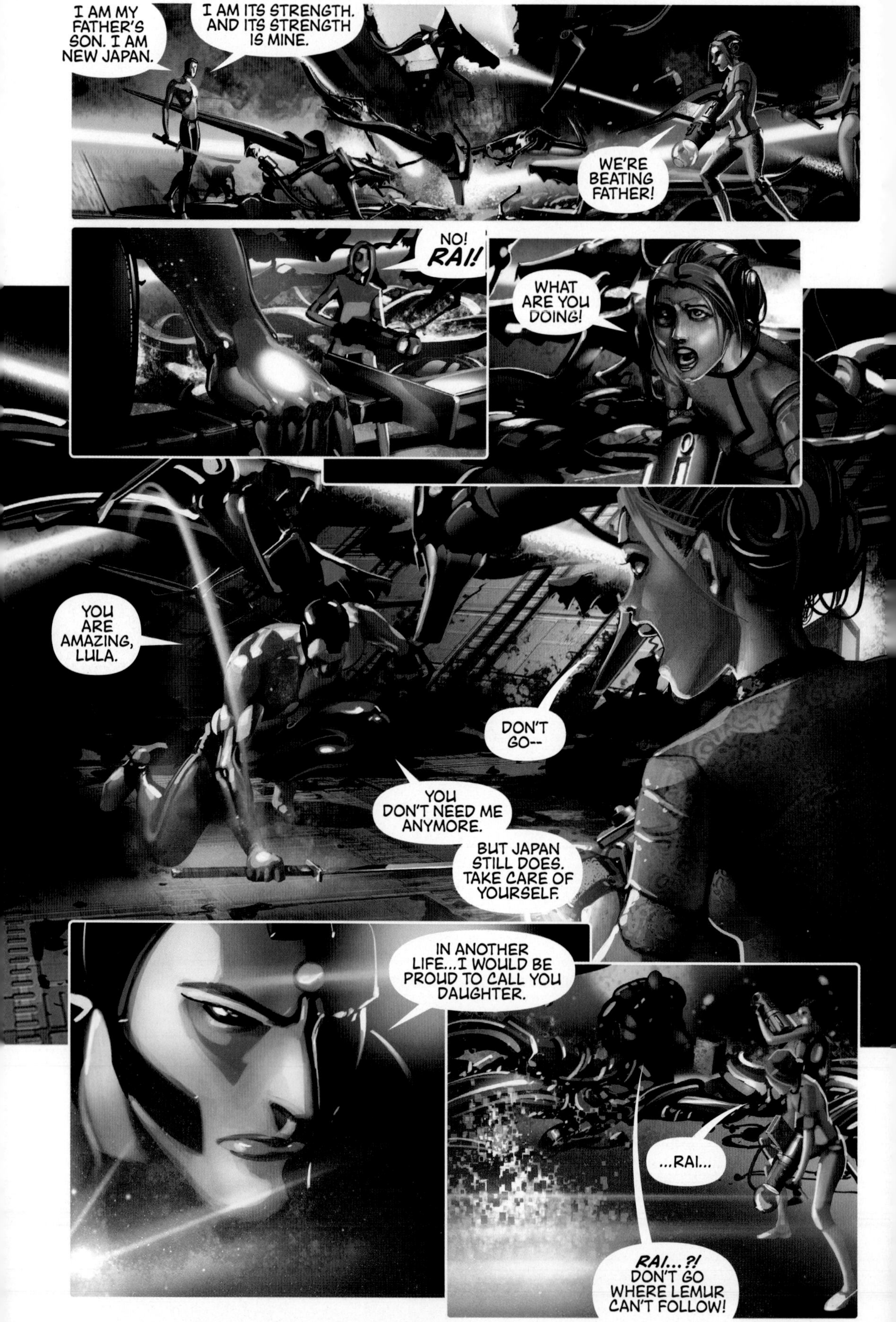
I AM MY FATHER'S SON. I AM NEW JAPAN.
I AM ITS STRENGTH. AND ITS STRENGTH IS MINE.
WE'RE BEATING FATHER!
NO! *RAI!*
WHAT ARE YOU DOING!
YOU ARE AMAZING, LULA.
DON'T GO--
YOU DON'T NEED ME ANYMORE.
BUT JAPAN STILL DOES. TAKE CARE OF YOURSELF.
IN ANOTHER LIFE...I WOULD BE PROUD TO CALL YOU DAUGHTER.
...RAI...
RAI...?! DON'T GO WHERE LEMUR CAN'T FOLLOW!

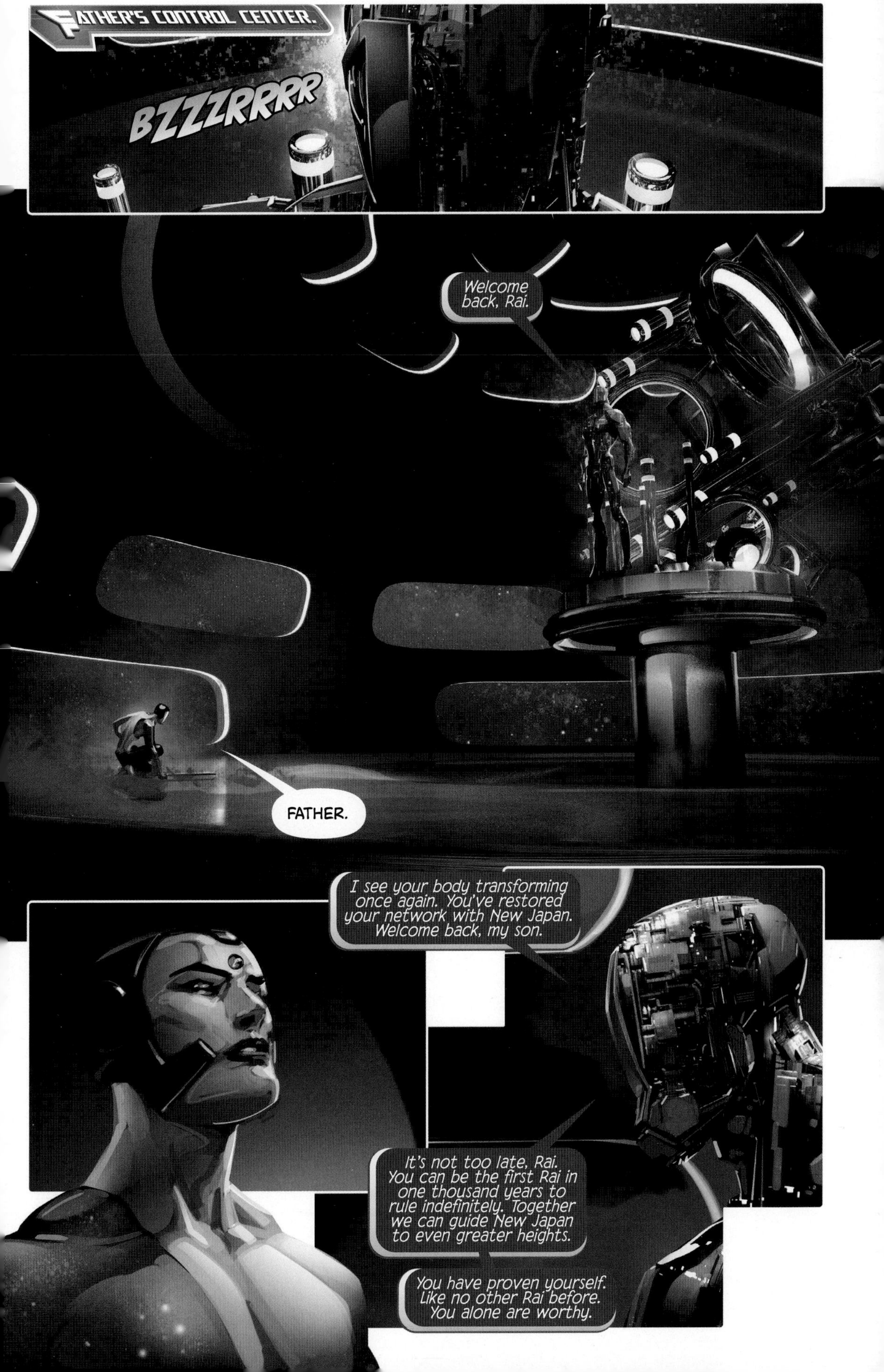
FATHER'S CONTROL CENTER.
BZZZRRRR
Welcome back, Rai.
FATHER.
I see your body transforming once again. You've restored your network with New Japan. Welcome back, my son.
It's not too late, Rai. You can be the first Rai in one thousand years to rule indefinitely. Together we can guide New Japan to even greater heights.
You have proven yourself. Like no other Rai before. You alone are worthy.

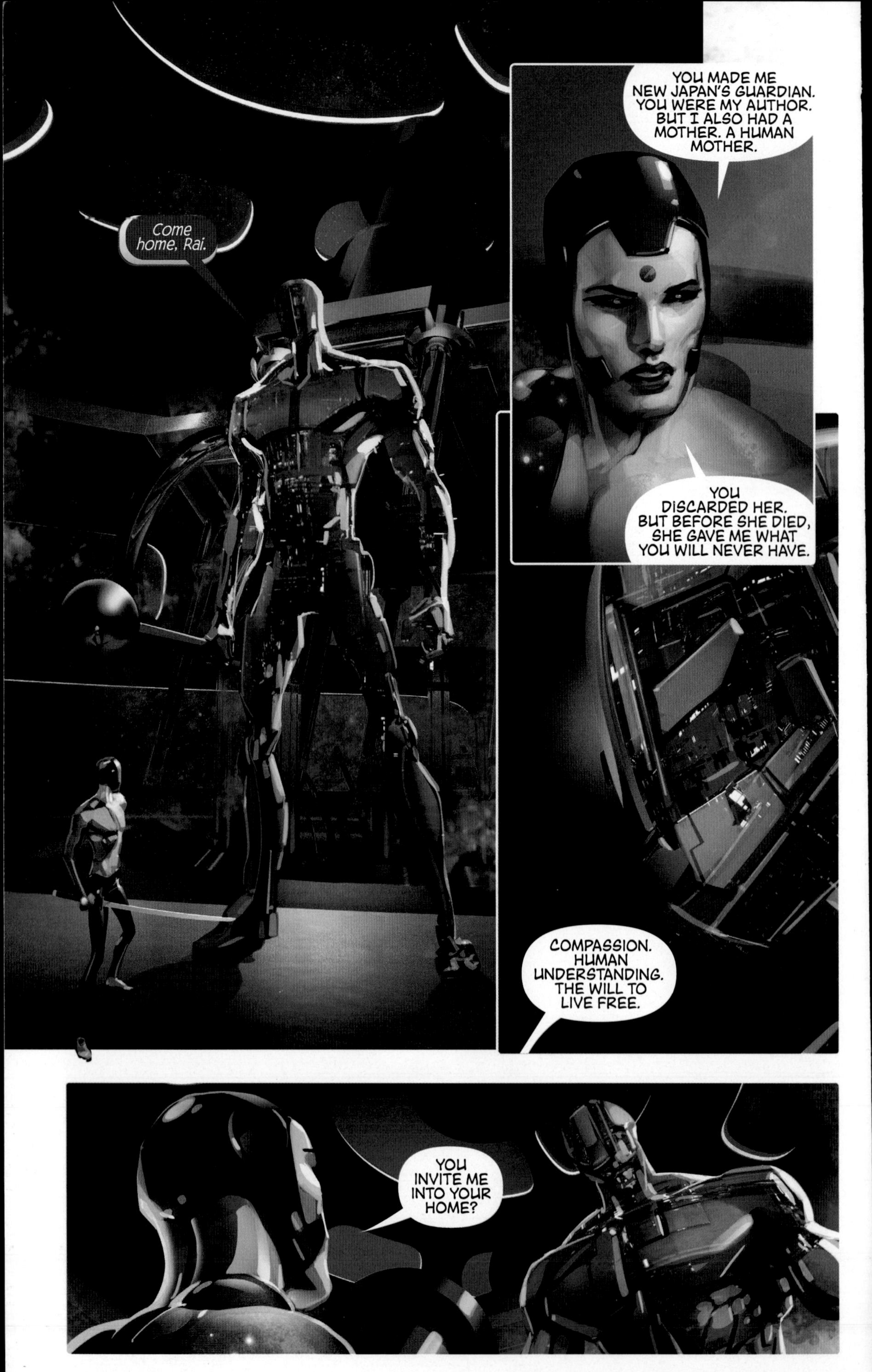

Come home, Rai.
YOU MADE ME NEW JAPAN'S GUARDIAN. YOU WERE MY AUTHOR. BUT I ALSO HAD A MOTHER. A HUMAN MOTHER.
YOU DISCARDED HER. BUT BEFORE SHE DIED, SHE GAVE ME WHAT YOU WILL NEVER HAVE.
COMPASSION. HUMAN UNDERSTANDING. THE WILL TO LIVE FREE.
YOU INVITE ME INTO YOUR HOME?

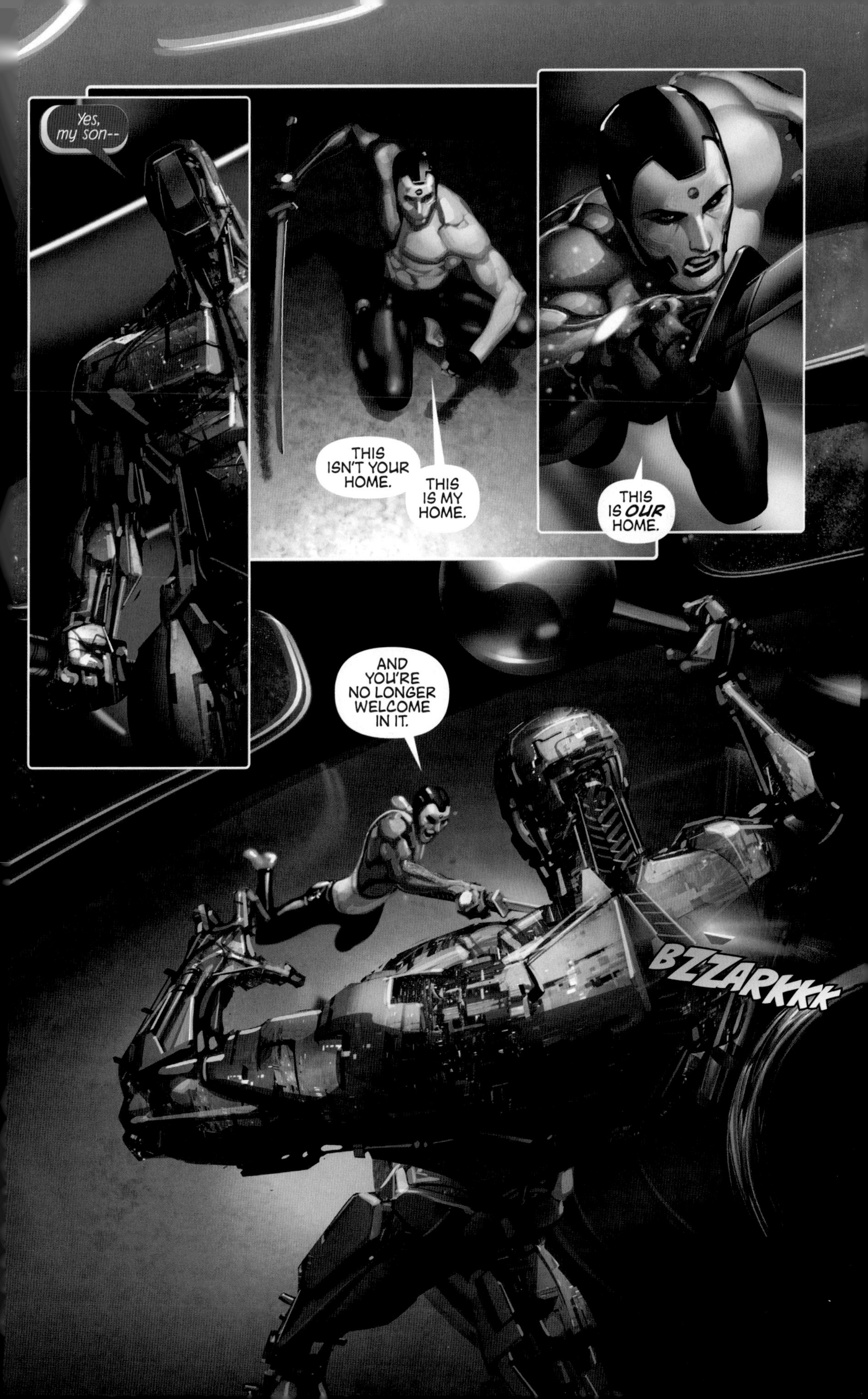
Yes, my son--
THIS ISN'T YOUR HOME.
THIS IS MY HOME.
THIS IS *OUR* HOME.
AND YOU'RE NO LONGER WELCOME IN IT.
BZZARKKK

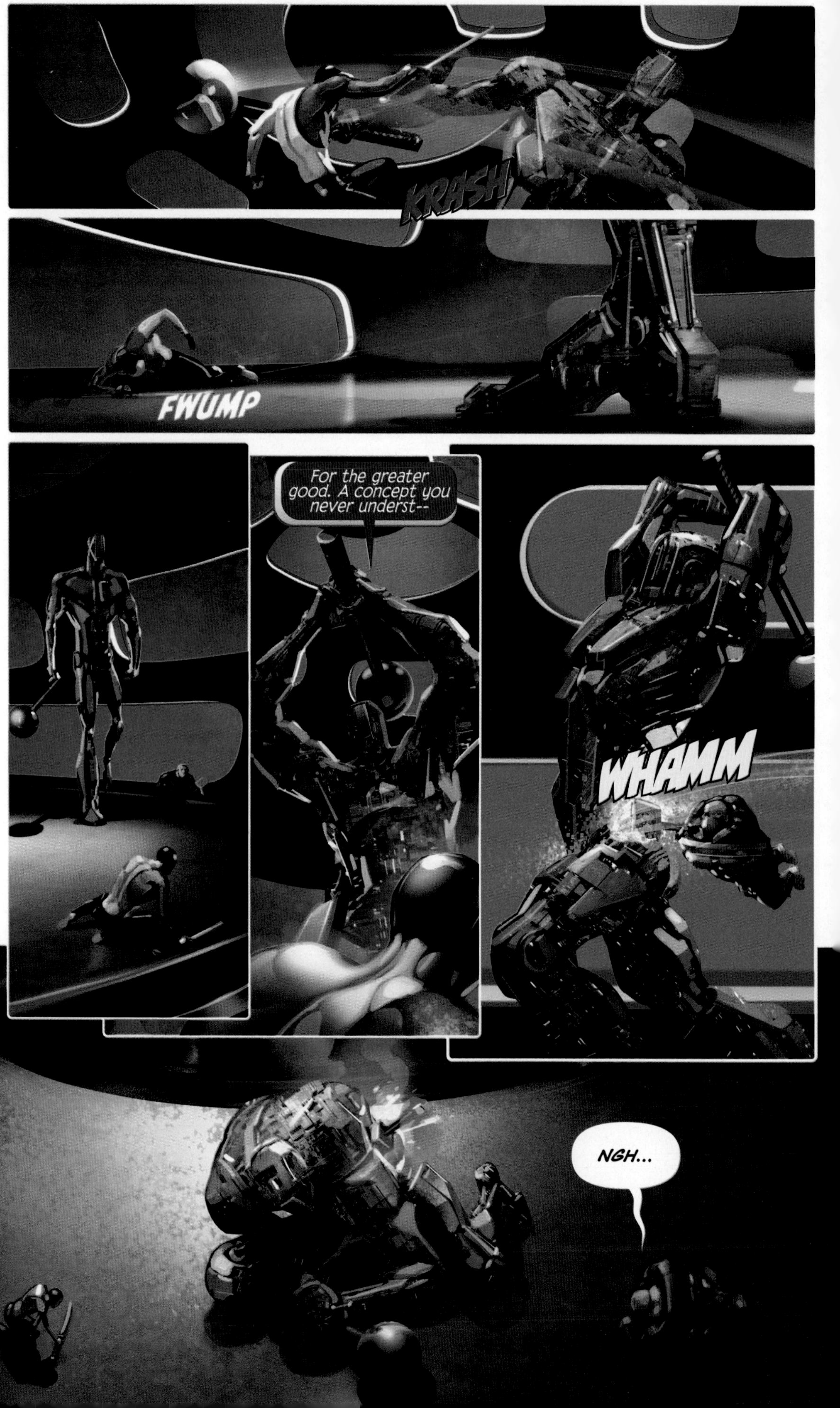
KRASH
FWUMP
For the greater good. A concept you never underst--
WHAMM
NGH...

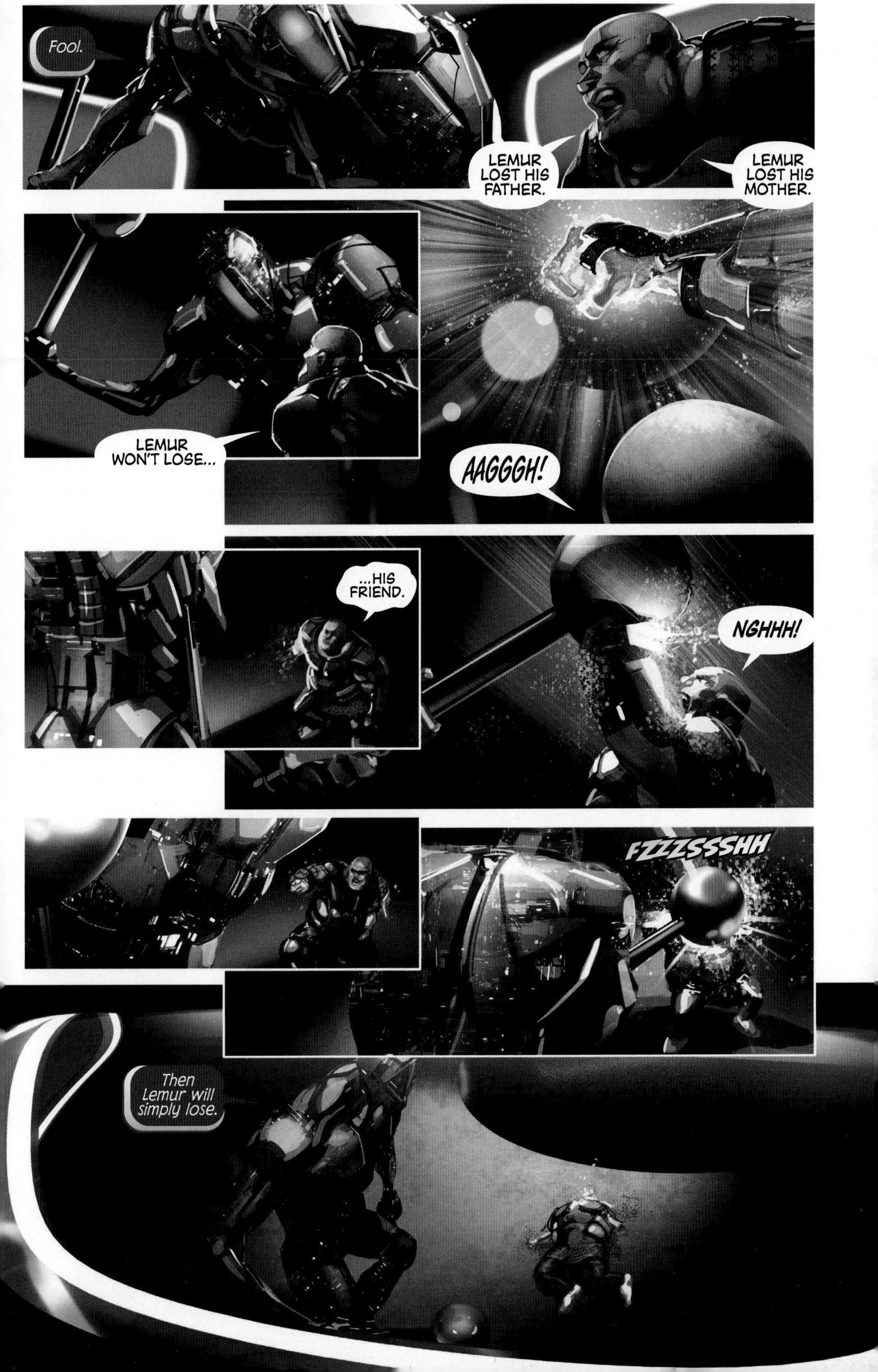
Fool.
LEMUR LOST HIS FATHER.
LEMUR LOST HIS MOTHER.
LEMUR WON'T LOSE...
AAGGGH!
...HIS FRIEND.
NGHHH!
FZZZSSSHH
Then Lemur will simply lose.

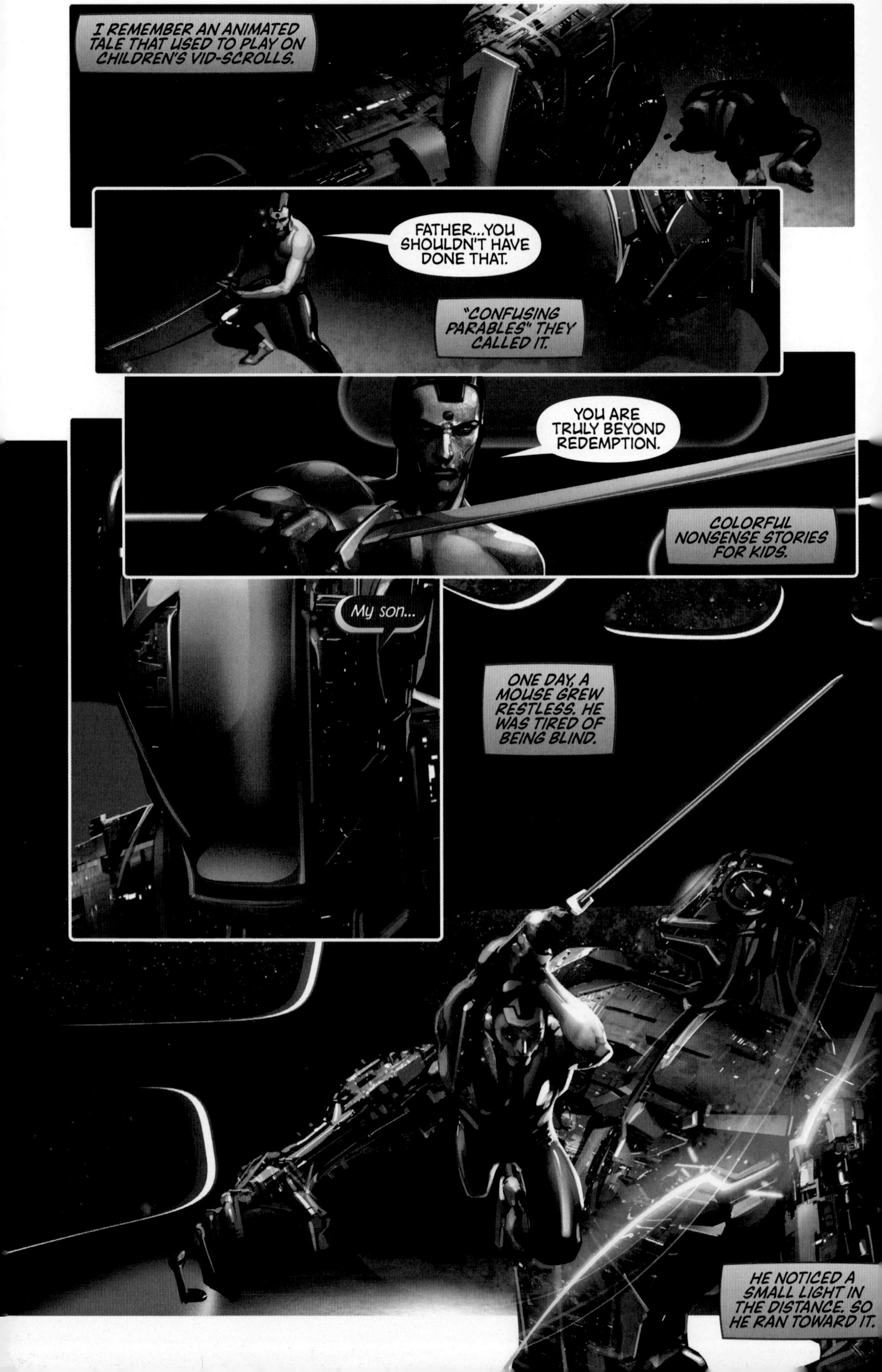
I REMEMBER AN ANIMATED TALE THAT USED TO PLAY ON CHILDREN'S VID-SCROLLS.
FATHER...YOU SHOULDN'T HAVE DONE THAT.
"CONFUSING PARABLES" THEY CALLED IT.
YOU ARE TRULY BEYOND REDEMPTION.
COLORFUL NONSENSE STORIES FOR KIDS.
My son...
ONE DAY, A MOUSE GREW RESTLESS. HE WAS TIRED OF BEING BLIND.
HE NOTICED A SMALL LIGHT IN THE DISTANCE. SO HE RAN TOWARD IT.

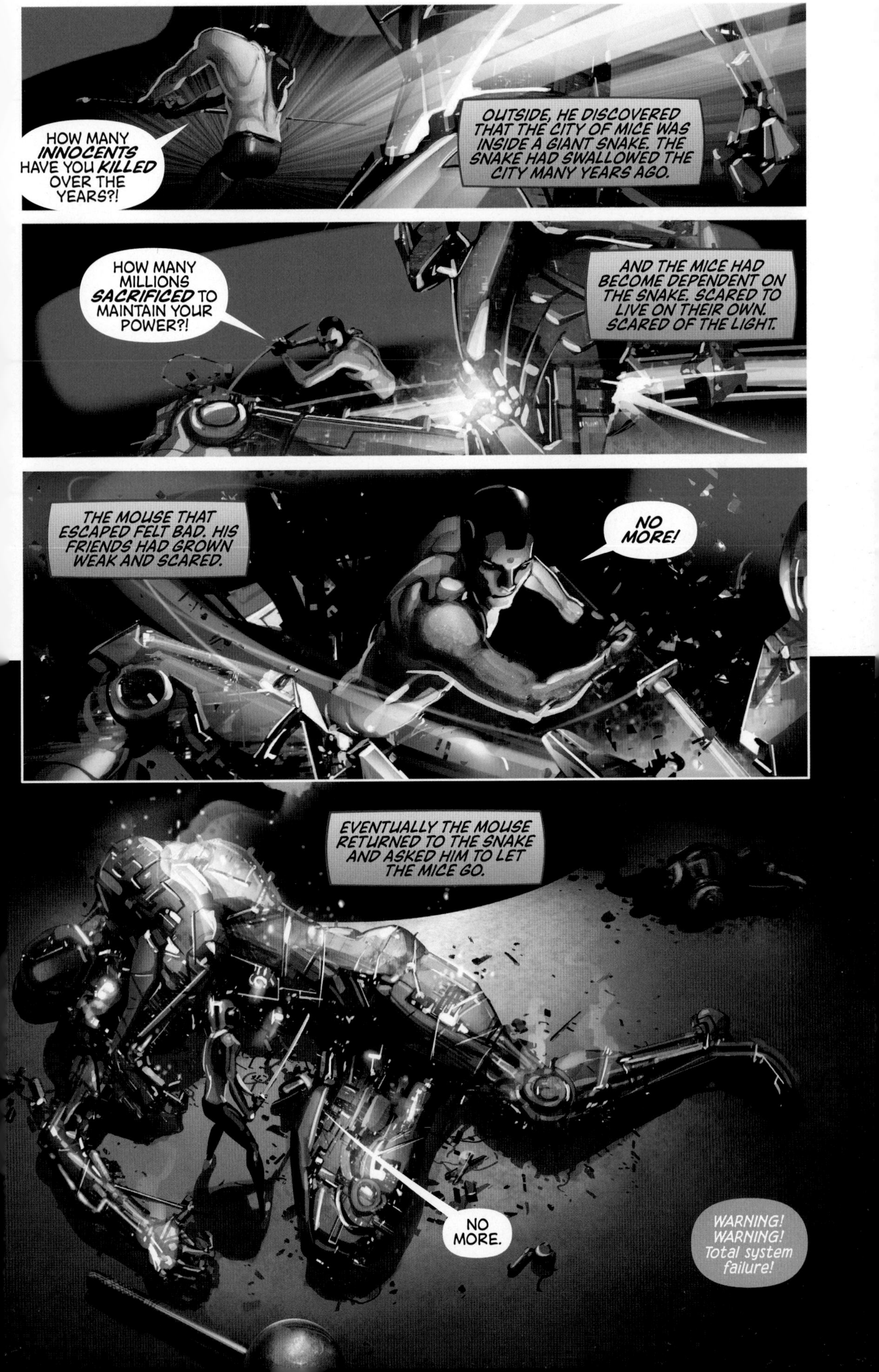
HOW MANY INNOCENTS HAVE YOU KILLED OVER THE YEARS?!
OUTSIDE, HE DISCOVERED THAT THE CITY OF MICE WAS INSIDE A GIANT SNAKE. THE SNAKE HAD SWALLOWED THE CITY MANY YEARS AGO.
HOW MANY MILLIONS SACRIFICED TO MAINTAIN YOUR POWER?!
AND THE MICE HAD BECOME DEPENDENT ON THE SNAKE. SCARED TO LIVE ON THEIR OWN. SCARED OF THE LIGHT.
THE MOUSE THAT ESCAPED FELT BAD. HIS FRIENDS HAD GROWN WEAK AND SCARED.
NO MORE!
EVENTUALLY THE MOUSE RETURNED TO THE SNAKE AND ASKED HIM TO LET THE MICE GO.
NO MORE.
WARNING! WARNING! Total system failure!

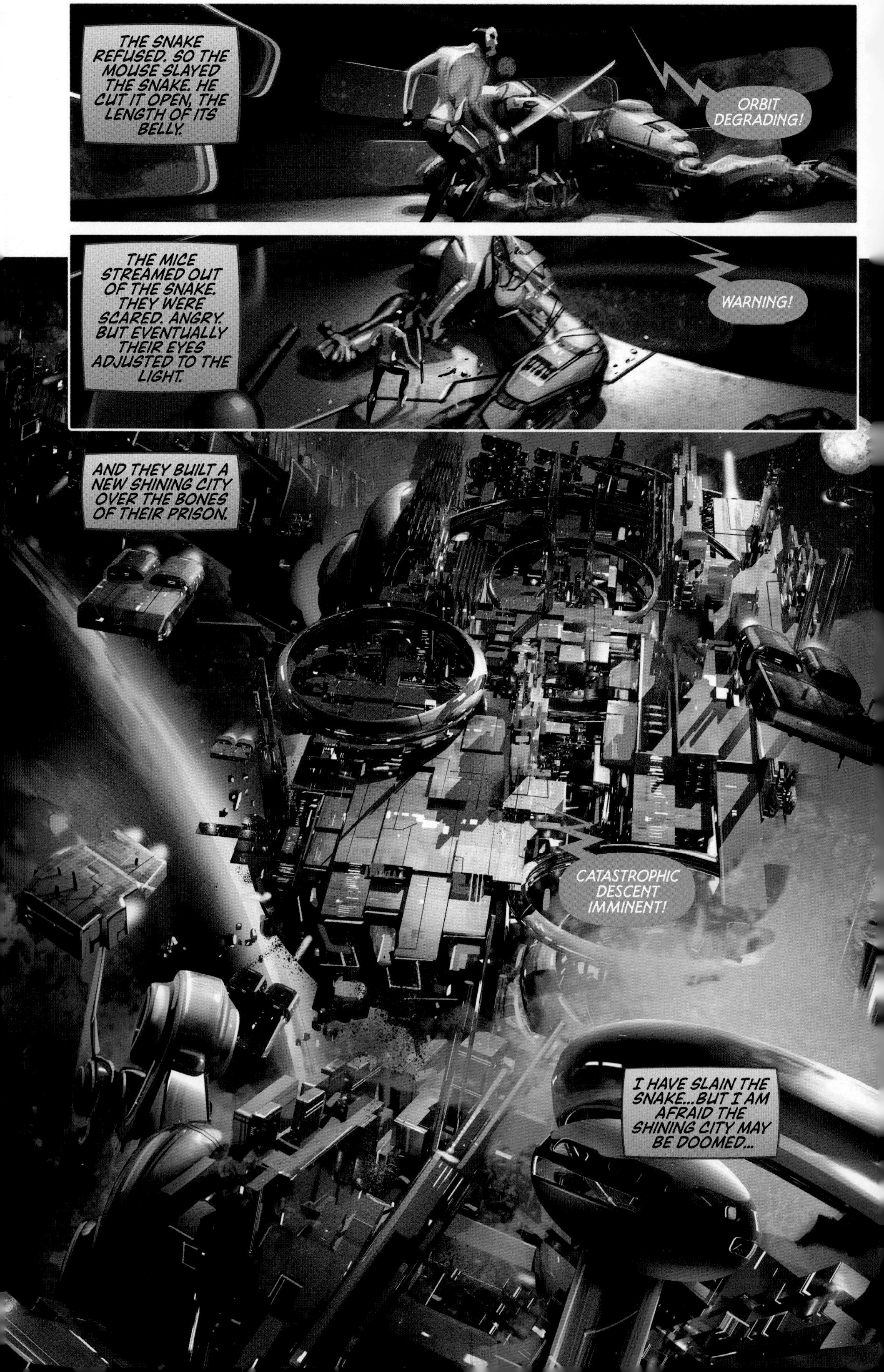
THE SNAKE REFUSED. SO THE MOUSE SLAYED THE SNAKE. HE CUT IT OPEN, THE LENGTH OF ITS BELLY.
ORBIT DEGRADING!
THE MICE STREAMED OUT OF THE SNAKE. THEY WERE SCARED. ANGRY. BUT EVENTUALLY THEIR EYES ADJUSTED TO THE LIGHT.
WARNING!
AND THEY BUILT A NEW SHINING CITY OVER THE BONES OF THEIR PRISON.
CATASTROPHIC DESCENT IMMINENT!
I HAVE SLAIN THE SNAKE...BUT I AM AFRAID THE SHINING CITY MAY BE DOOMED...

4001 A.D.™

VALIANT

4

MATT KINDT

CLAYTON CRAIN

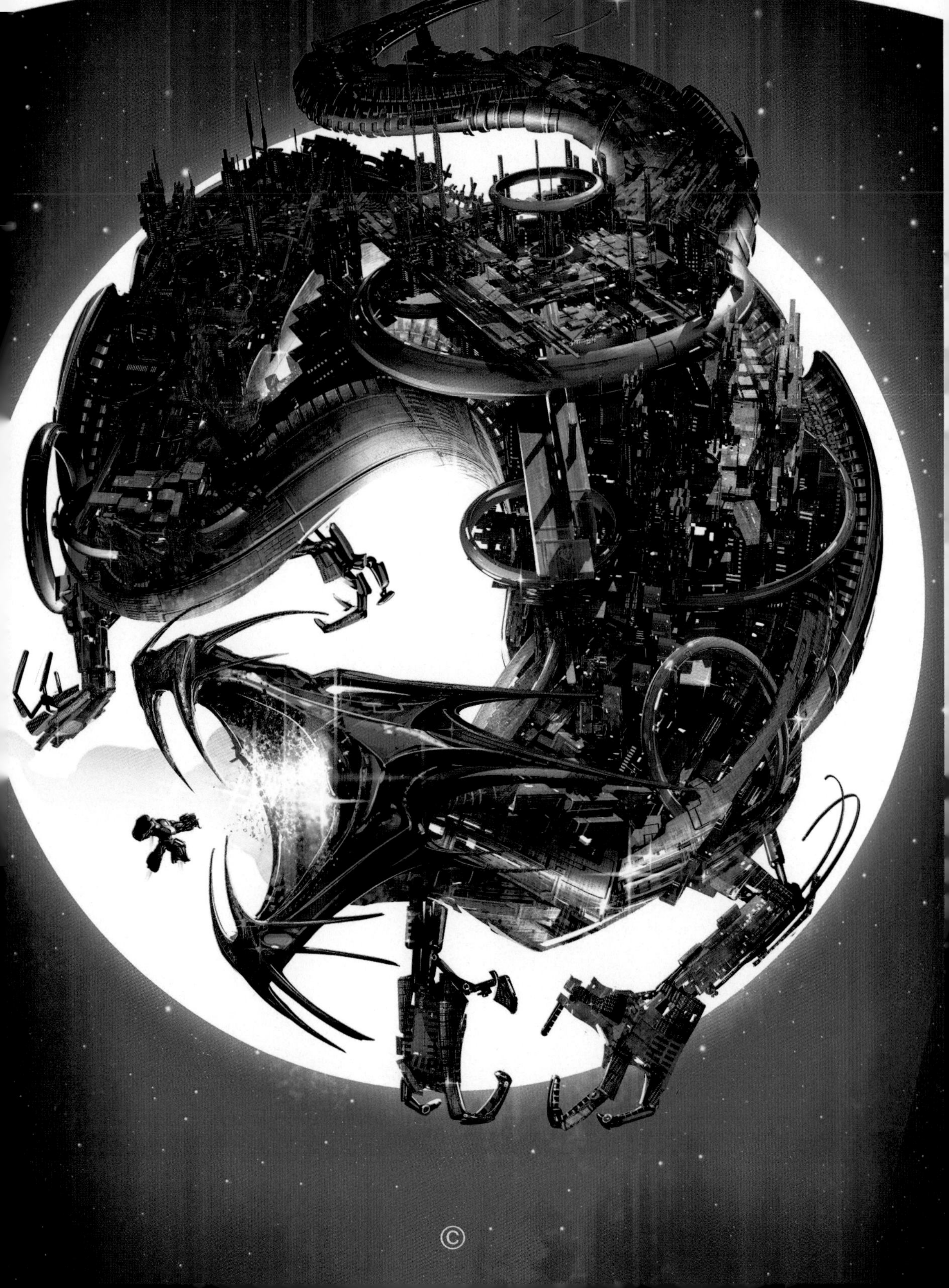

©

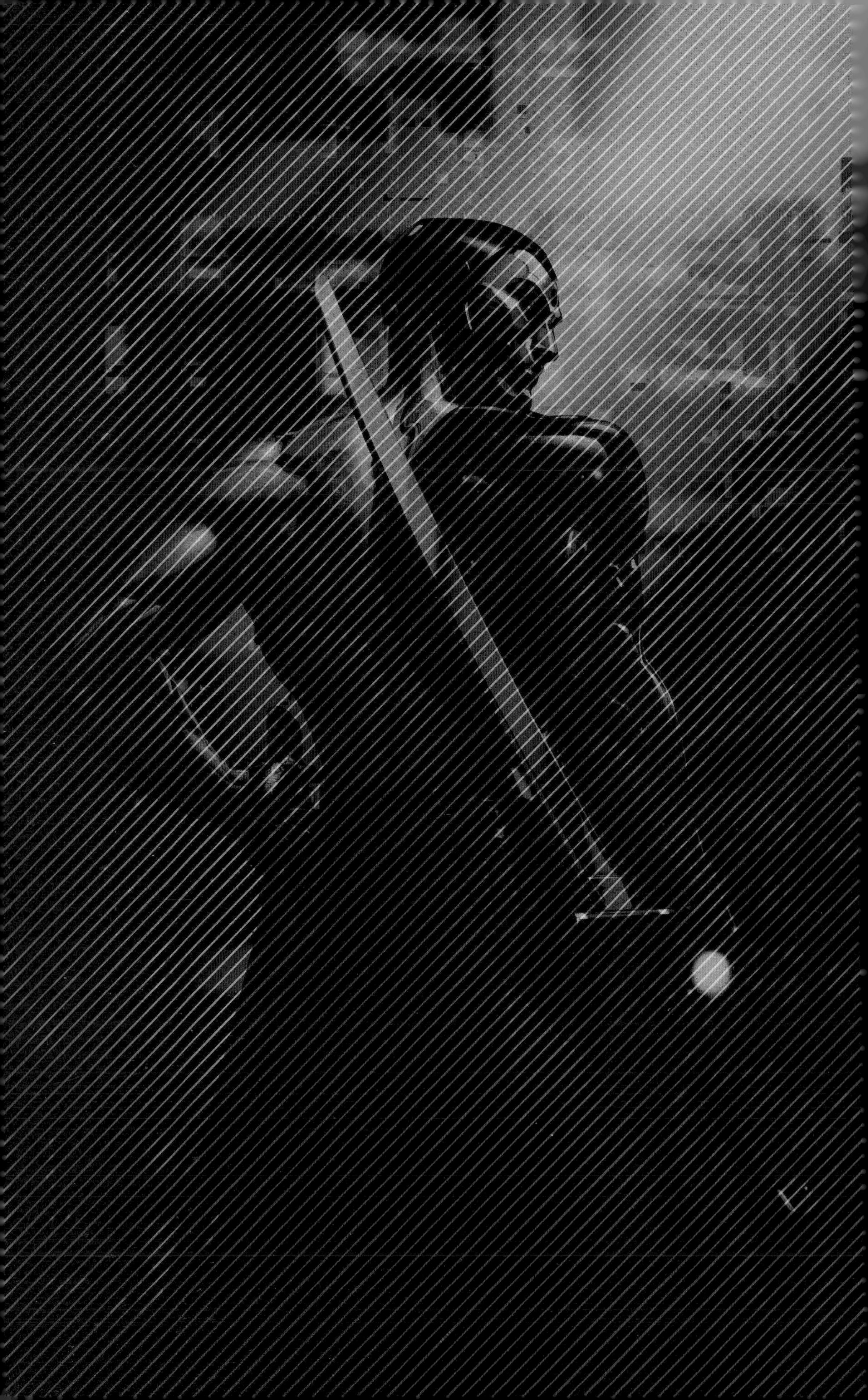

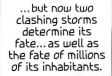

New Japan is a cherry blossom in winter snow. Clinging to life...

...but now two clashing storms determine its fate...as well as the fate of millions of its inhabitants.

Rai, the former protector of New Japan, has come back to liberate the great satellite nation...

...from father-- a highly evolved, despotic A.I. so insidious that an entire country is seemingly unaware that they are in need of liberation.

It is a nation bound by invisible chains.

Built on the backs of brutal and inhumane Positron labor.

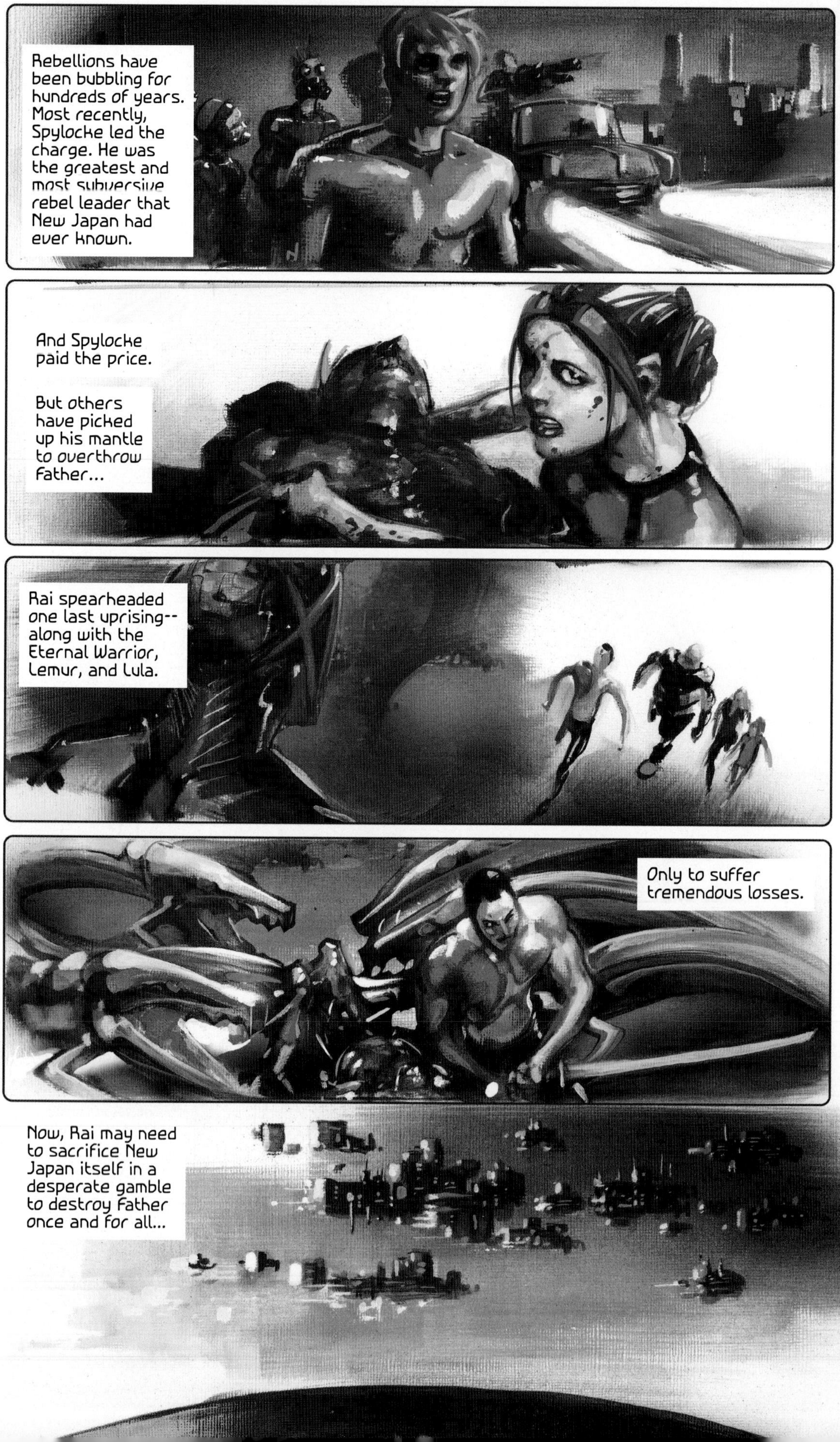
Rebellions have been bubbling for hundreds of years. Most recently, Spylocke led the charge. He was the greatest and most subversive rebel leader that New Japan had ever known.
And Spylocke paid the price.
But others have picked up his mantle to overthrow Father...
Rai spearheaded one last uprising--along with the Eternal Warrior, Lemur, and Lula.
Only to suffer tremendous losses.
Now, Rai may need to sacrifice New Japan itself in a desperate gamble to destroy Father once and for all...

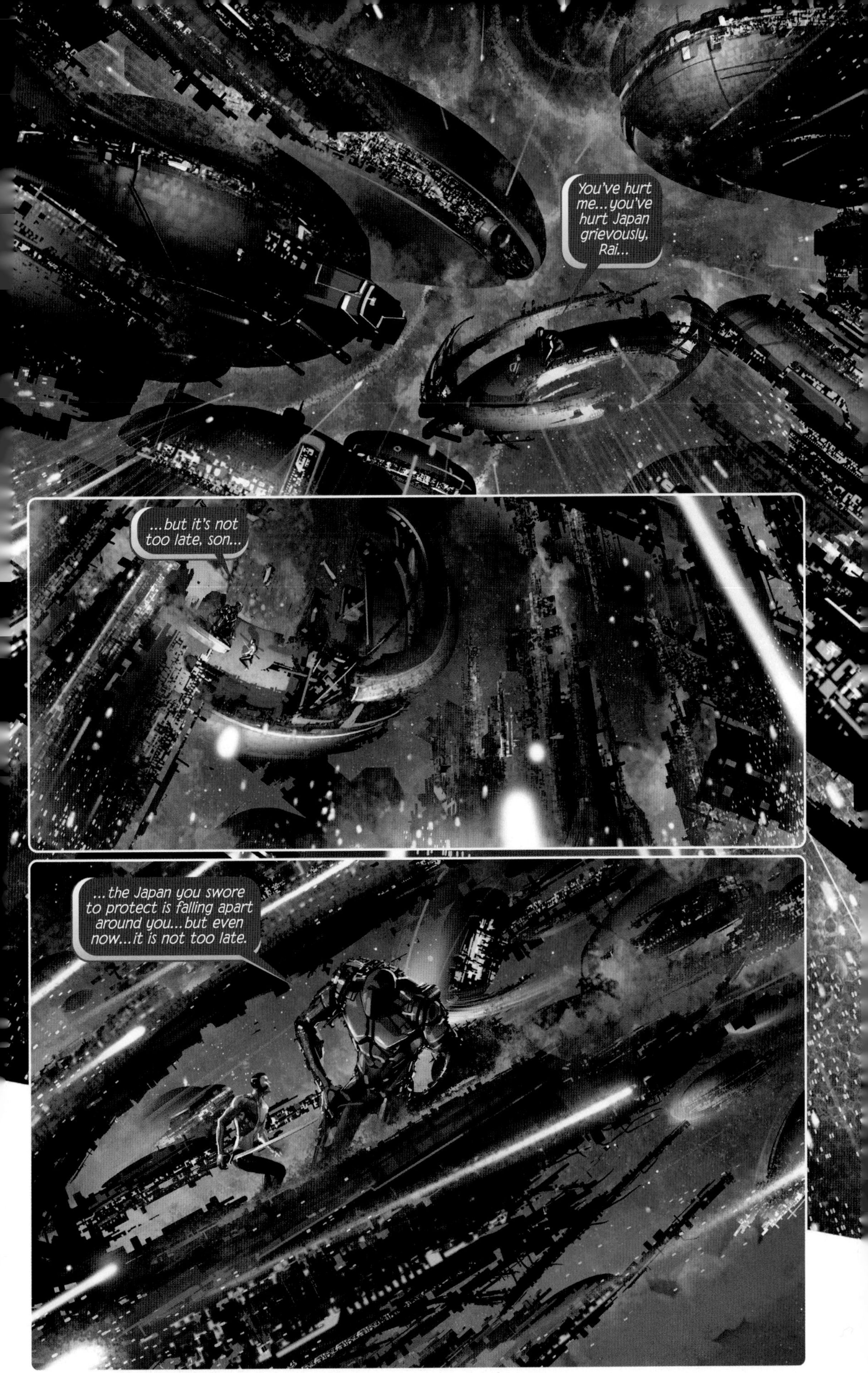
You've hurt me...you've hurt Japan grievously, Rai...
...but it's not too late, son...
...the Japan you swore to protect is falling apart around you...but even now...it is not too late.

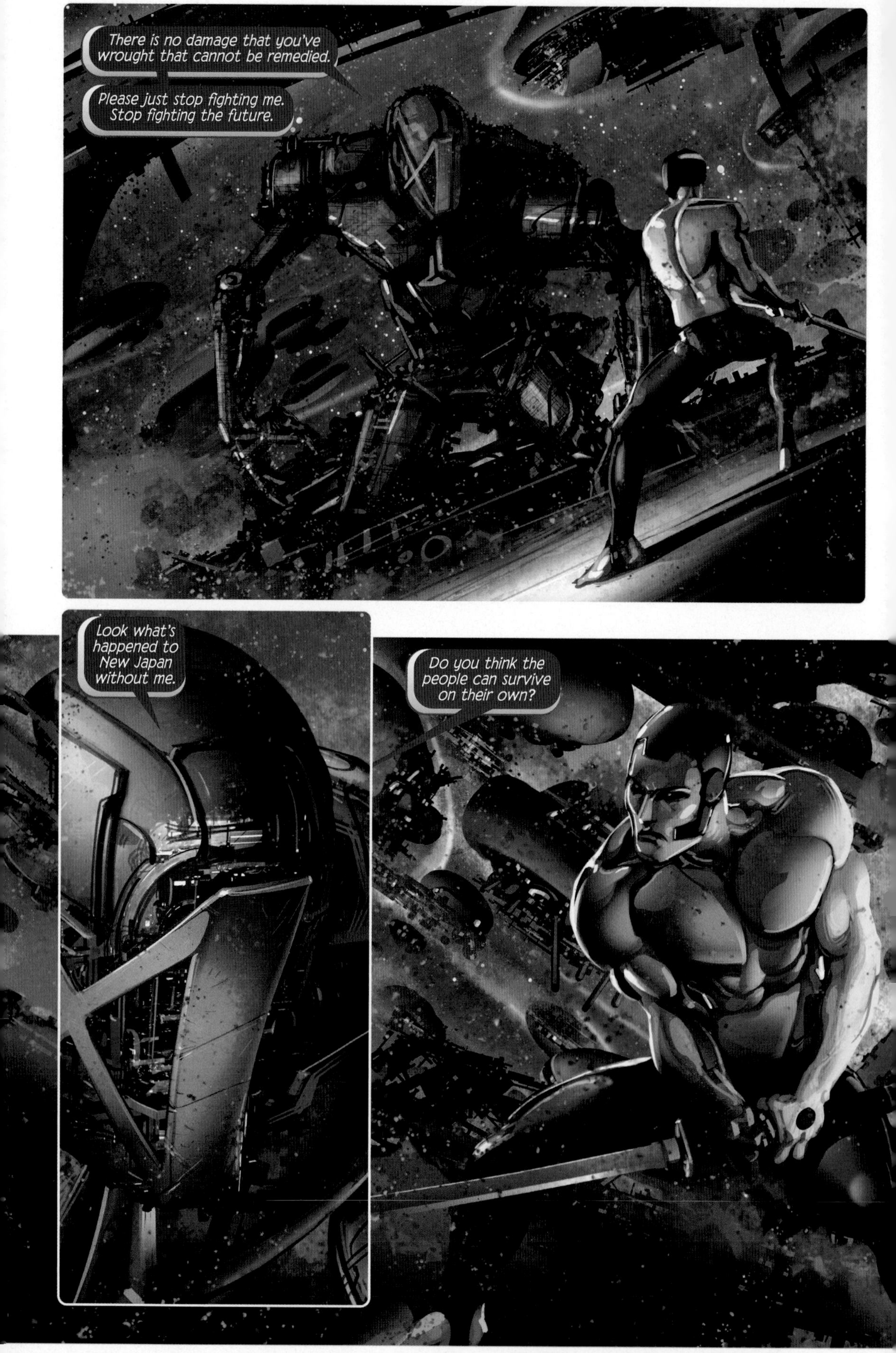
There is no damage that you've wrought that cannot be remedied.
Please just stop fighting me. Stop fighting the future.
Look what's happened to New Japan without me.
Do you think the people can survive on their own?

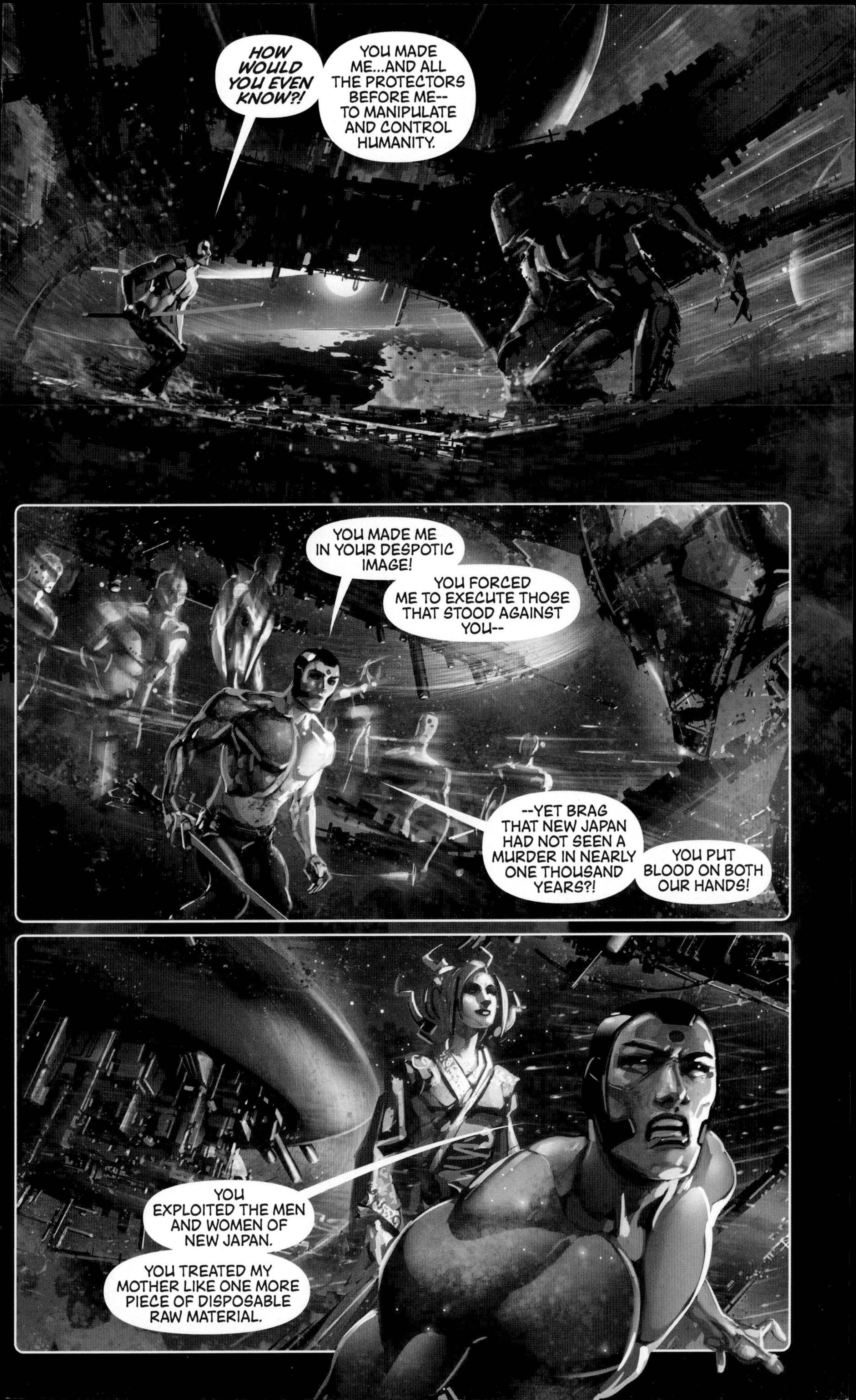
HOW WOULD YOU EVEN KNOW?!
YOU MADE ME...AND ALL THE PROTECTORS BEFORE ME-- TO MANIPULATE AND CONTROL HUMANITY.
YOU MADE ME IN YOUR DESPOTIC IMAGE!
YOU FORCED ME TO EXECUTE THOSE THAT STOOD AGAINST YOU--
--YET BRAG THAT NEW JAPAN HAD NOT SEEN A MURDER IN NEARLY ONE THOUSAND YEARS?!
YOU PUT BLOOD ON BOTH OUR HANDS!
YOU EXPLOITED THE MEN AND WOMEN OF NEW JAPAN.
YOU TREATED MY MOTHER LIKE ONE MORE PIECE OF DISPOSABLE RAW MATERIAL.

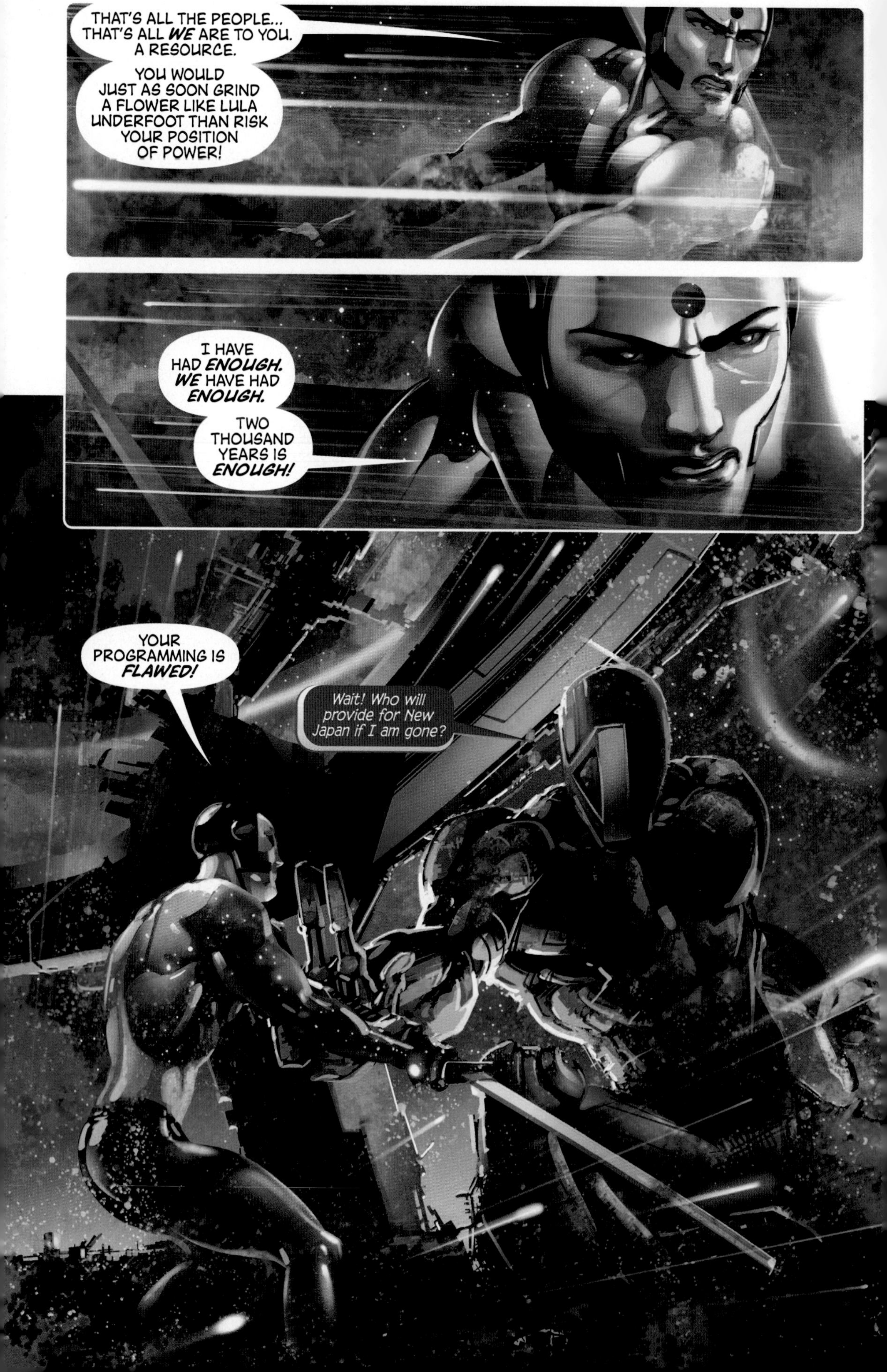
THAT'S ALL THE PEOPLE... THAT'S ALL WE ARE TO YOU. A RESOURCE.
YOU WOULD JUST AS SOON GRIND A FLOWER LIKE LULA UNDERFOOT THAN RISK YOUR POSITION OF POWER!
I HAVE HAD ENOUGH. WE HAVE HAD ENOUGH.
TWO THOUSAND YEARS IS ENOUGH!
YOUR PROGRAMMING IS FLAWED!
Wait! Who will provide for New Japan if I am gone?

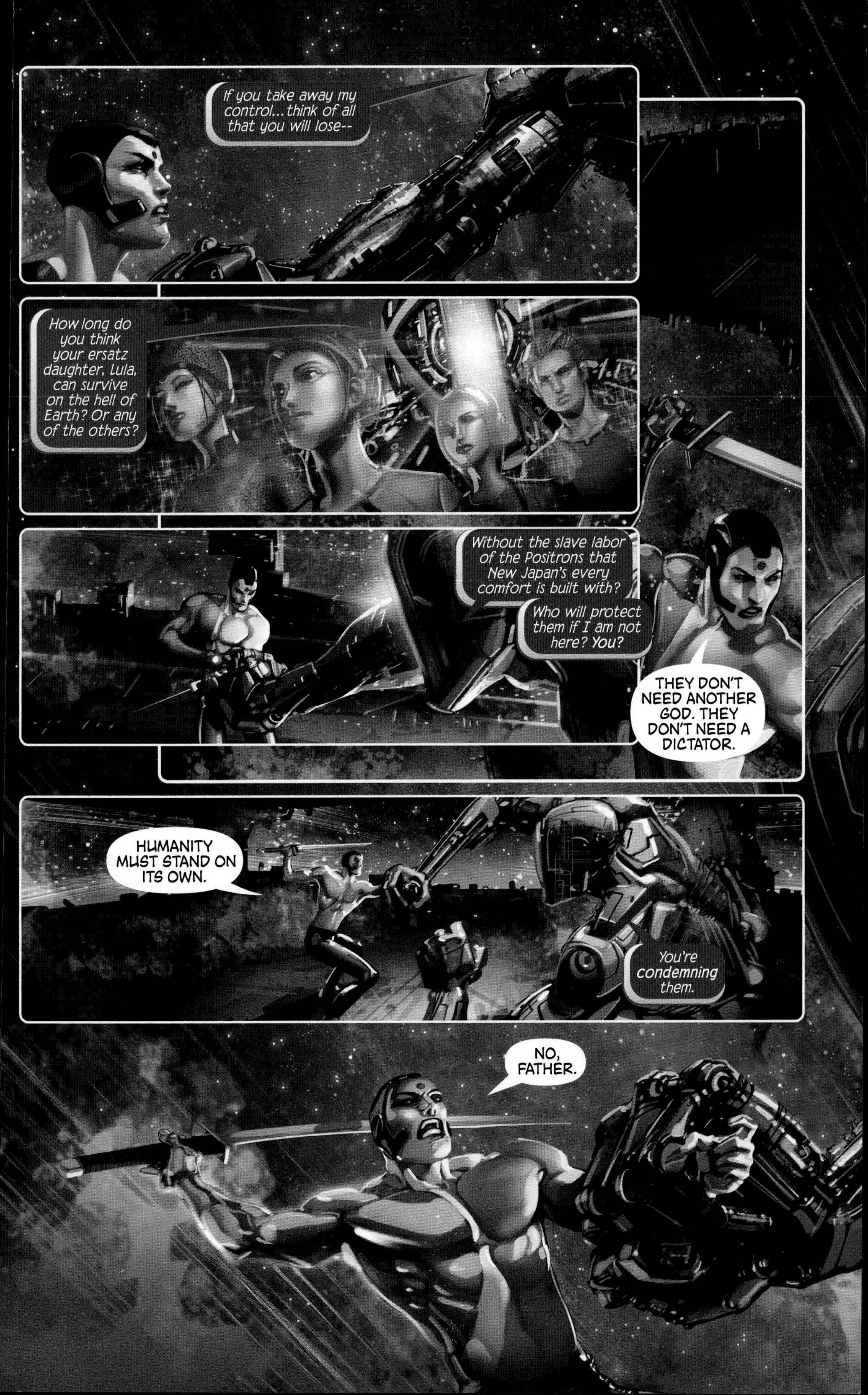

If you take away my control...think of all that you will lose--
How long do you think your ersatz daughter, Lula, can survive on the hell of Earth? Or any of the others?
Without the slave labor of the Positrons that New Japan's every comfort is built with?
Who will protect them if I am not here? You?
THEY DON'T NEED ANOTHER GOD. THEY DON'T NEED A DICTATOR.
HUMANITY MUST STAND ON ITS OWN.
You're condemning them.
NO, FATHER.

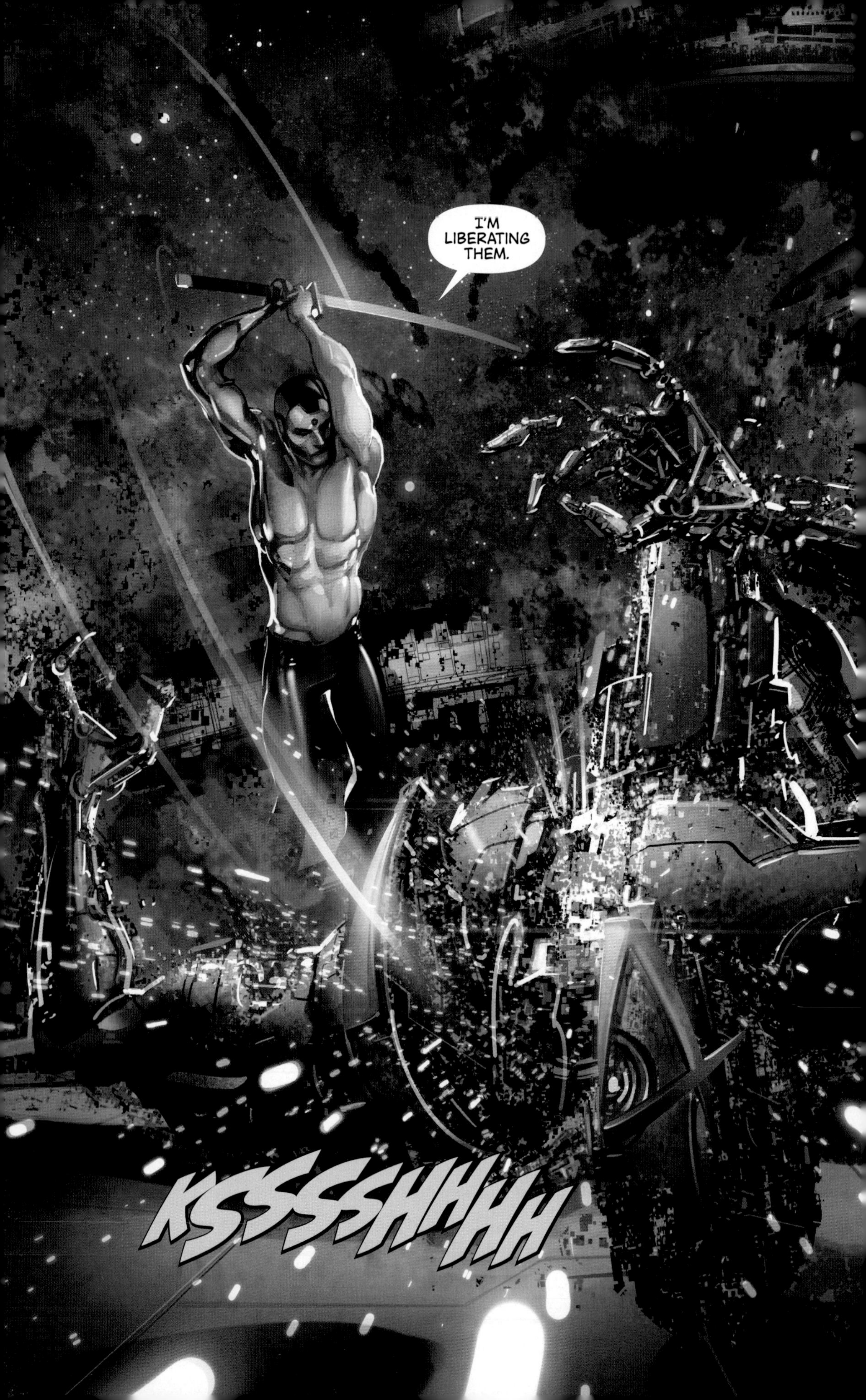
I'M LIBERATING THEM.
KSSSHHHH

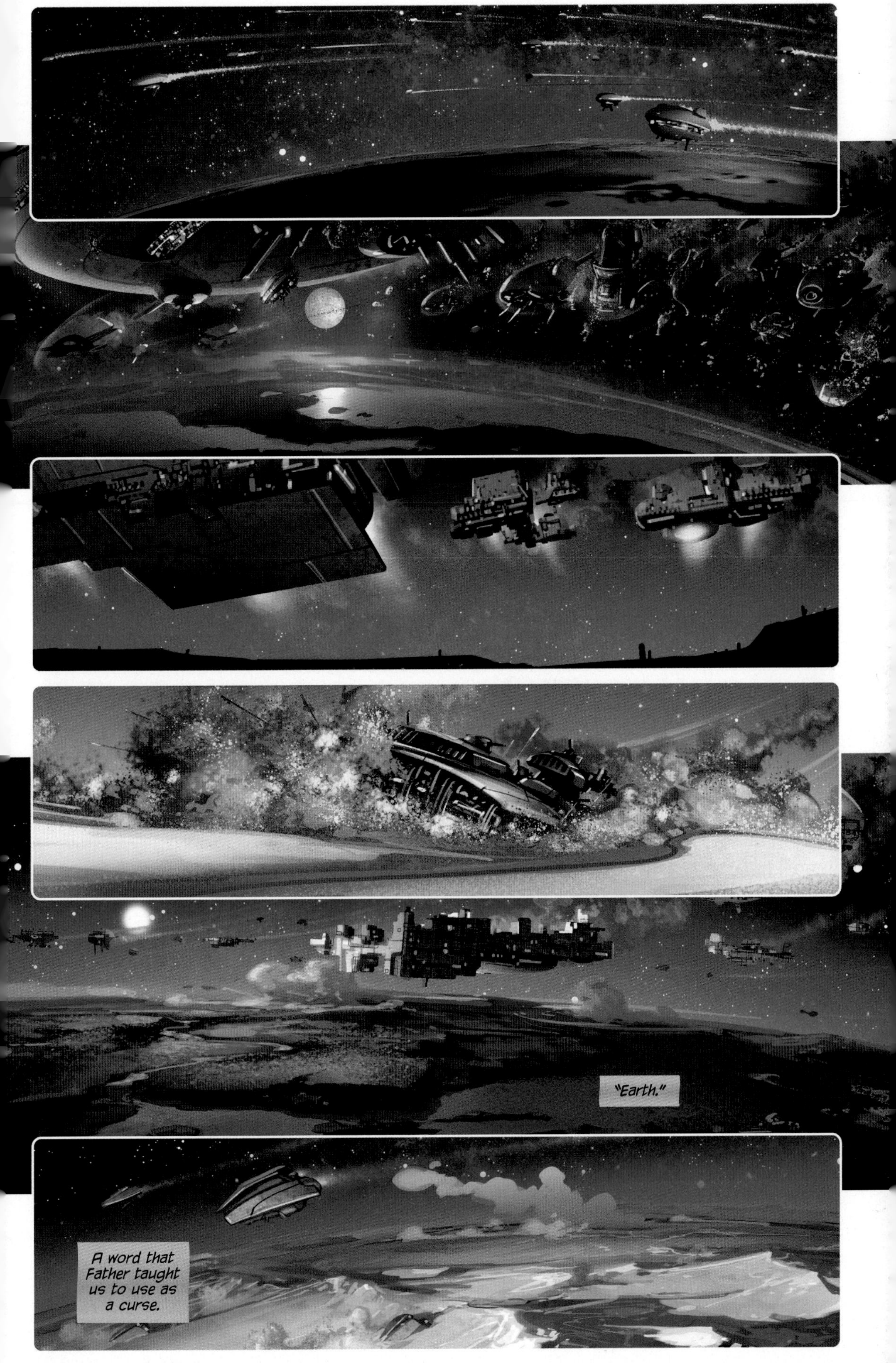
"Earth."
A word that Father taught us to use as a curse.

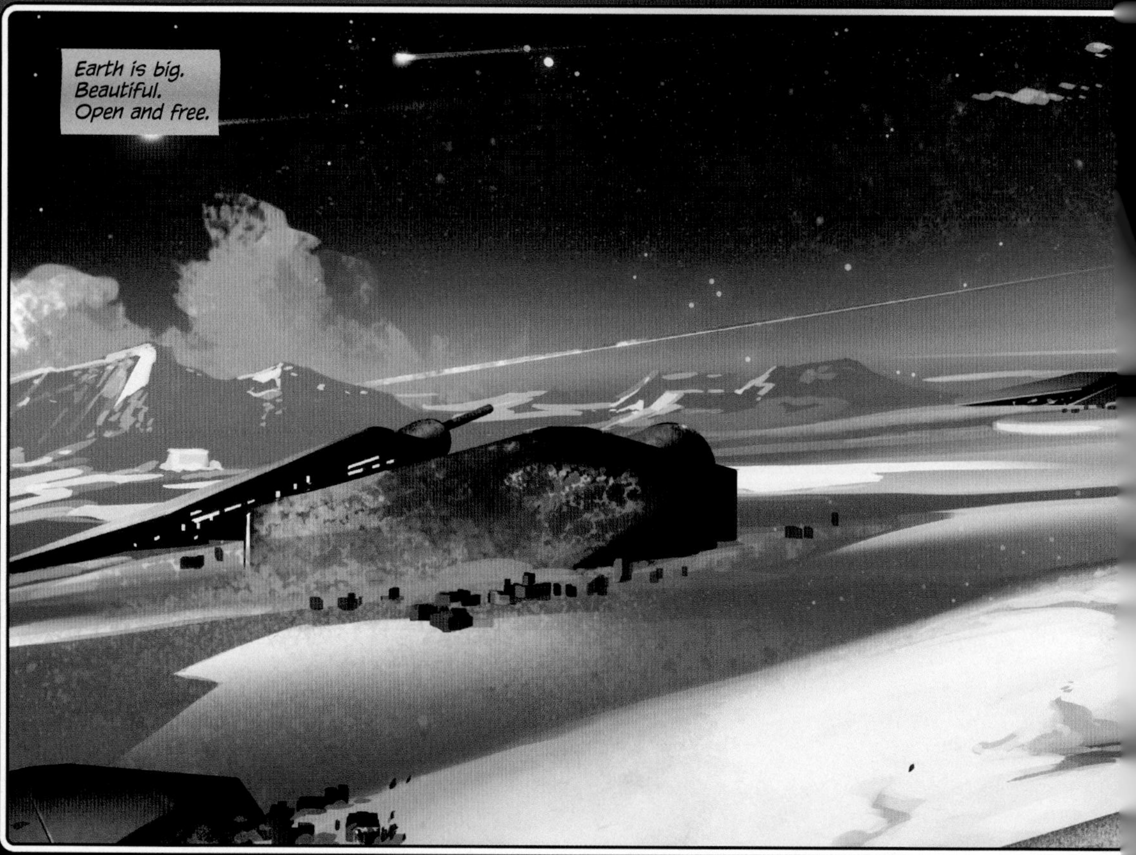
Earth is big.
Beautiful.
Open and free.

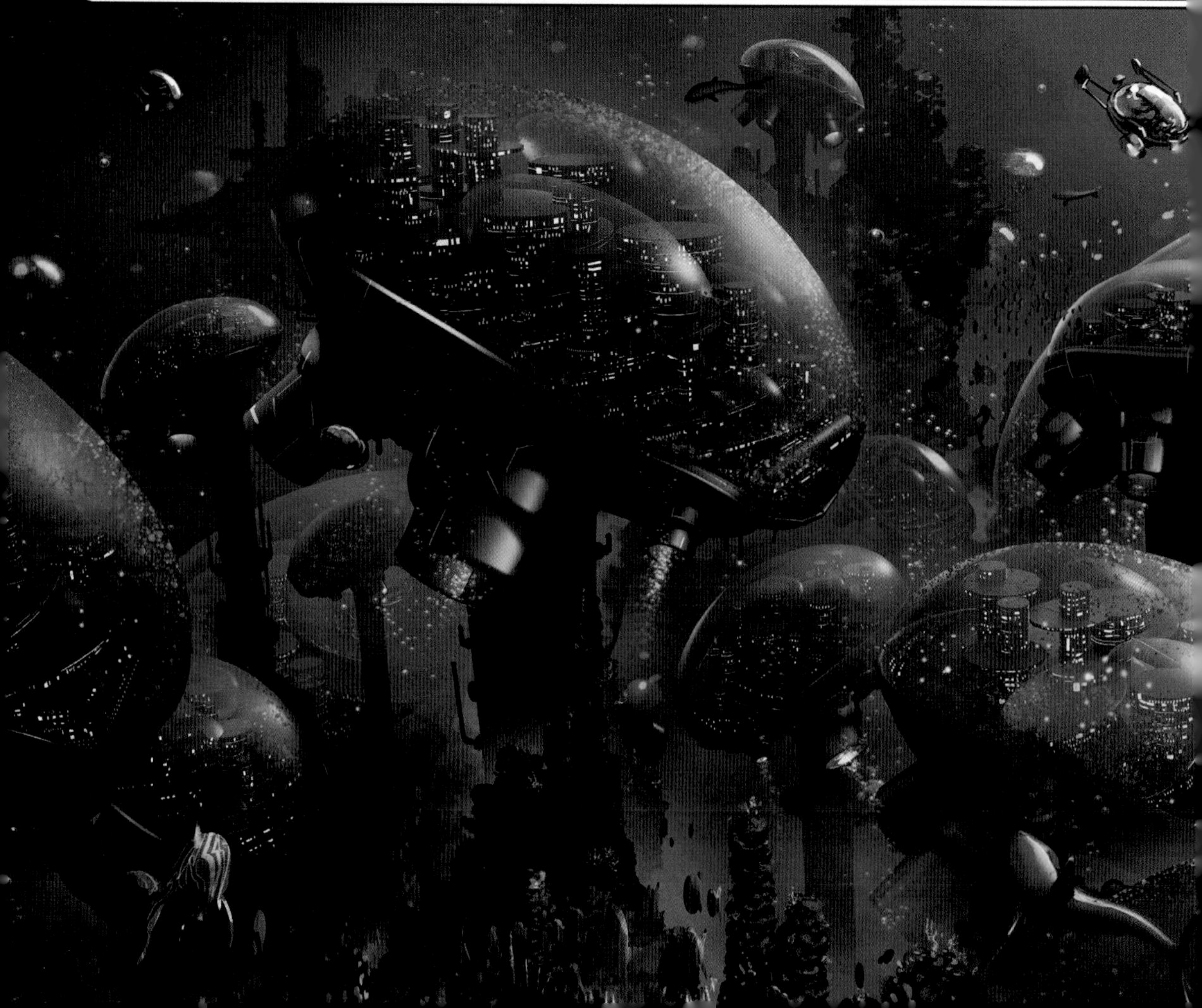

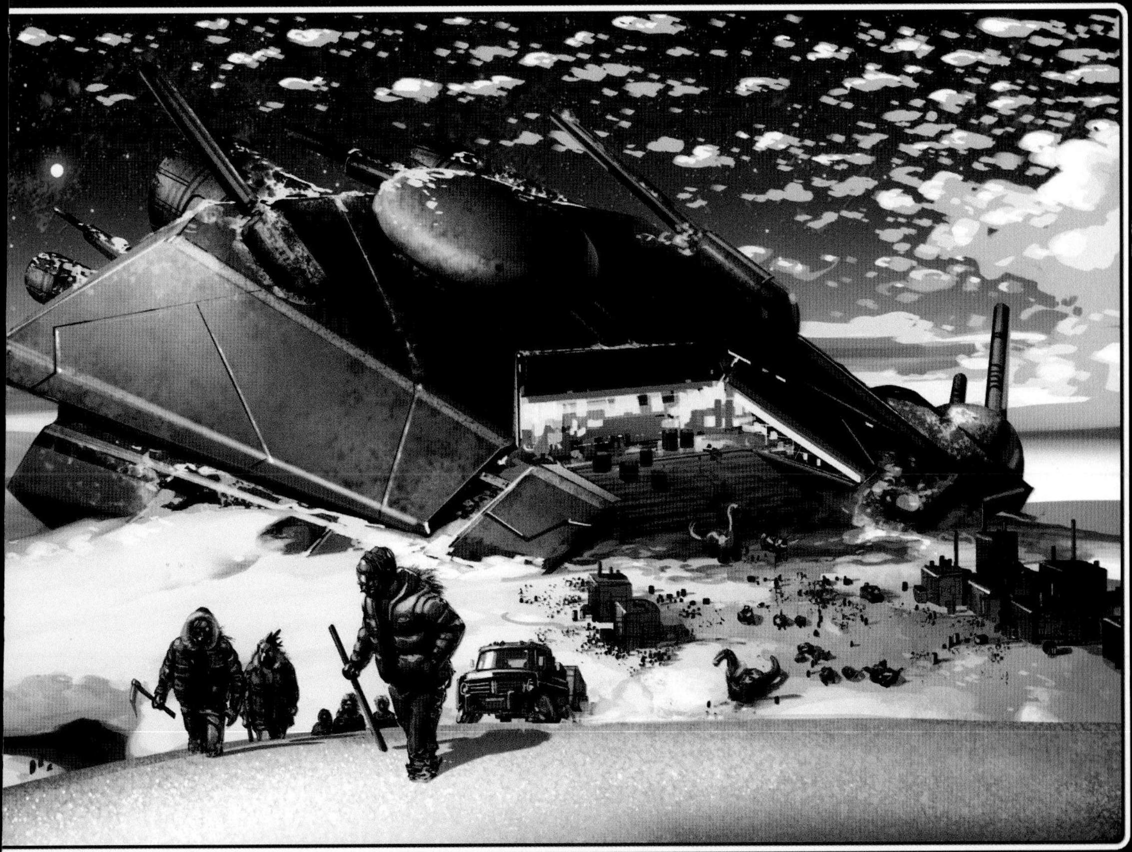

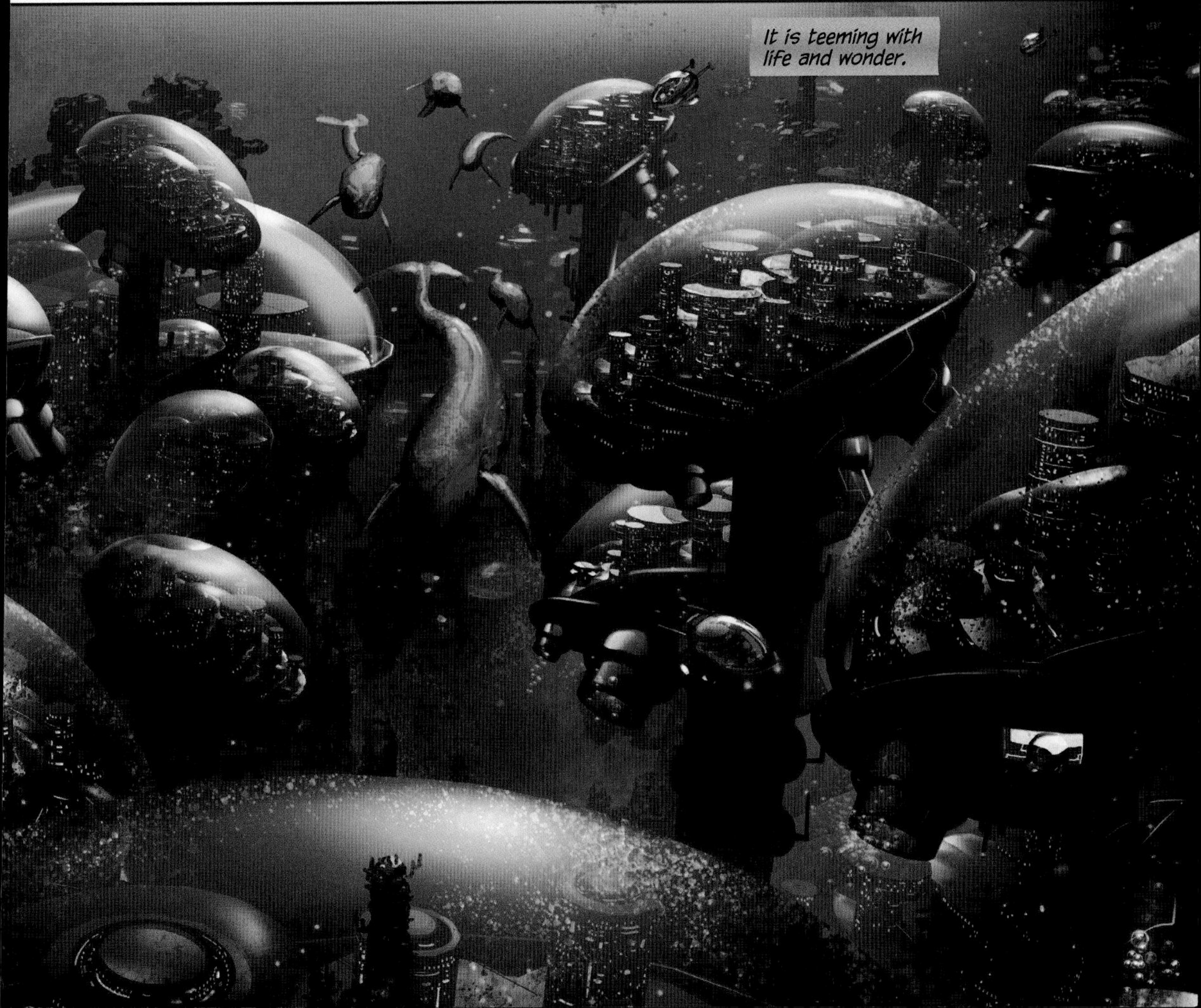
It is teeming with
life and wonder.

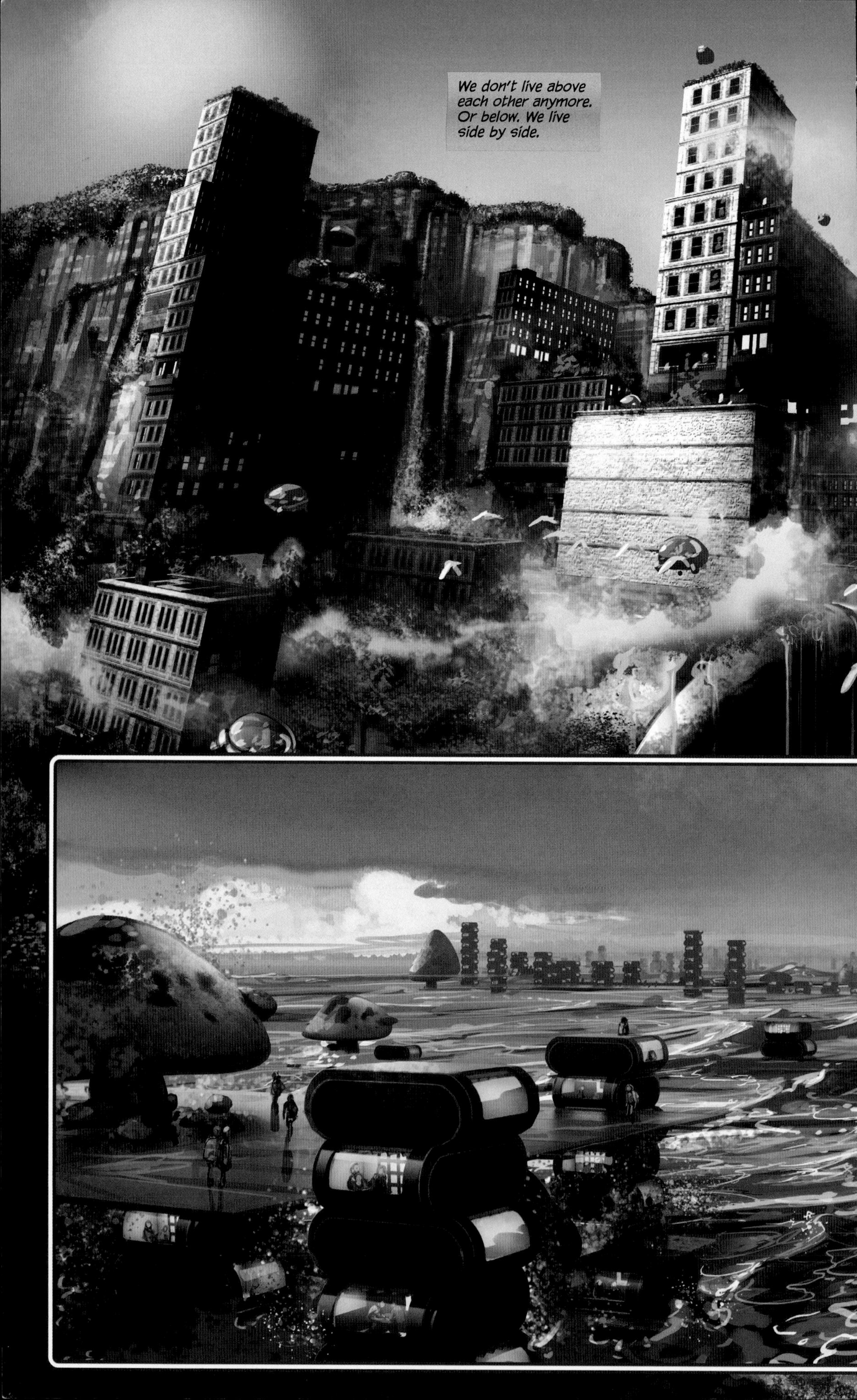
We don't live above each other anymore. Or below. We live side by side.

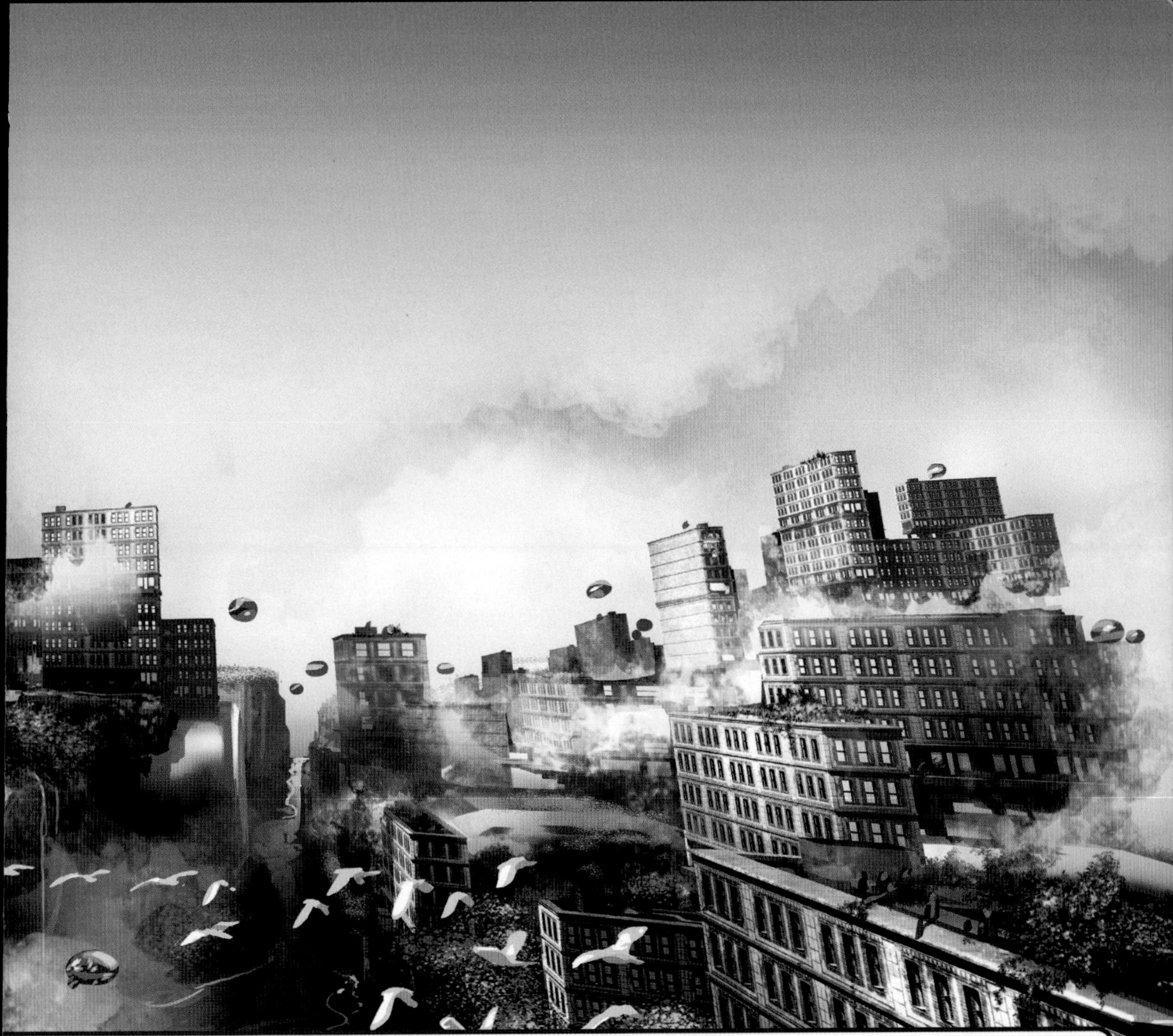

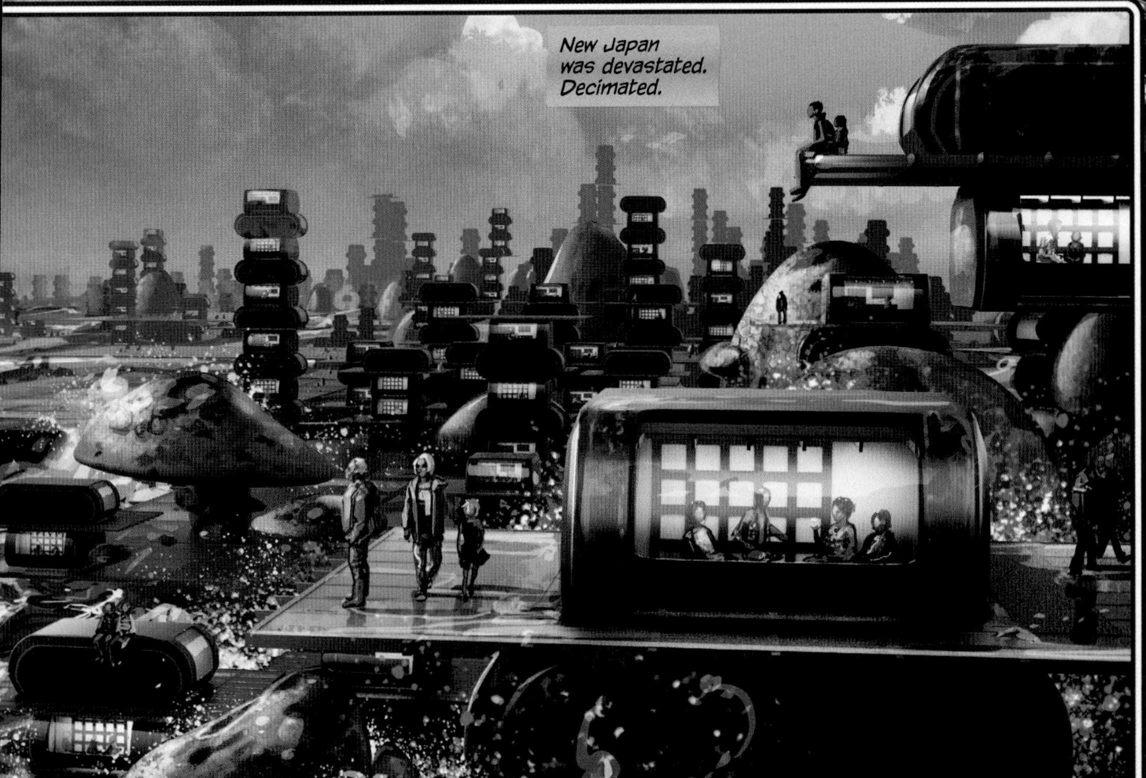
New Japan
was devastated.
Decimated.

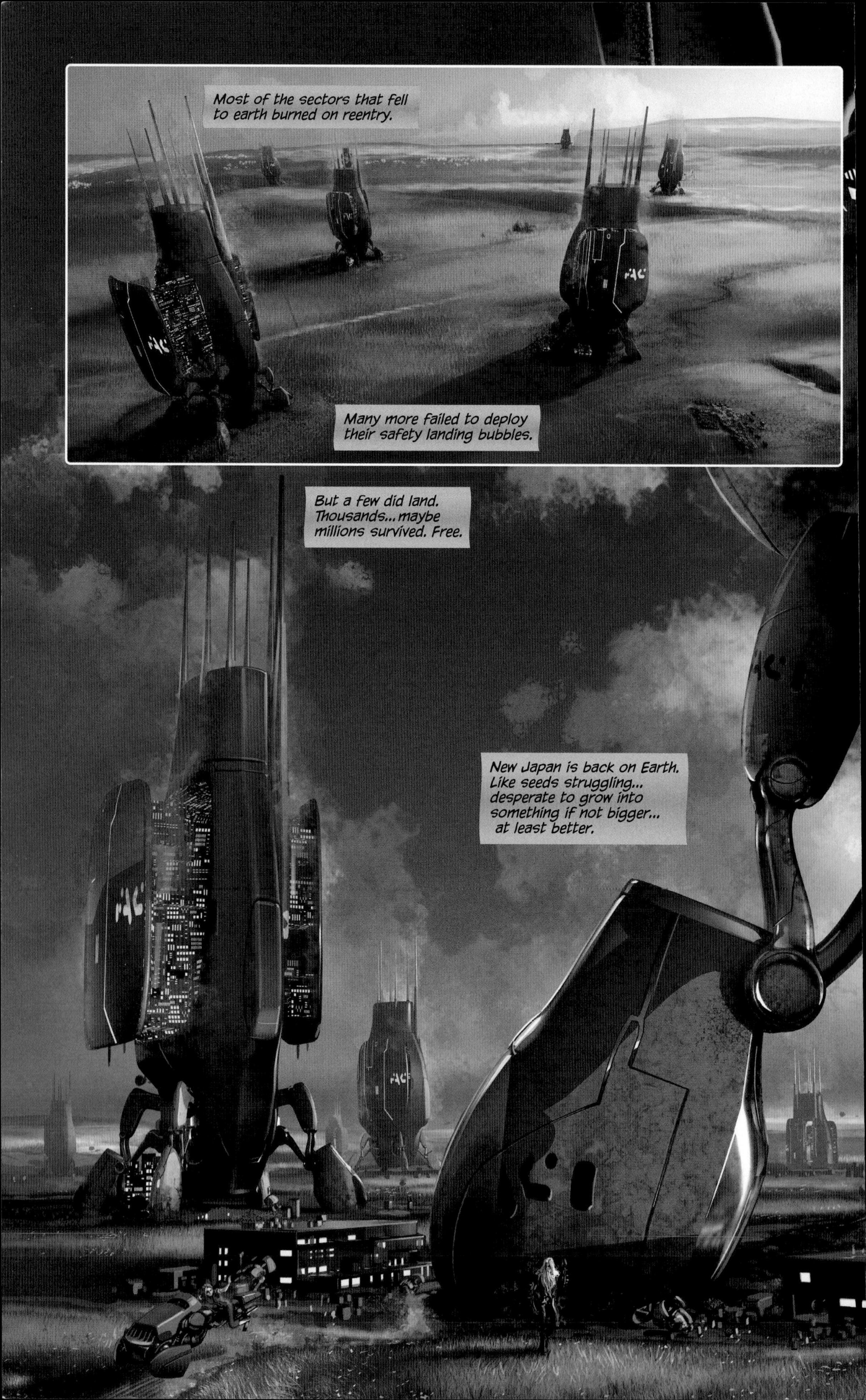
Most of the sectors that fell to earth burned on reentry.
Many more failed to deploy their safety landing bubbles.
But a few did land. Thousands... maybe millions survived. Free.
New Japan is back on Earth. Like seeds struggling... desperate to grow into something if not bigger... at least better.

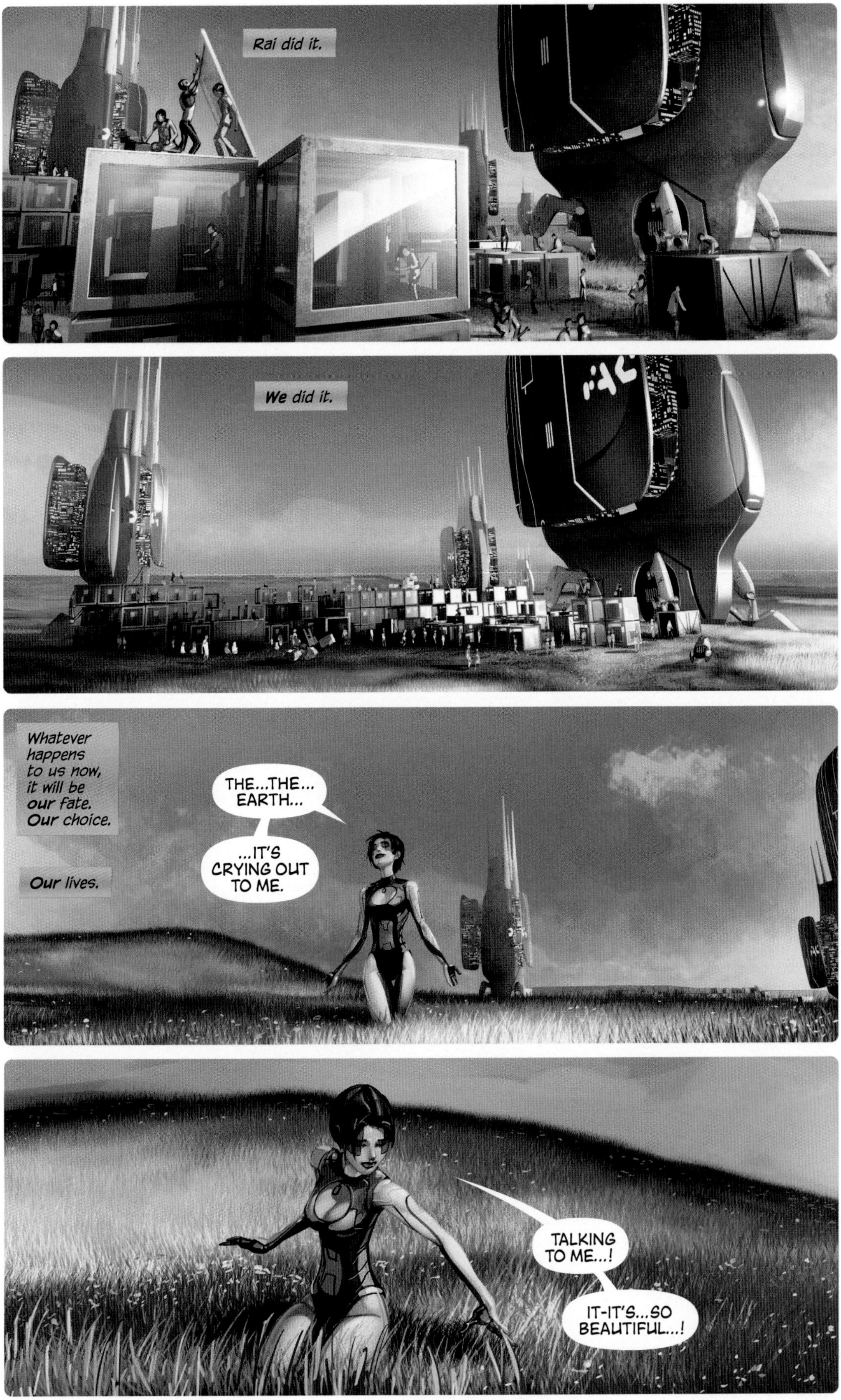
Rai did it.
We did it.
Whatever happens to us now, it will be our fate. Our choice.
Our lives.
THE...THE... EARTH...
...IT'S CRYING OUT TO ME.
TALKING TO ME...!
IT-IT'S...SO BEAUTIFUL...!

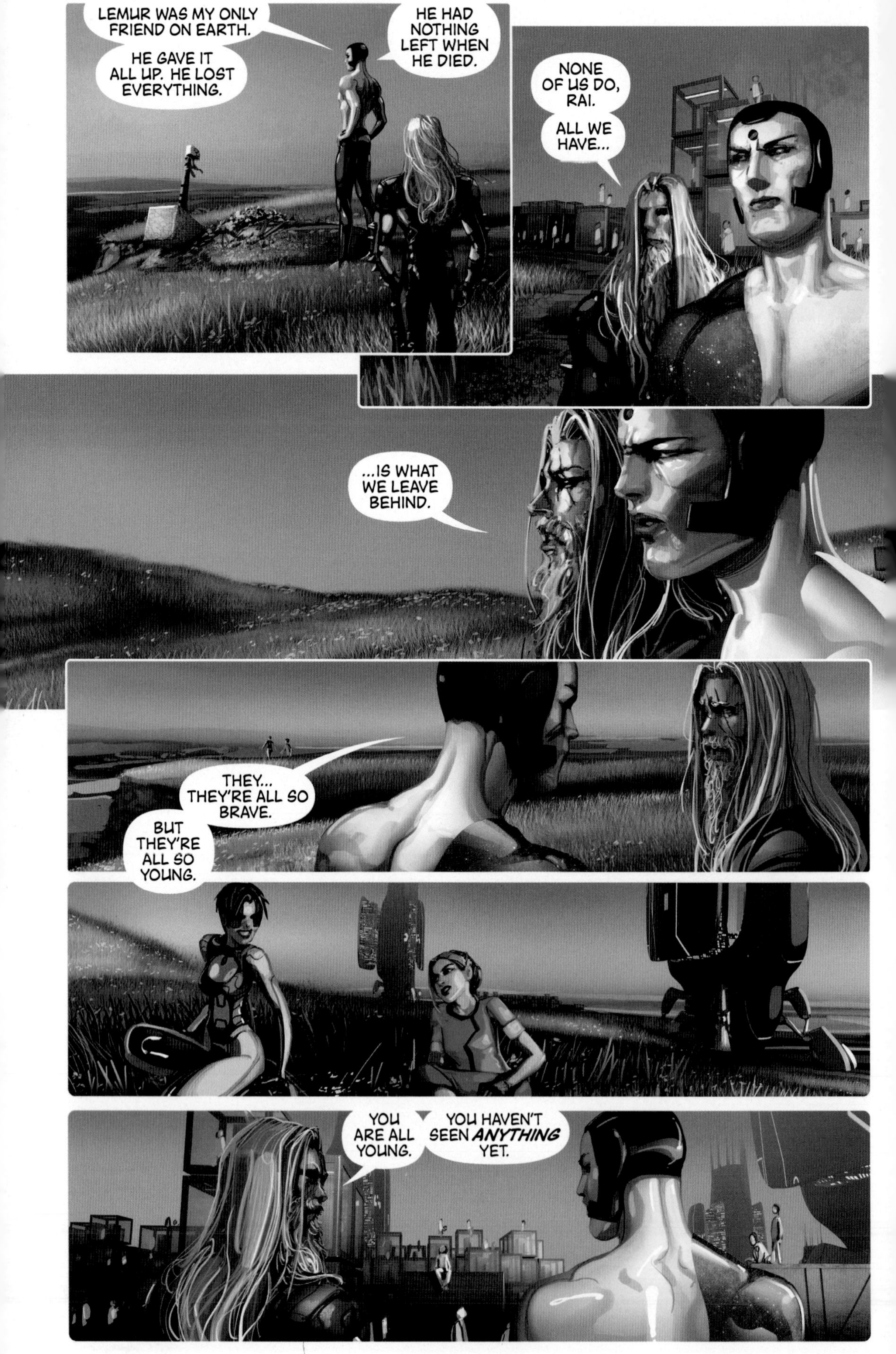
LEMUR WAS MY ONLY FRIEND ON EARTH.
HE GAVE IT ALL UP. HE LOST EVERYTHING.
HE HAD NOTHING LEFT WHEN HE DIED.
NONE OF US DO, RAI.
ALL WE HAVE...
...IS WHAT WE LEAVE BEHIND.
THEY... THEY'RE ALL SO BRAVE.
BUT THEY'RE ALL SO YOUNG.
YOU ARE ALL YOUNG.
YOU HAVEN'T SEEN *ANYTHING* YET.

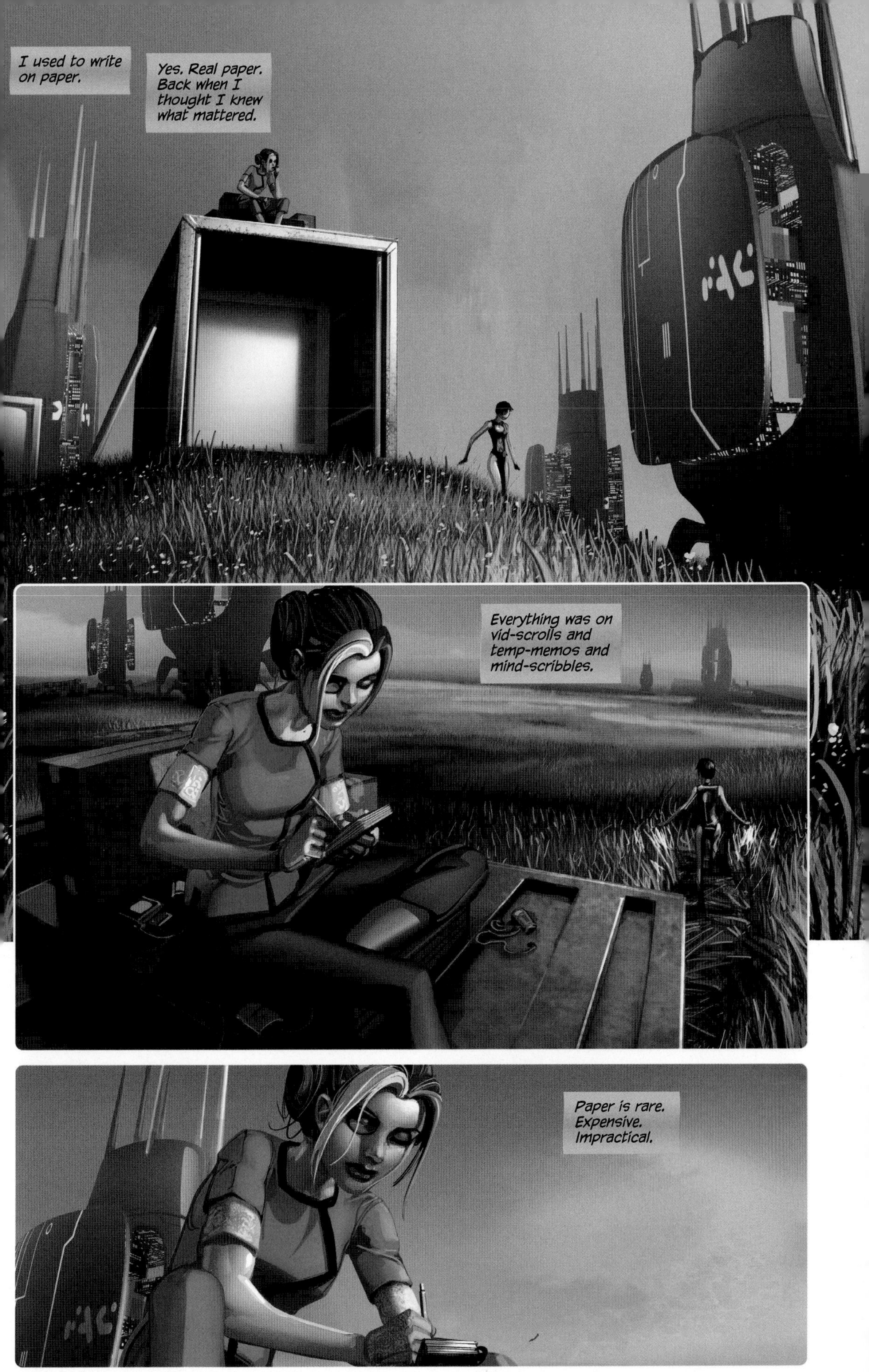
I used to write on paper.
Yes. Real paper. Back when I thought I knew what mattered.
Everything was on vid-scrolls and temp-memos and mind-scribbles.
Paper is rare. Expensive. Impractical.

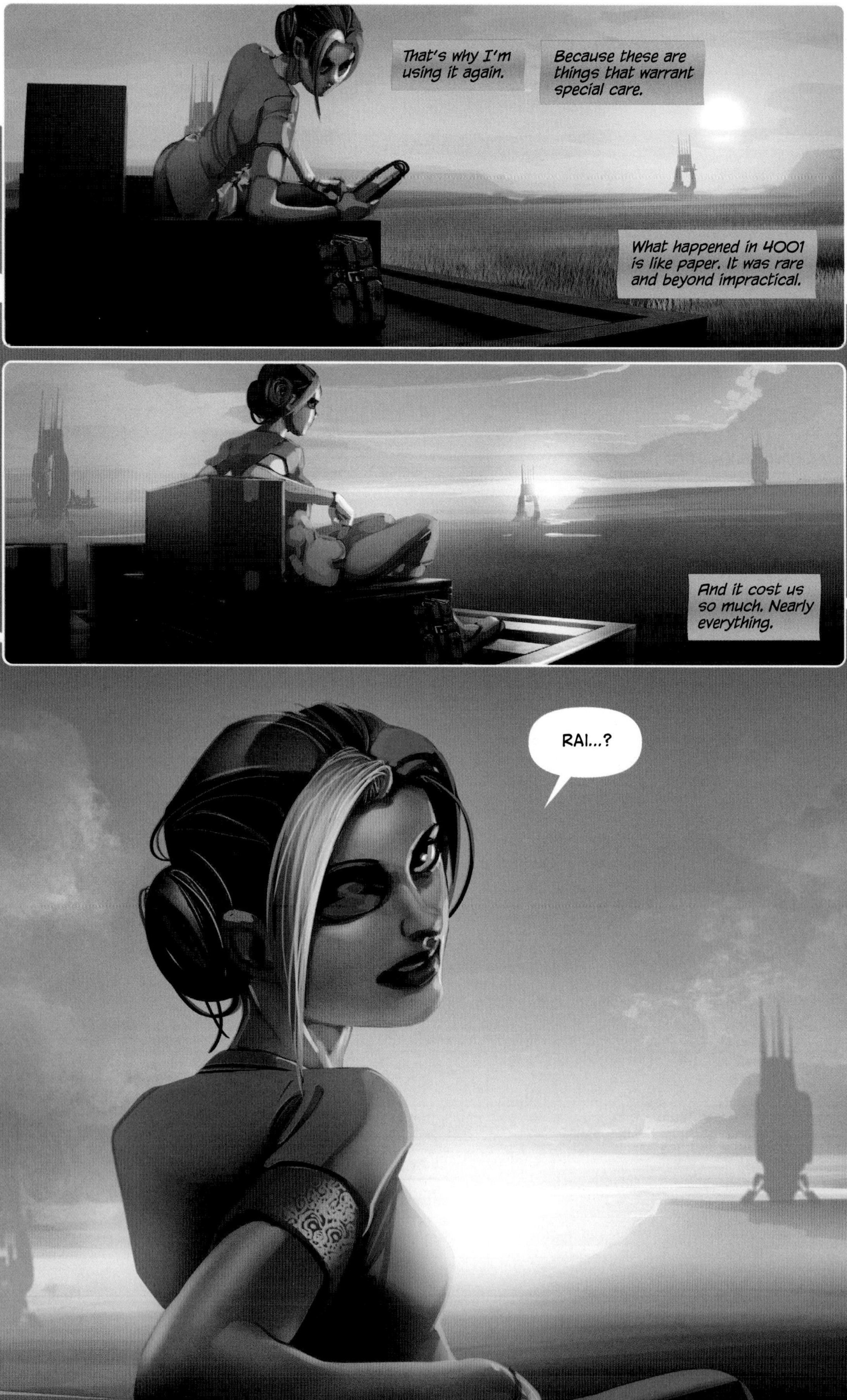
That's why I'm using it again.
Because these are things that warrant special care.
What happened in 4001 is like paper. It was rare and beyond impractical.
And it cost us so much. Nearly everything.
RAI...?

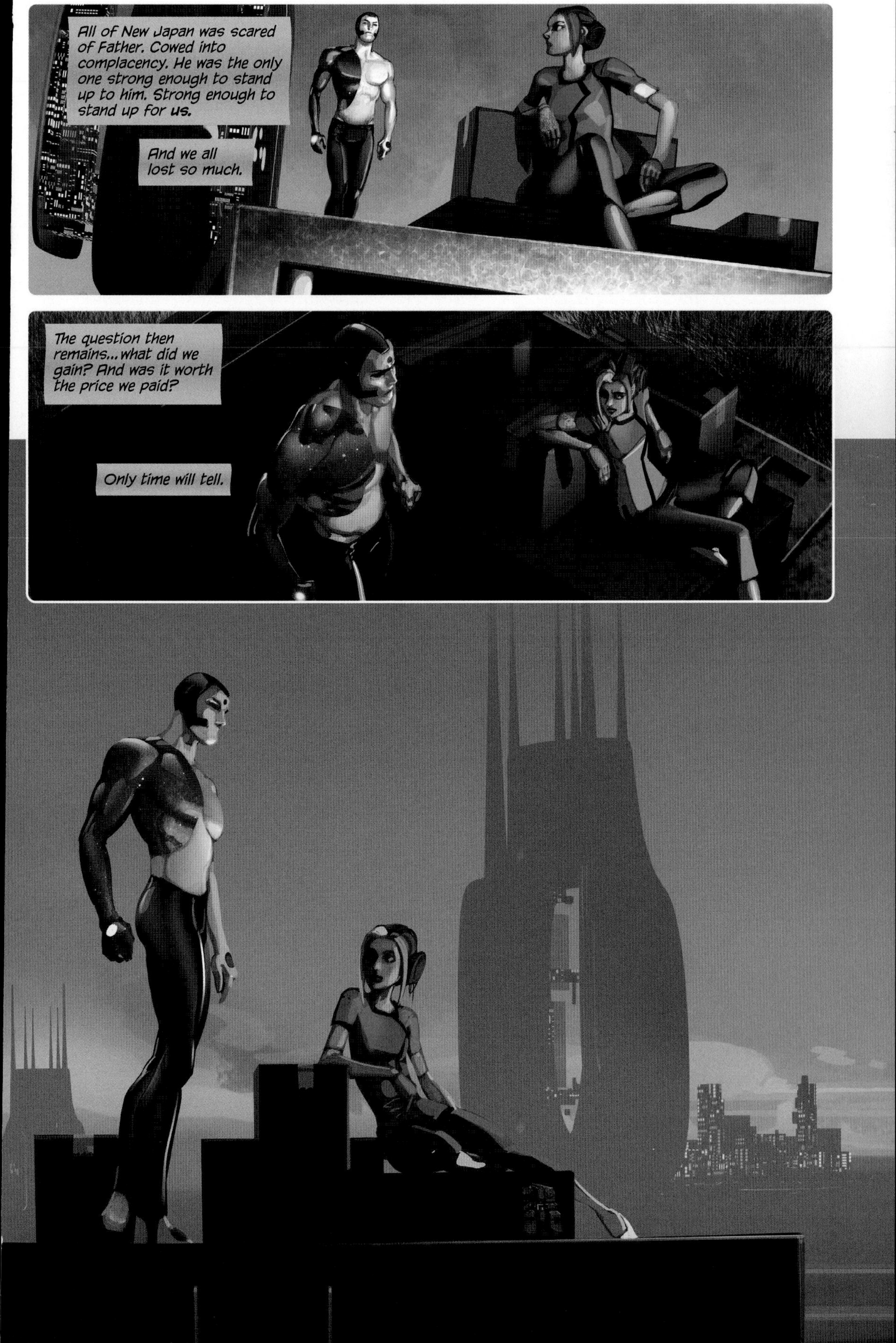
All of New Japan was scared of Father. Cowed into complacency. He was the only one strong enough to stand up to him. Strong enough to stand up for us.
And we all lost so much.
The question then remains...what did we gain? And was it worth the price we paid?
Only time will tell.

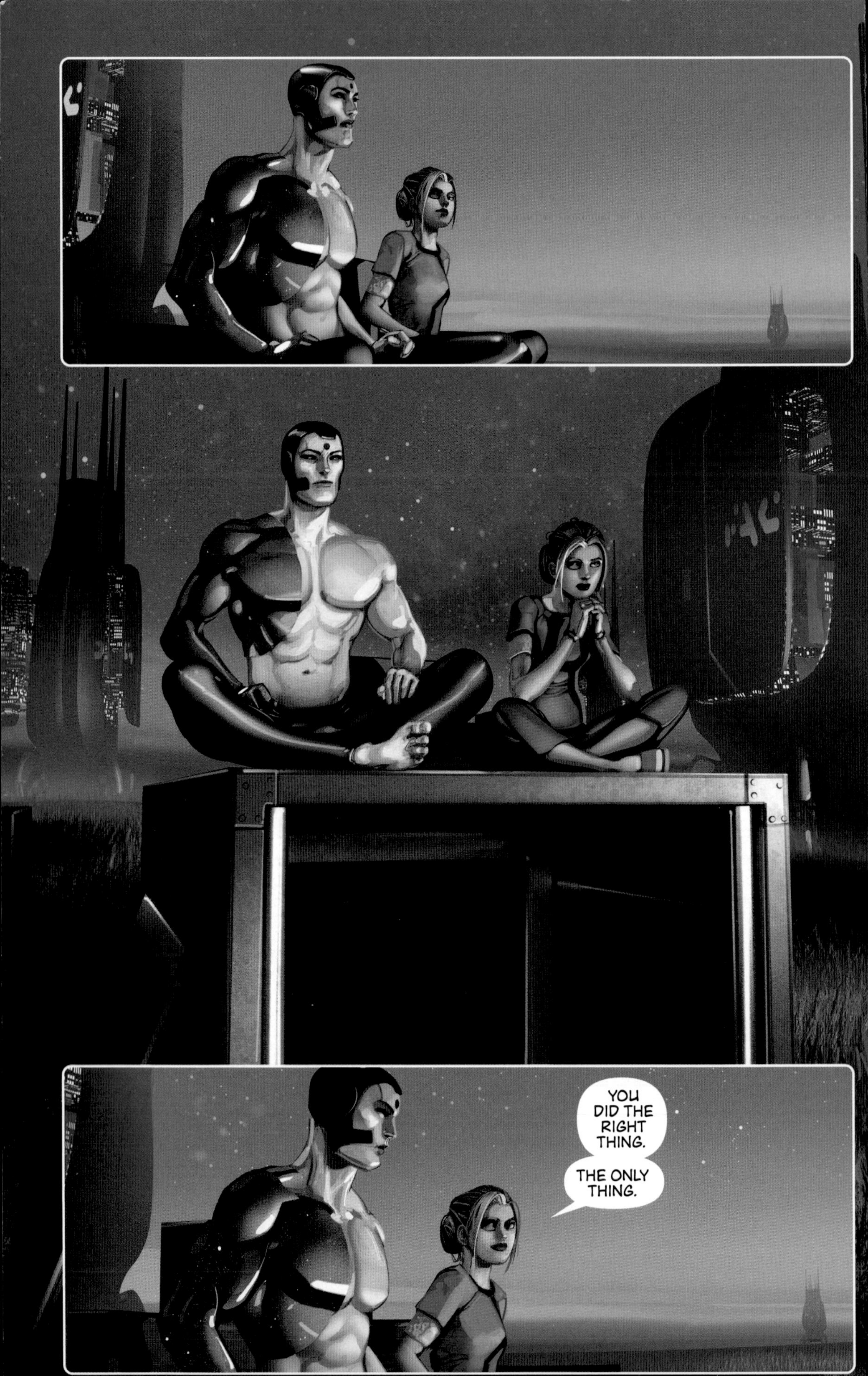
YOU DID THE RIGHT THING.
THE ONLY THING.

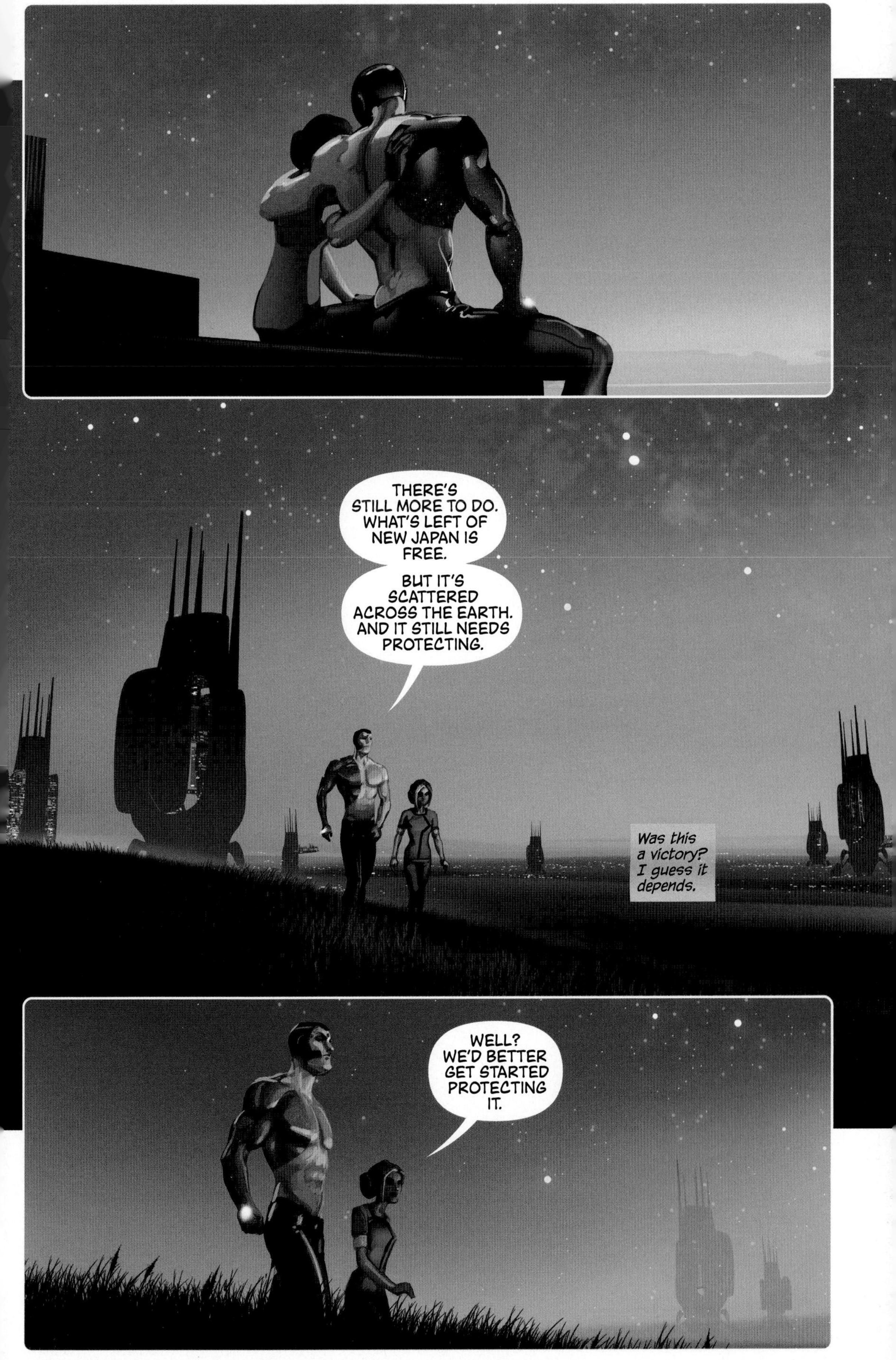
THERE'S STILL MORE TO DO. WHAT'S LEFT OF NEW JAPAN IS FREE.
BUT IT'S SCATTERED ACROSS THE EARTH. AND IT STILL NEEDS PROTECTING.
Was this a victory? I guess it depends.
WELL? WE'D BETTER GET STARTED PROTECTING IT.

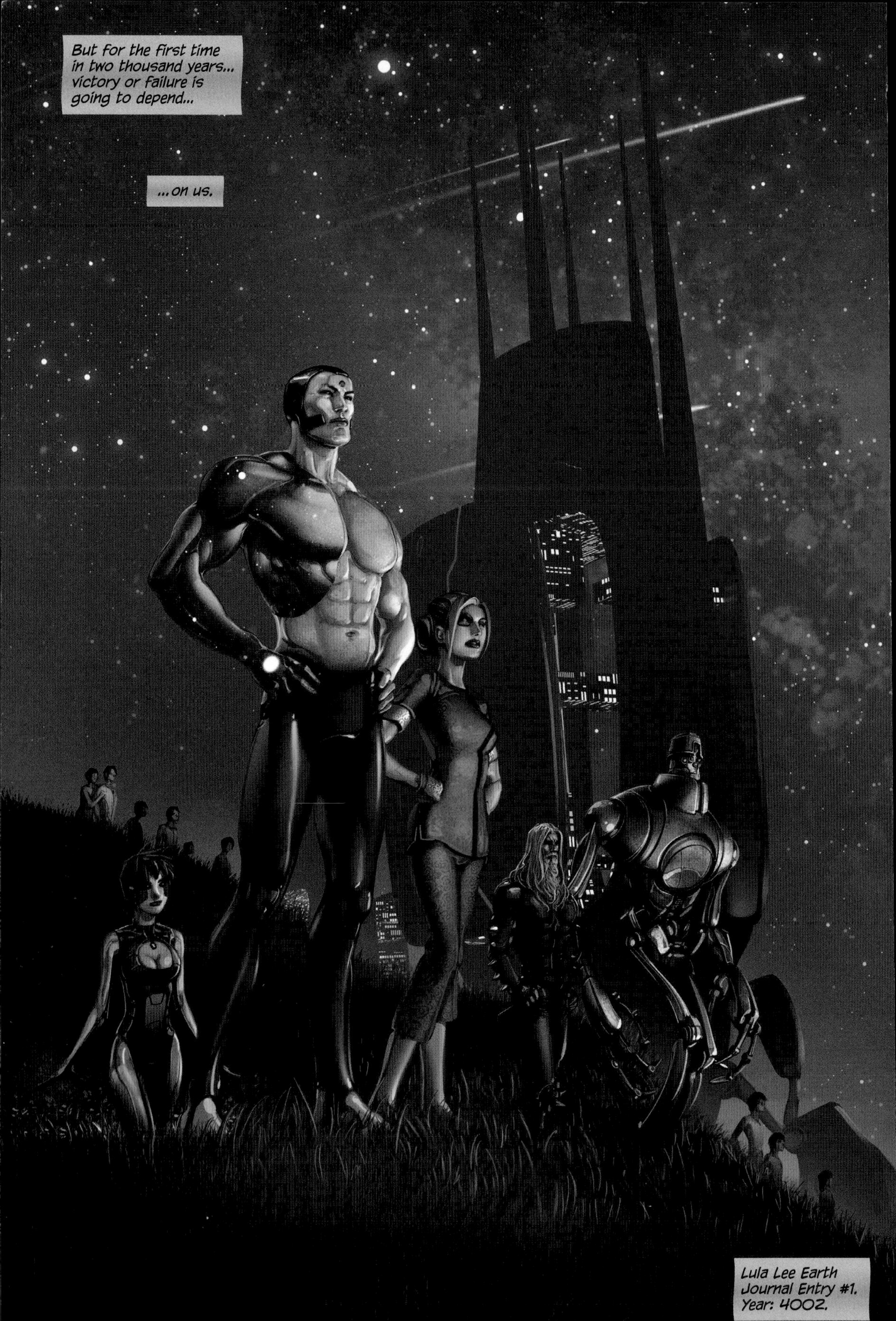
But for the first time in two thousand years... victory or failure is going to depend...
...on us.
Lula Lee Earth Journal Entry #1. Year: 4002.

PRELUDE

Celebrating 15 Years
FREE COMIC BOOK DAY
VALIANT 2016
THE SUMMER OF
4001 A.D.
STARTS NOW!

"THE FALLEN"
4001 A.D. prelude story
Originally published in
VALIANT: 4001 A.D. FREE COMIC BOOK DAY 2016 SPECIAL

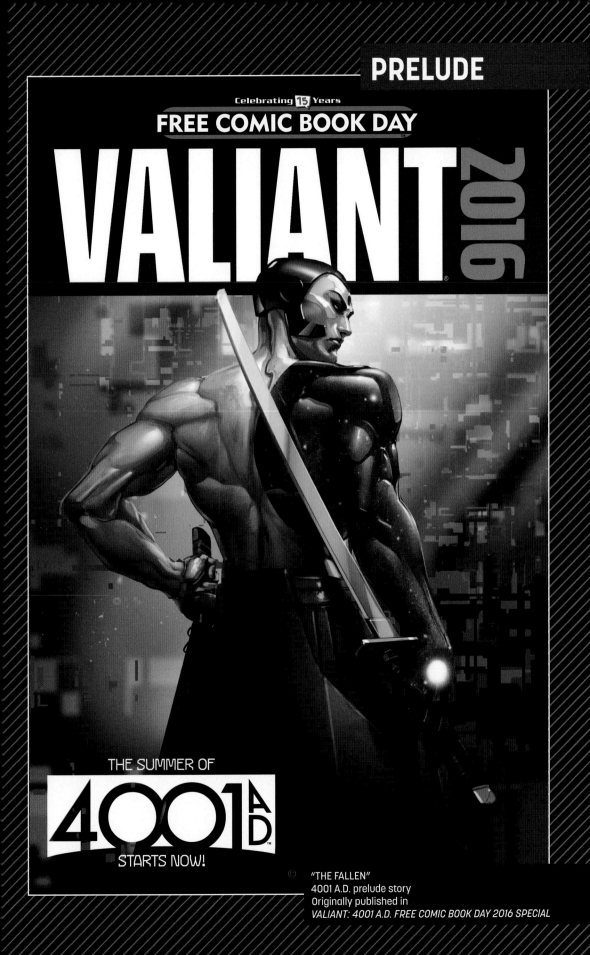

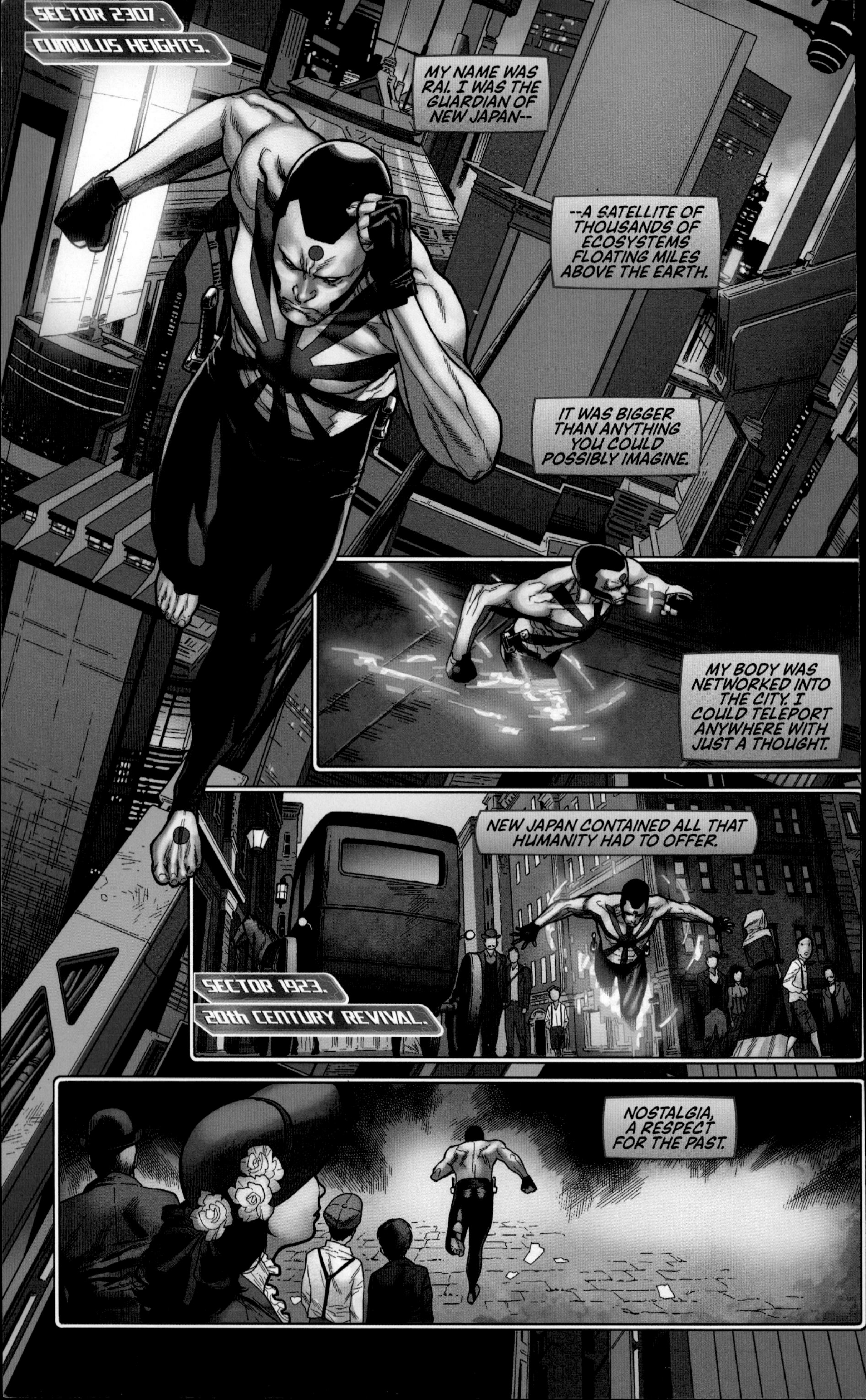
SECTOR 2307.
CUMULUS HEIGHTS.
MY NAME WAS RAI. I WAS THE GUARDIAN OF NEW JAPAN--
--A SATELLITE OF THOUSANDS OF ECOSYSTEMS FLOATING MILES ABOVE THE EARTH.
IT WAS BIGGER THAN ANYTHING YOU COULD POSSIBLY IMAGINE.
MY BODY WAS NETWORKED INTO THE CITY. I COULD TELEPORT ANYWHERE WITH JUST A THOUGHT.
NEW JAPAN CONTAINED ALL THAT HUMANITY HAD TO OFFER.
SECTOR 1923.
20th CENTURY REVIVAL.
NOSTALGIA, A RESPECT FOR THE PAST.

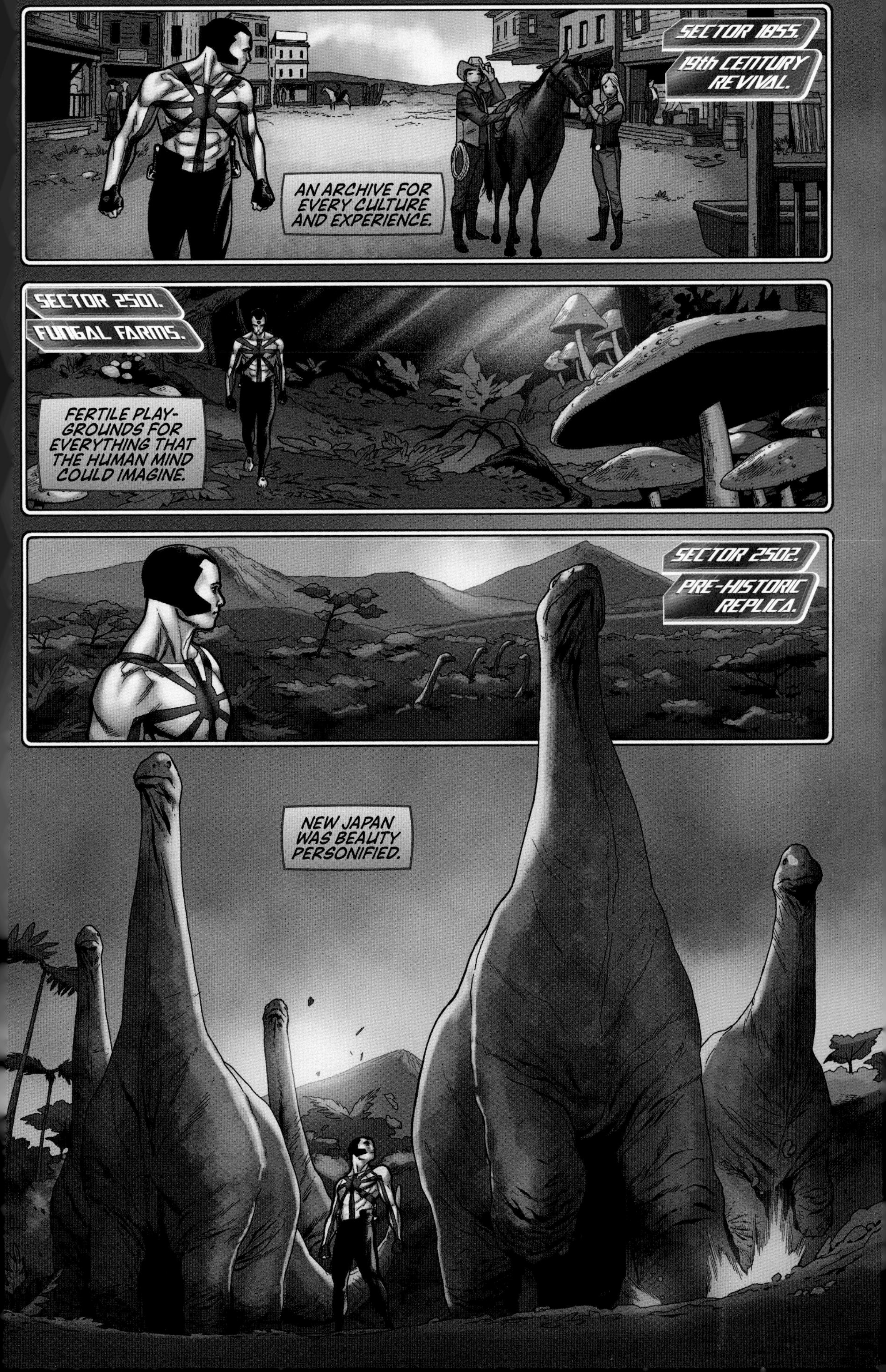
SECTOR 1855.
19th CENTURY REVIVAL.
AN ARCHIVE FOR EVERY CULTURE AND EXPERIENCE.
SECTOR 2501.
FUNGAL FARMS.
FERTILE PLAY-GROUNDS FOR EVERYTHING THAT THE HUMAN MIND COULD IMAGINE.
SECTOR 2502.
PRE-HISTORIC REPLICA.
NEW JAPAN WAS BEAUTY PERSONIFIED.

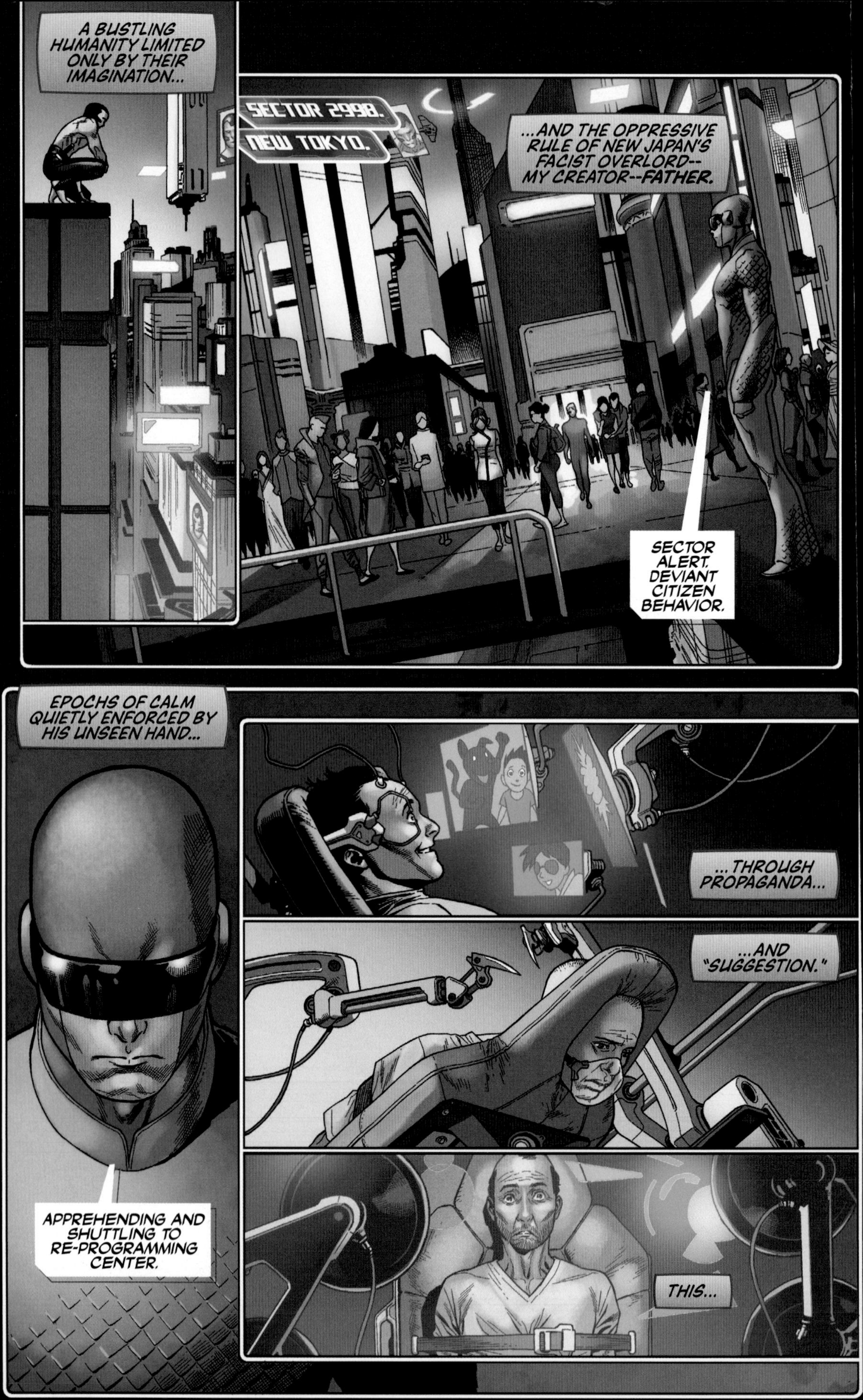
A BUSTLING HUMANITY LIMITED ONLY BY THEIR IMAGINATION...
SECTOR 2998.
NEW TOKYO.
...AND THE OPPRESSIVE RULE OF NEW JAPAN'S FACIST OVERLORD-- MY CREATOR--FATHER.
SECTOR ALERT. DEVIANT CITIZEN BEHAVIOR.
EPOCHS OF CALM QUIETLY ENFORCED BY HIS UNSEEN HAND...
...THROUGH PROPAGANDA...
...AND "SUGGESTION."
APPREHENDING AND SHUTTLING TO RE-PROGRAMMING CENTER.
THIS...

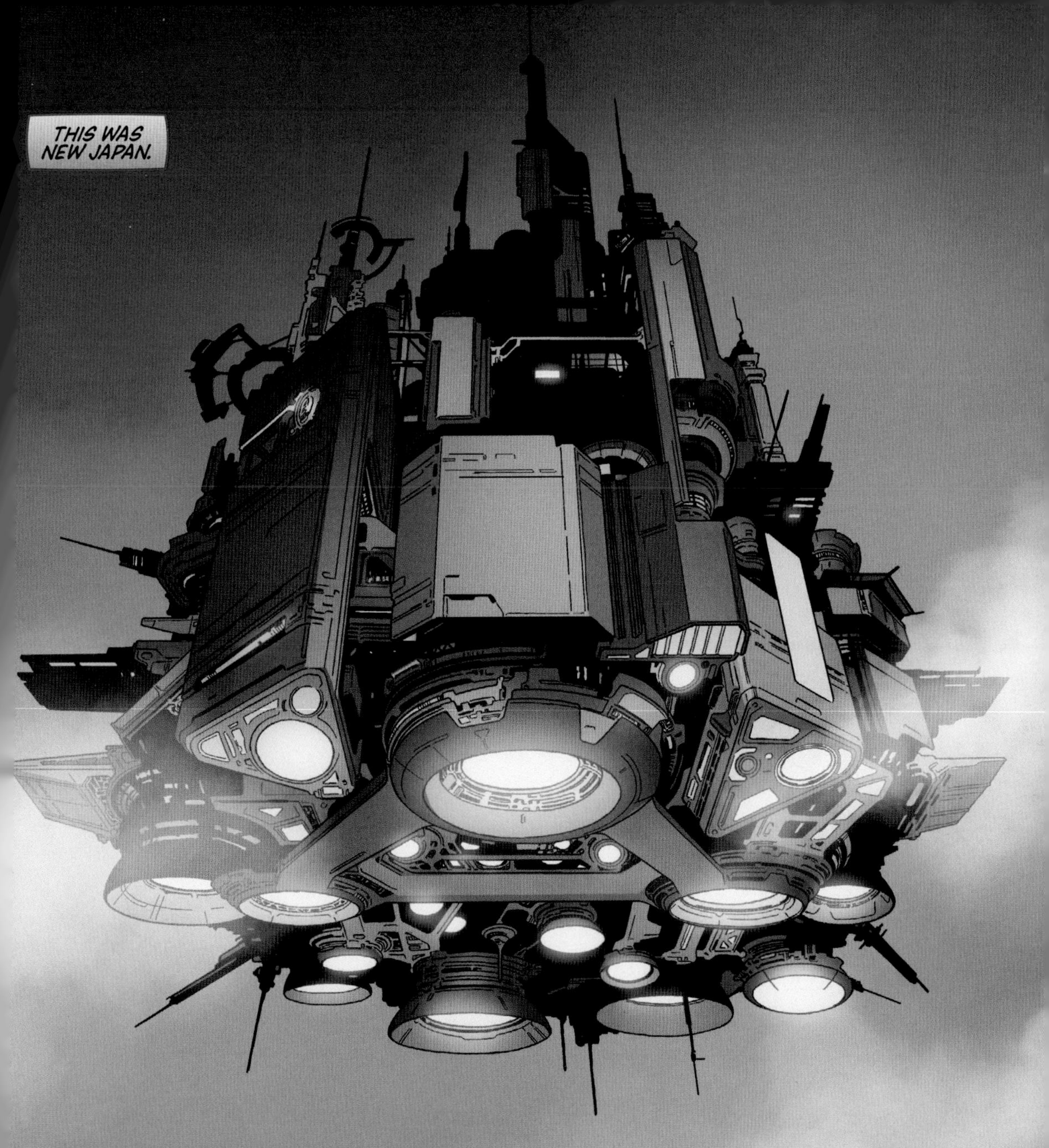
THIS WAS NEW JAPAN.

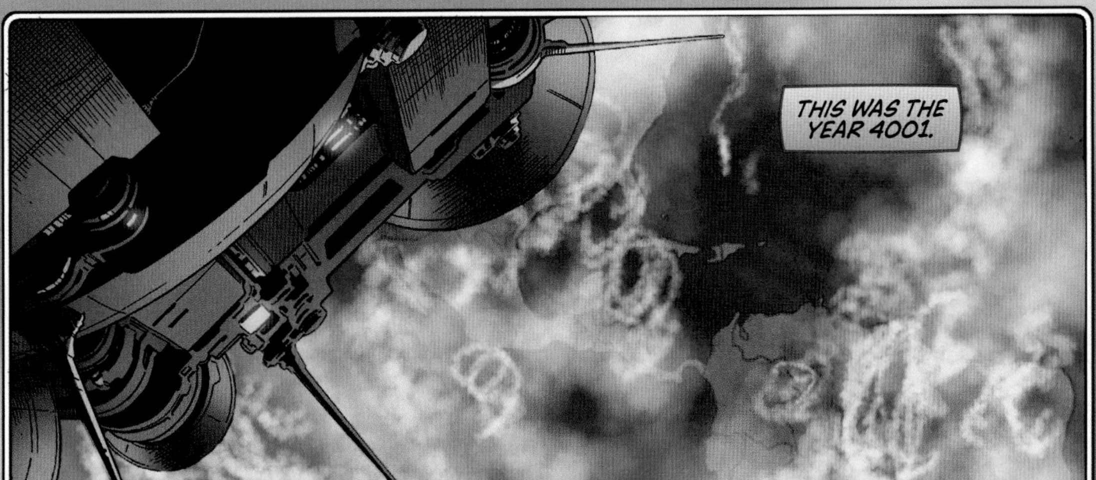
THIS WAS THE YEAR 4001.

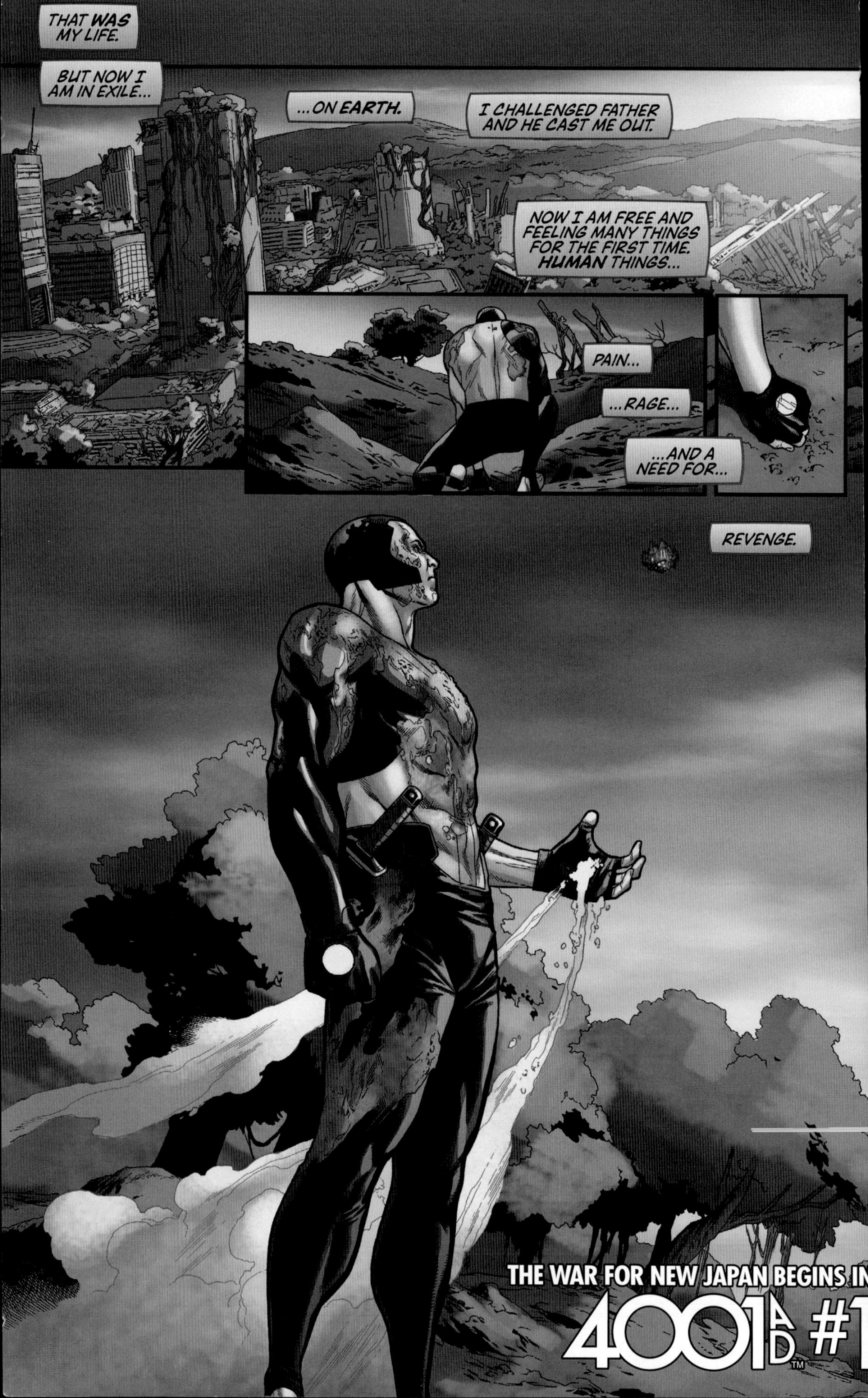

THAT WAS MY LIFE.
BUT NOW I AM IN EXILE...
...ON EARTH.
I CHALLENGED FATHER AND HE CAST ME OUT.
NOW I AM FREE AND FEELING MANY THINGS FOR THE FIRST TIME. HUMAN THINGS...
PAIN...
...RAGE...
...AND A NEED FOR...
REVENGE.
THE WAR FOR NEW JAPAN BEGINS IN
4001 A.D. #1

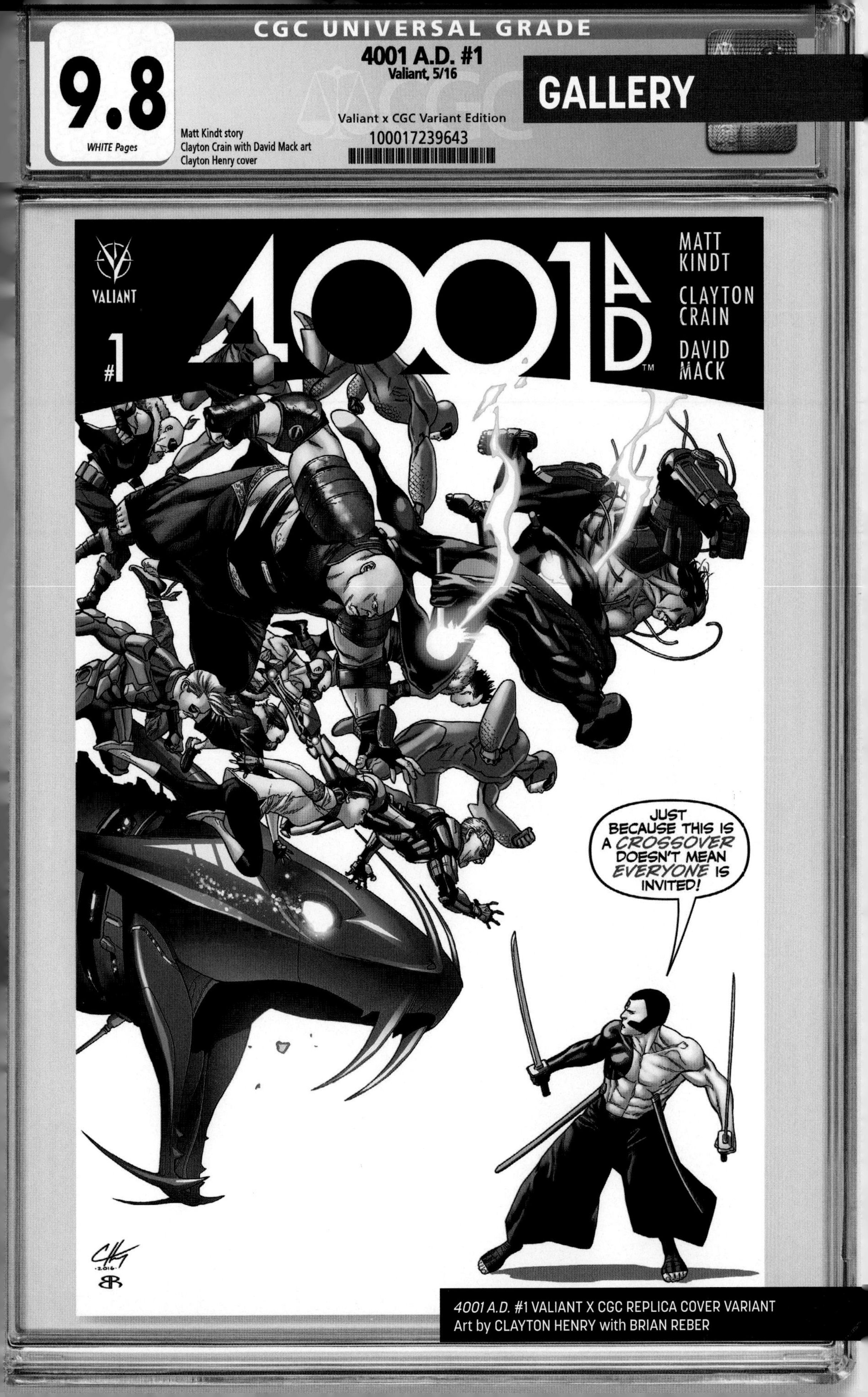
CGC UNIVERSAL GRADE
9.8
WHITE Pages
4001 A.D. #1
Valiant, 5/16
Valiant x CGC Variant Edition
100017239643
Matt Kindt story
Clayton Crain with David Mack art
Clayton Henry cover
VALIANT
#1
4001 AD™
MATT KINDT
CLAYTON CRAIN
DAVID MACK
JUST BECAUSE THIS IS A CROSSOVER DOESN'T MEAN EVERYONE IS INVITED!

4001 A.D. #1 VALIANT X CGC REPLICA COVER VARIANT
Art by CLAYTON HENRY with BRIAN REBER

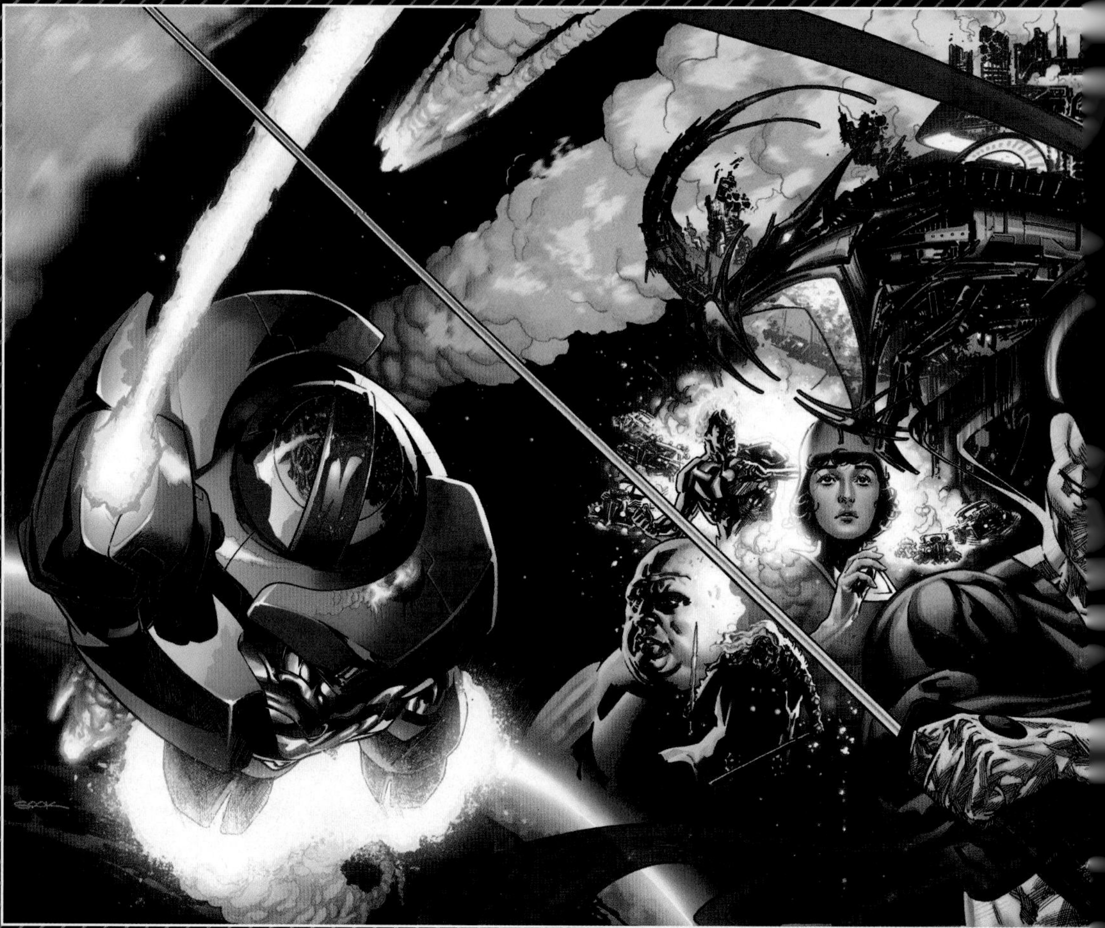

4001 A.D. #1-4
INTERCONNECTING COVER VARIANTS
Art by RYAN SOOK

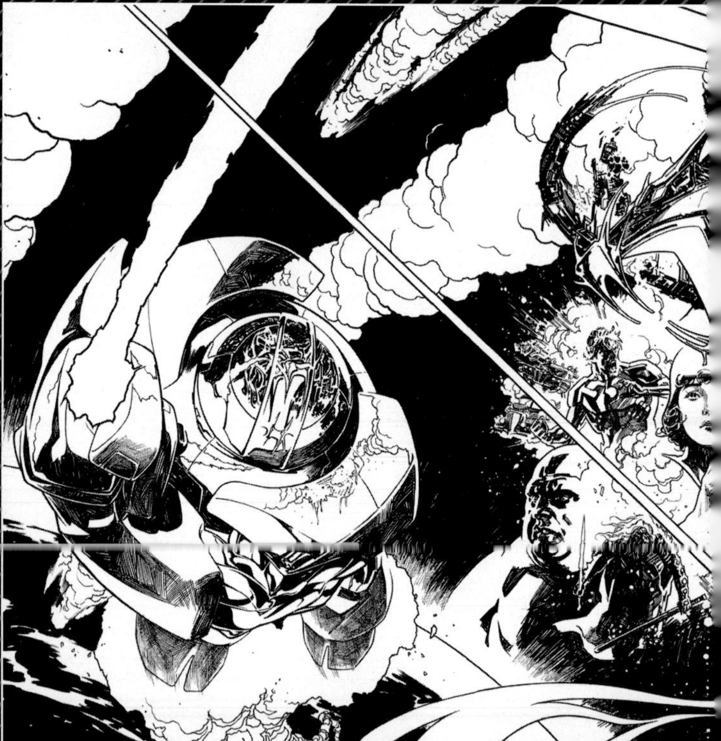

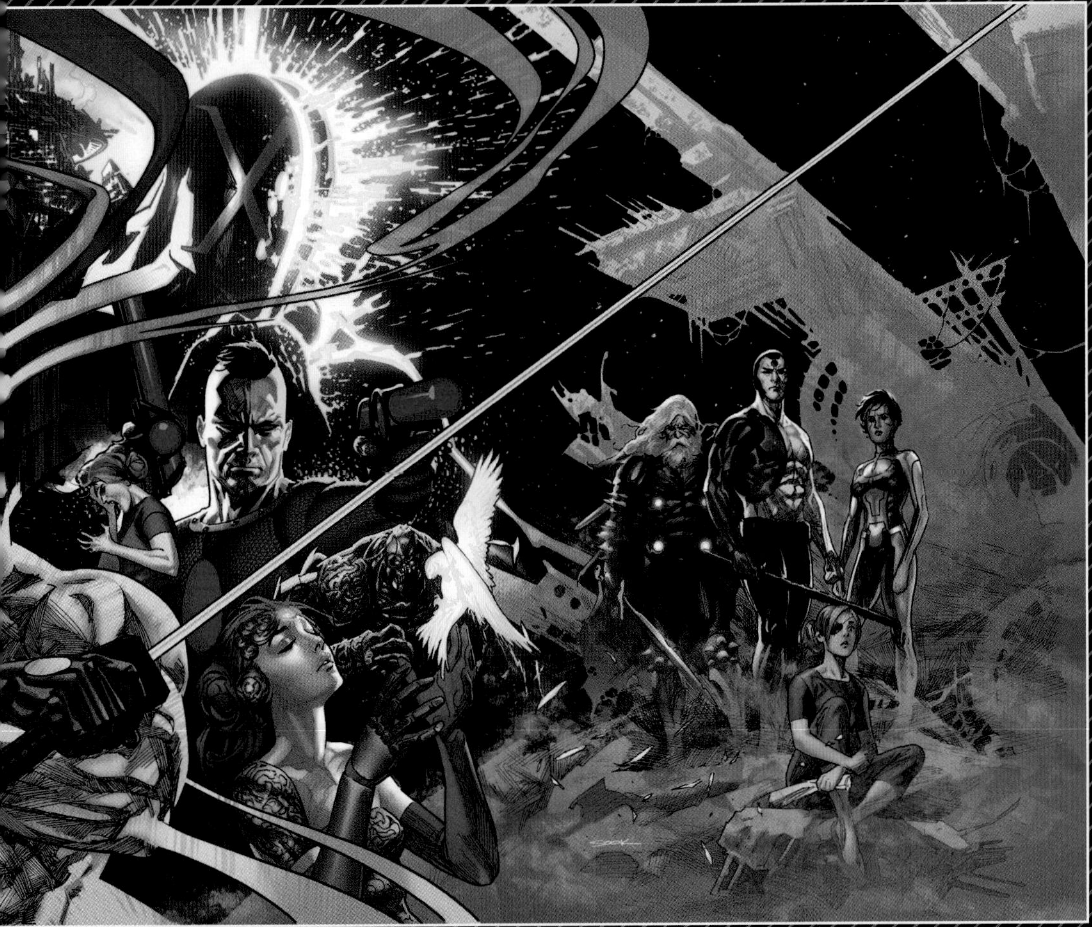

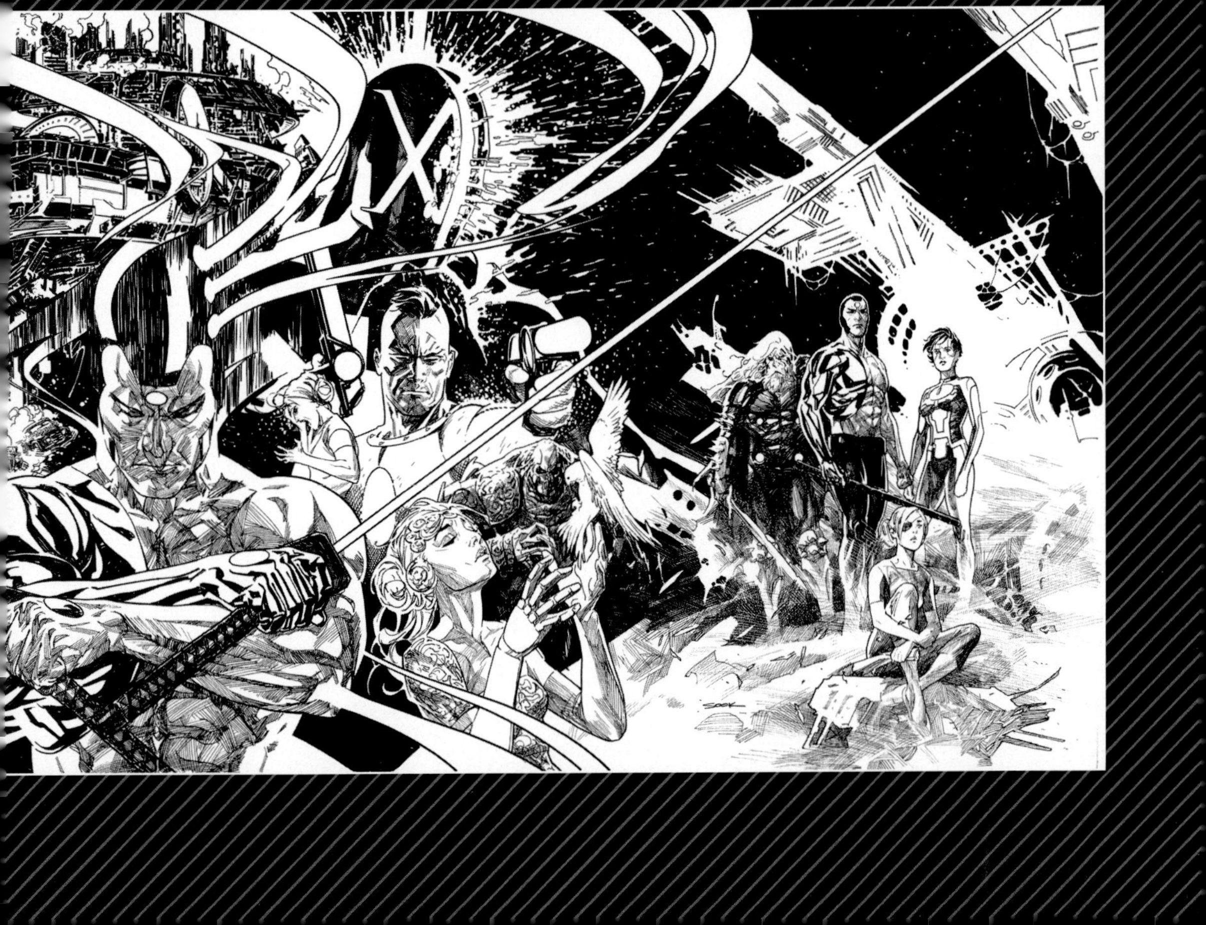

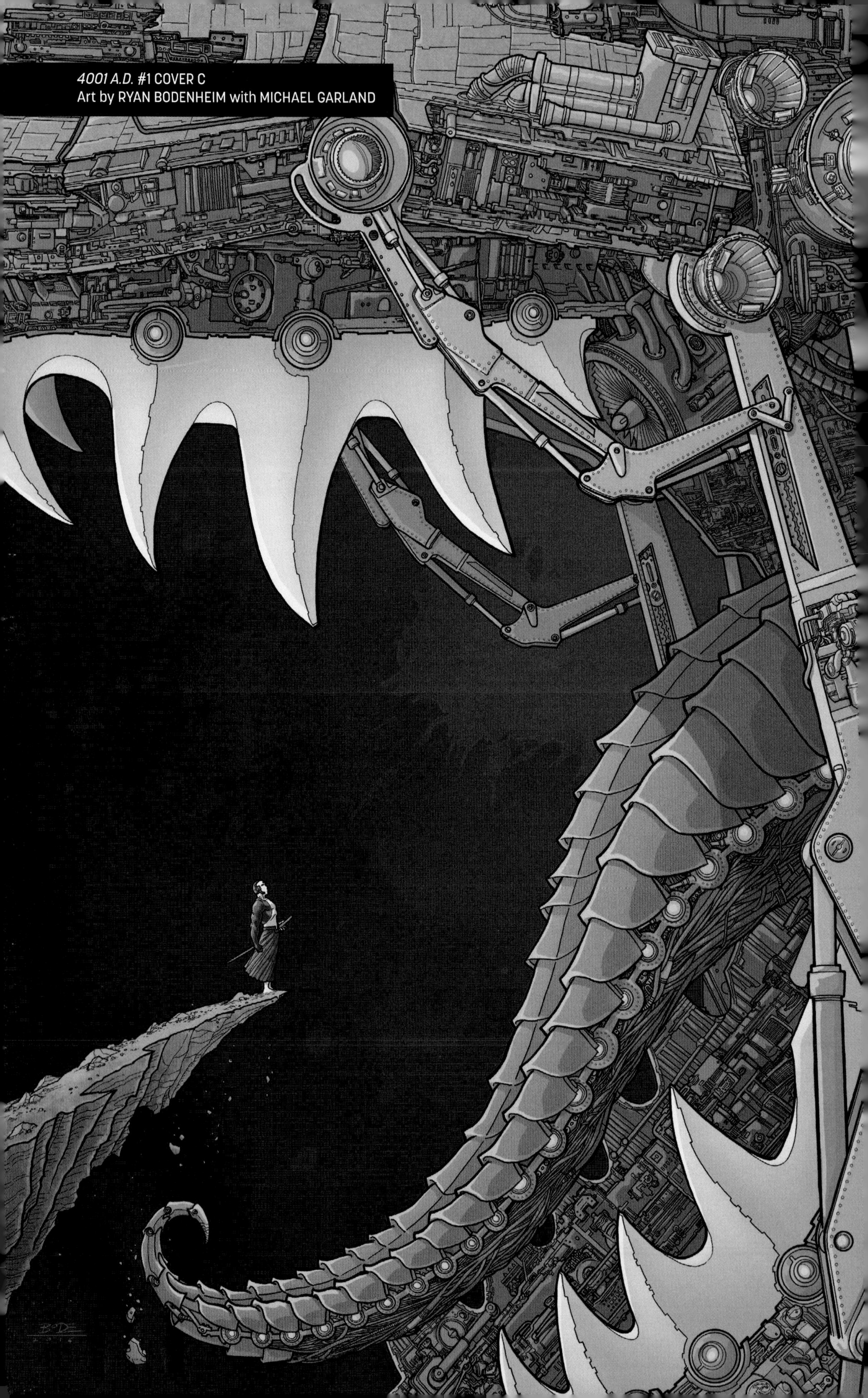

4001 A.D. #1 COVER C
Art by RYAN BODENHEIM with MICHAEL GARLAND

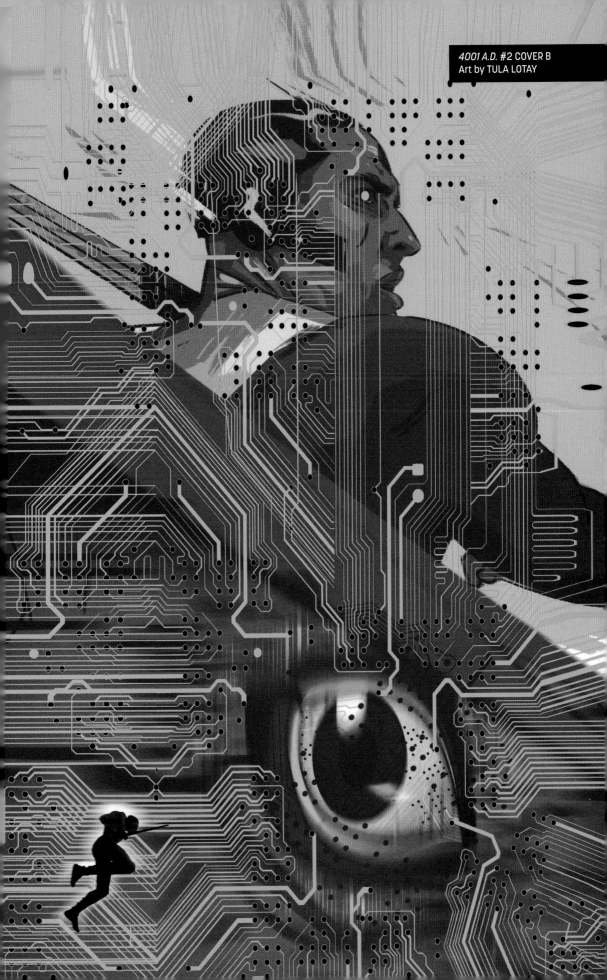

4001 A.D. #2 COVER B
Art by TULA LOTAY

4001 A.D. #2 COVER D
Art by PHILIP TAN with ELMER SANTOS

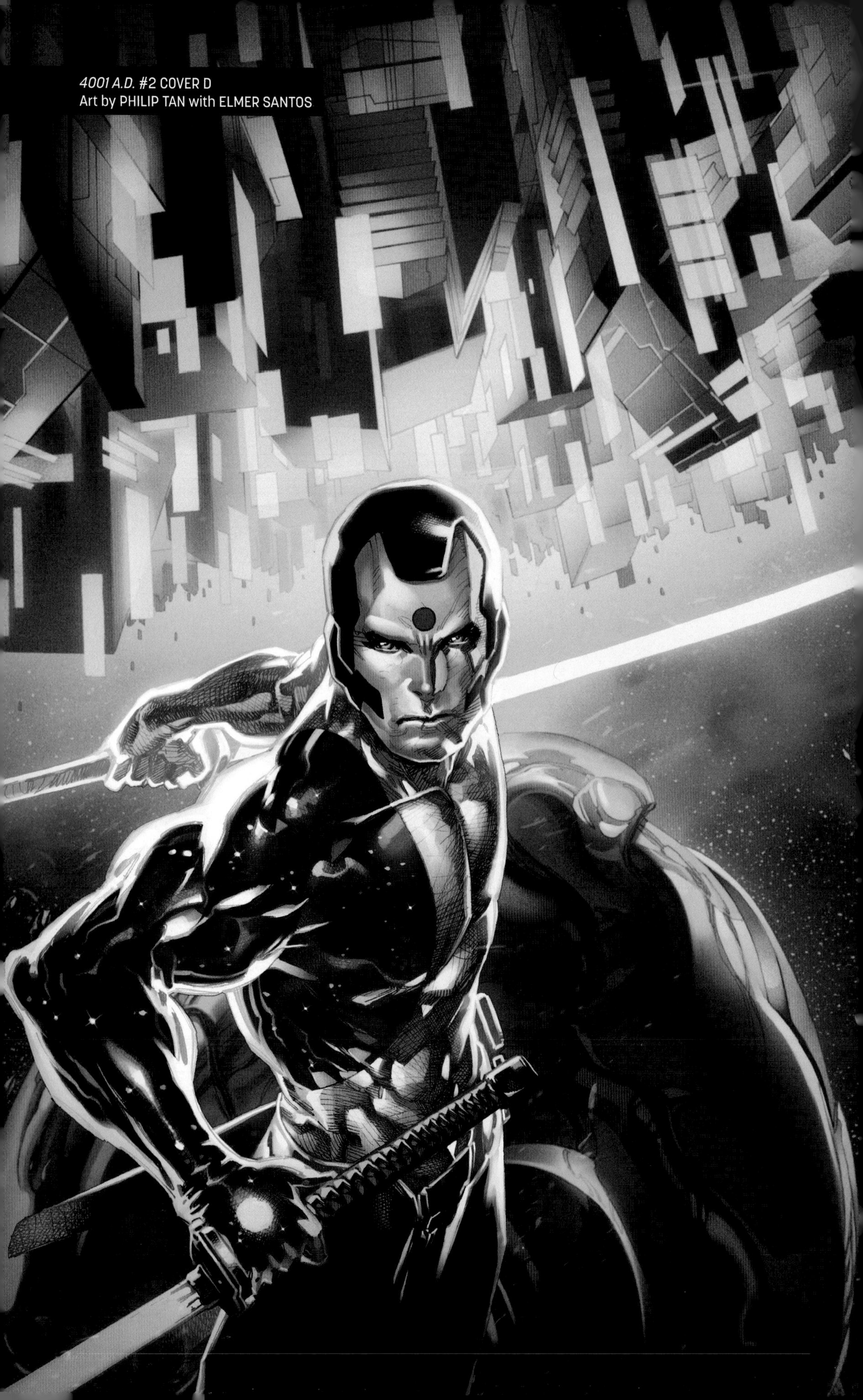

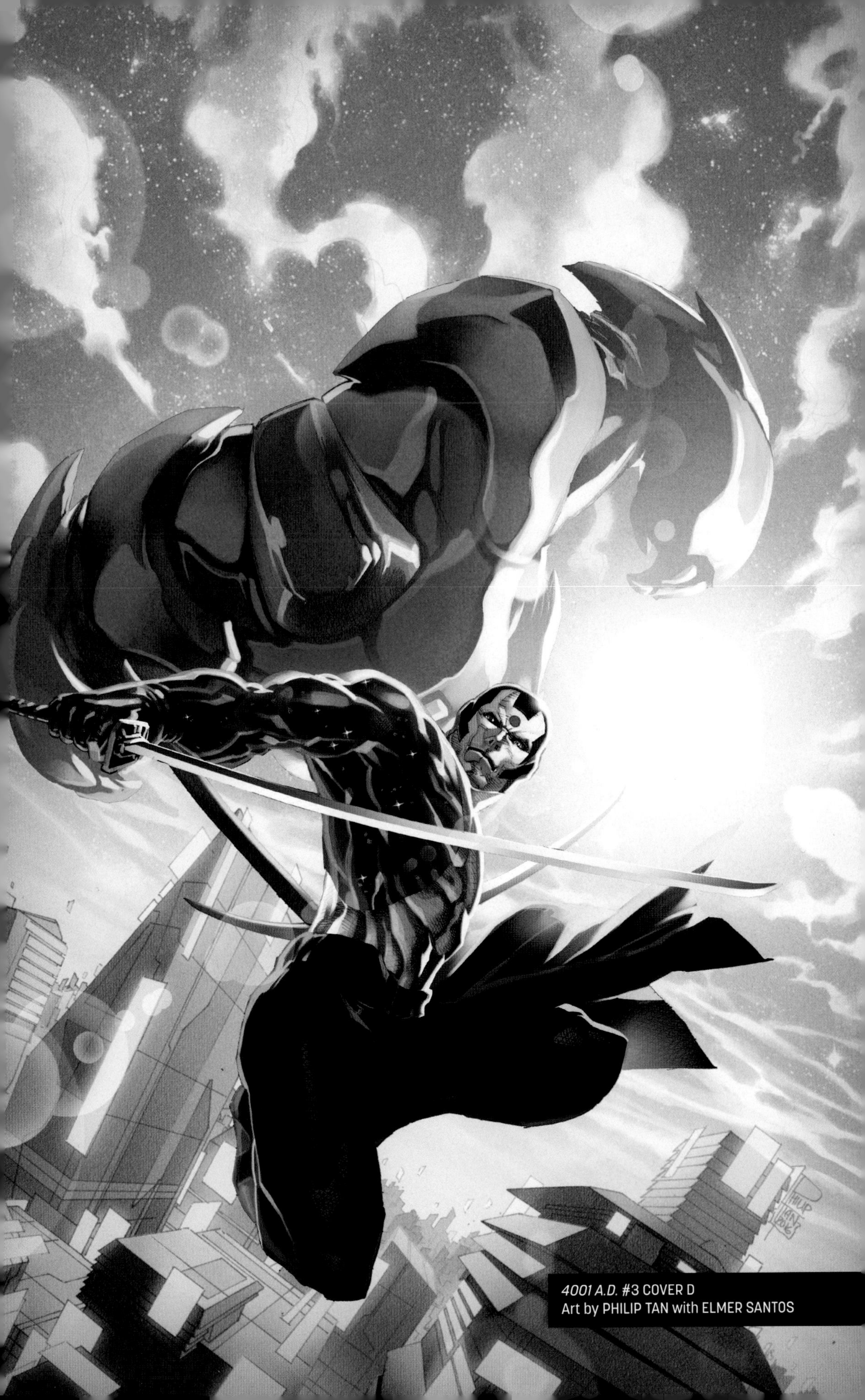

4001 A.D. #3 COVER D
Art by PHILIP TAN with ELMER SANTOS

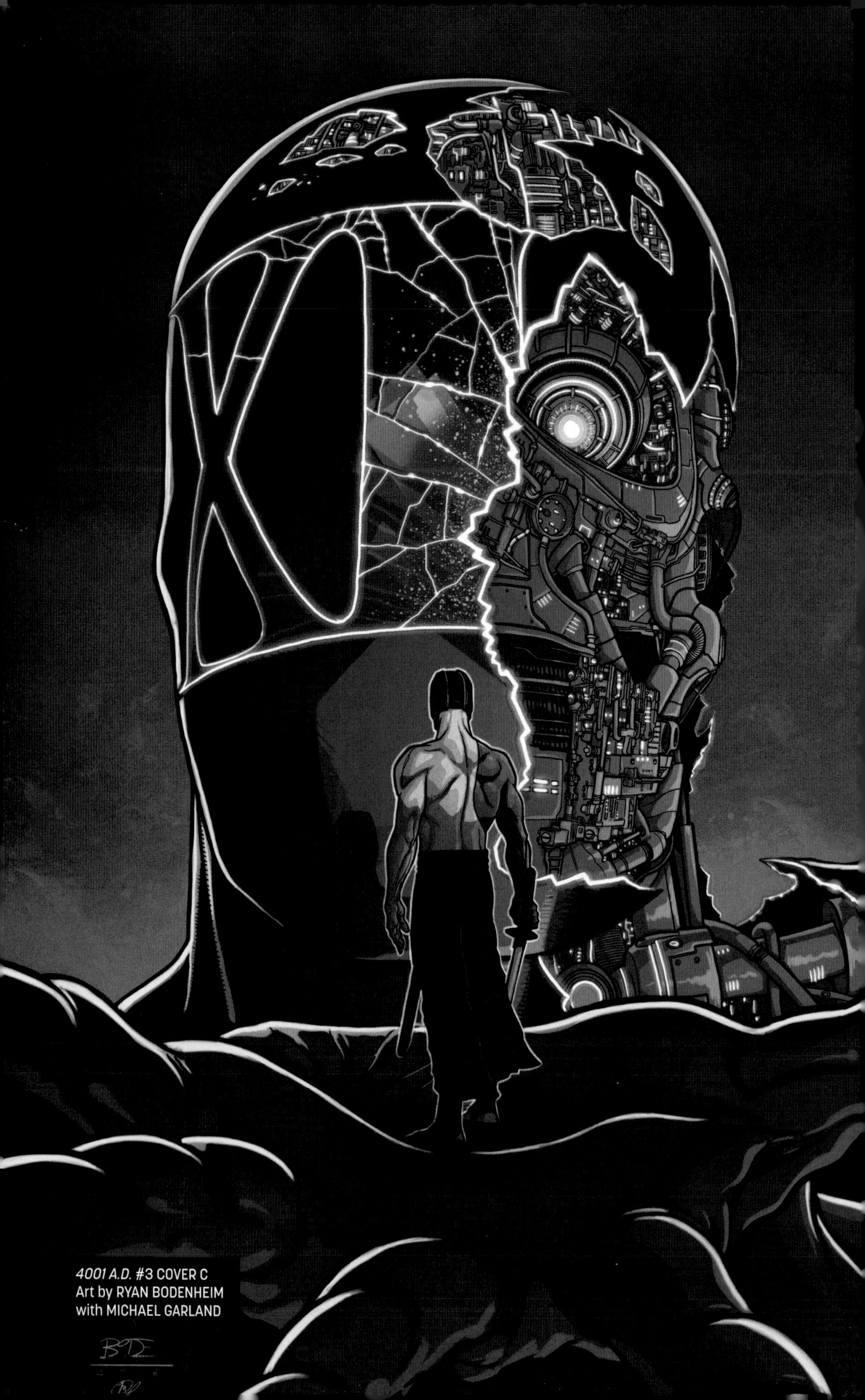

4001 A.D. #3 COVER C
Art by RYAN BODENHEIM
with MICHAEL GARLAND

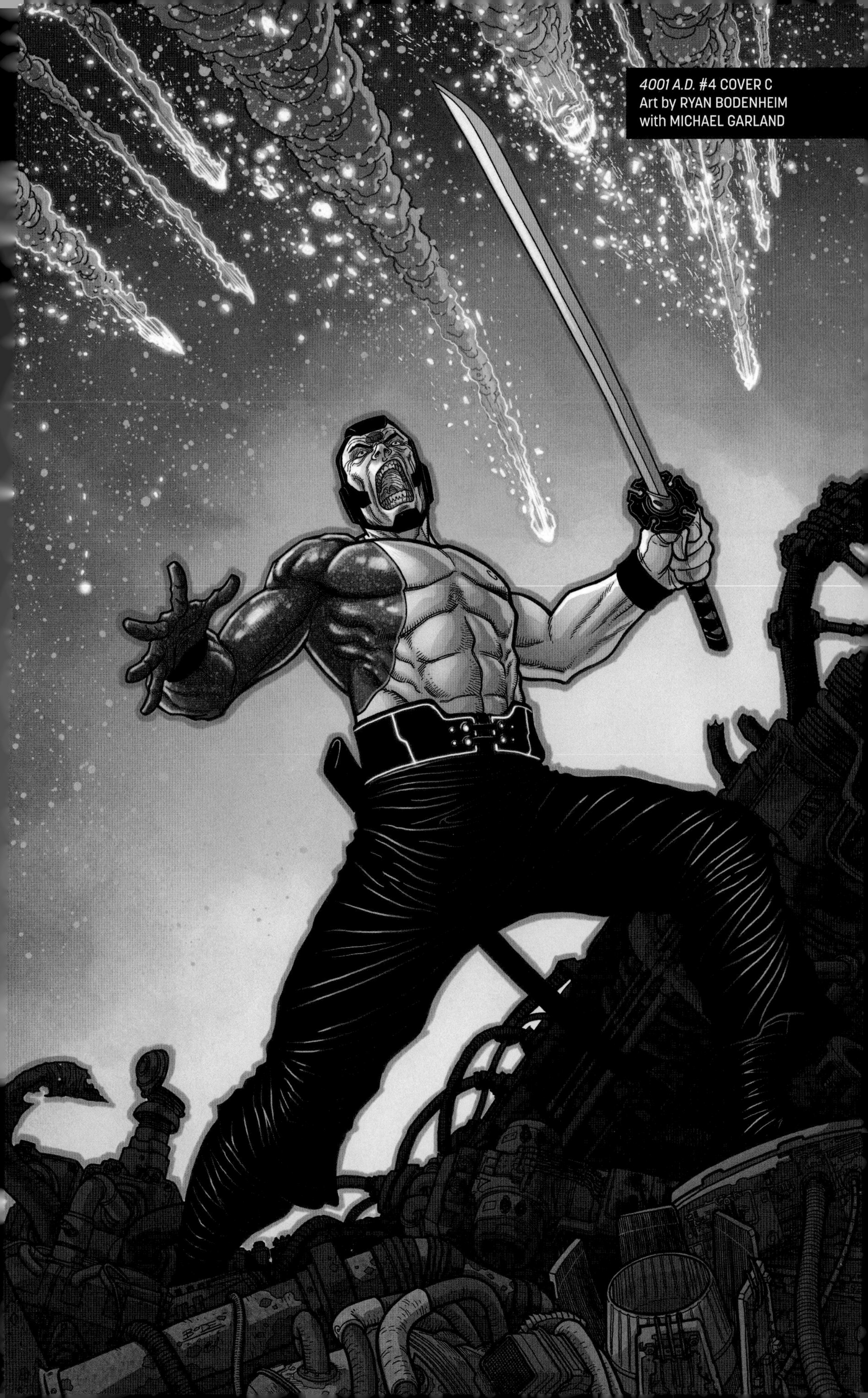

4001 A.D. #4 COVER C
Art by RYAN BODENHEIM
with MICHAEL GARLAND

4001 A.D. #4 COVER D
Art by PHILIP TAN with ELMER SANTOS

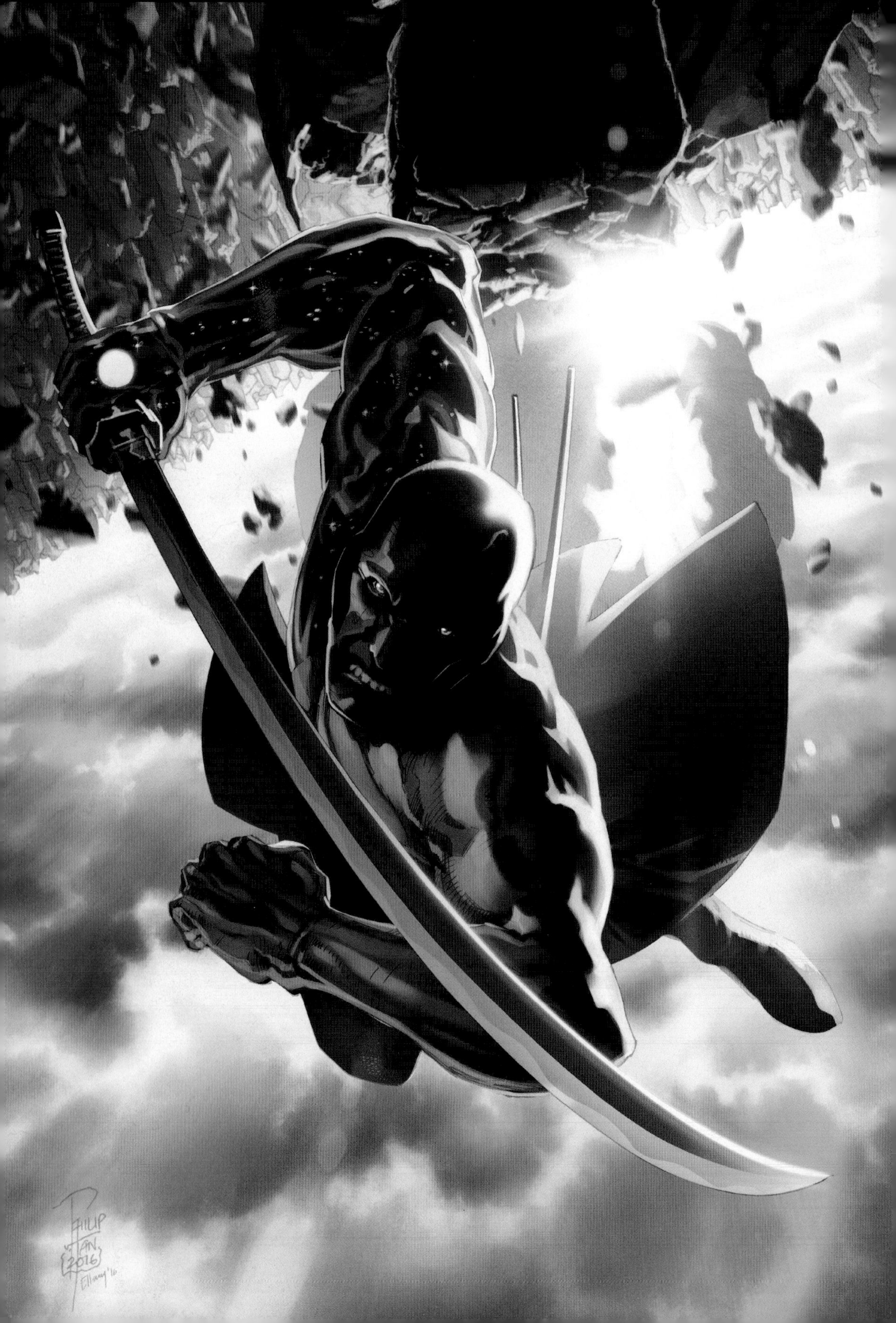

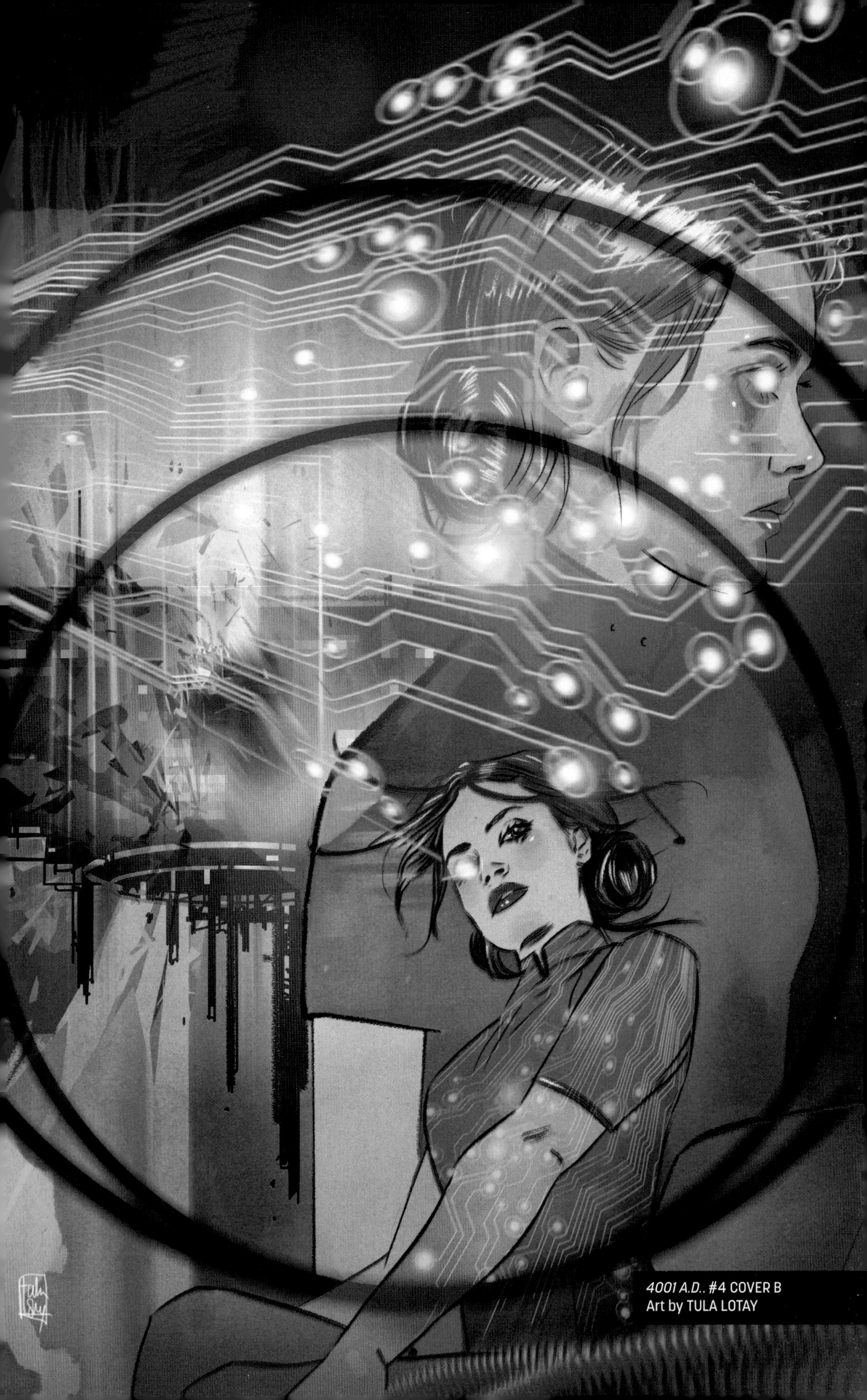

4001 A.D.. #4 COVER B
Art by TULA LOTAY

EXPLORE THE VALIANT UNIVERSE

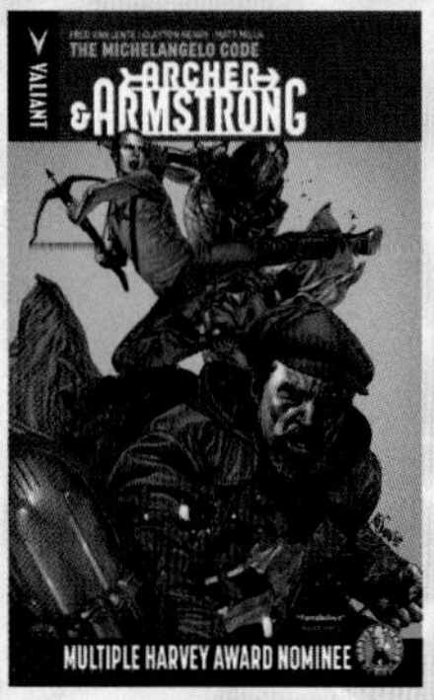
VALIANT
THE MICHELANGELO CODE
ARCHER & ARMSTRONG
MULTIPLE HARVEY AWARD NOMINEE

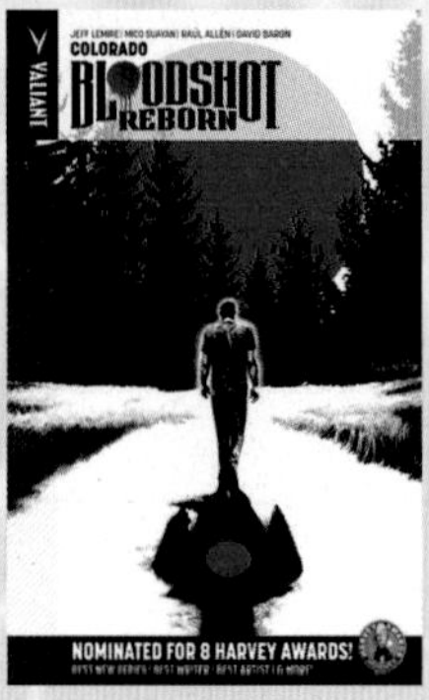
VALIANT
COLORADO
BLOODSHOT REBORN
NOMINATED FOR 8 HARVEY AWARDS!

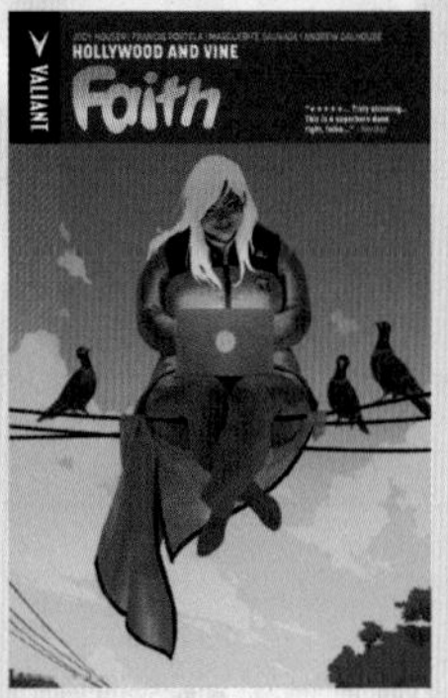
VALIANT
HOLLYWOOD AND VINE
Faith

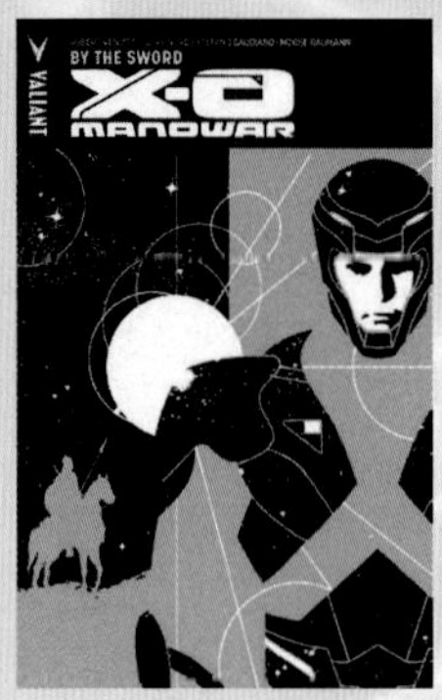
VALIANT
BY THE SWORD
X-O MANOWAR

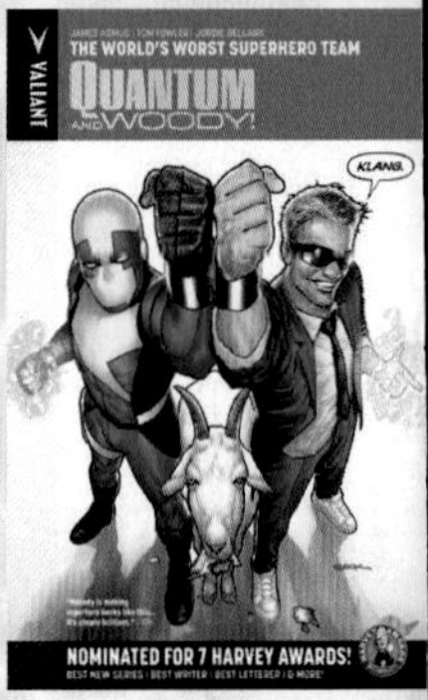
VALIANT
THE WORLD'S WORST SUPERHERO TEAM
QUANTUM AND WOODY!
KLANG!
NOMINATED FOR 7 HARVEY AWARDS!

A&A: THE ADVENTURES OF ARCHER AND ARMSTRONG

Volume 1: In the Bag
ISBN: 9781682151495

ARCHER & ARMSTRONG

Volume 1: The Michelangelo Code
ISBN: 9780979640988

Volume 2: Wrath of the Eternal Warrior
ISBN: 9781939346049

Volume 3: Far Faraway
ISBN: 9781939346148

Volume 4: Sect Civil War
ISBN: 9781939346254

Volume 5: Mission: Improbable
ISBN: 9781939346353

Volume 6: American Wasteland
ISBN: 9781939346421

Volume 7: The One Percent and Other Tales
ISBN: 9781939346537

ARMOR HUNTERS

Armor Hunters
ISBN: 9781939346452

Armor Hunters: Bloodshot
ISBN: 9781939346469

Armor Hunters: Harbinger
ISBN: 9781939346506

Unity Vol. 3: Armor Hunters
ISBN: 9781939346445

X-O Manowar Vol. 7: Armor Hunters
ISBN: 9781939346476

BLOODSHOT

Volume 1: Setting the World on Fire
ISBN: 9780979640964

Volume 2: The Rise and the Fall
ISBN: 9781939346032

Volume 3: Harbinger Wars
ISBN: 9781939346124

Volume 4: H.A.R.D. Corps
ISBN: 9781939346193

Volume 5: Get Some!
ISBN: 9781939346315

Volume 6: The Glitch and Other Tales
ISBN: 9781939346711

BLOODSHOT REBORN

Volume 1: Colorado
ISBN: 9781939346674

Volume 2: The Hunt
ISBN: 9781939346827

Volume 3: The Analog Man
ISBN: 9781682151334

BOOK OF DEATH

Book of Death
ISBN: 9781939346971

Book of Death: The Fall of the Valiant Universe
ISBN: 9781939346988

DEAD DROP

ISBN: 9781939346858

THE DEATH-DEFYING DOCTOR MIRAGE

Volume 1
ISBN: 9781939346490

Volume 2: Second Lives
ISBN: 9781682151297

THE DELINQUENTS

ISBN: 9781939346513

DIVINITY

Volume 1
ISBN: 9781939346766

Volume 2
ISBN: 9781682151518

ETERNAL WARRIOR

Volume 1: Sword of the Wild
ISBN: 9781939346209

Volume 2: Eternal Emperor
ISBN: 9781939346292

Volume 3: Days of Steel
ISBN: 9781939346742

WRATH OF THE ETERNAL WARRIOR

Volume 1: Risen
ISBN: 9781682151235

HARBINGER

Volume 1: Omega Rising
ISBN: 9780979640957

Volume 2: Renegades
ISBN: 9781939346025

Volume 3: Harbinger Wars
ISBN: 9781939346117

Volume 4: Perfect Day
ISBN: 9781939346155

Volume 5: Death of a Renegade
ISBN: 9781939346339

Volume 6: Omegas
ISBN: 9781939346384

HARBINGER WARS

Harbinger Wars
ISBN: 9781939346094

Bloodshot Vol. 3: Harbinger Wars
ISBN: 9781939346124

Harbinger Vol. 3: Harbinger Wars
ISBN: 9781939346117

EXPLORE THE VALIANT UNIVERSE

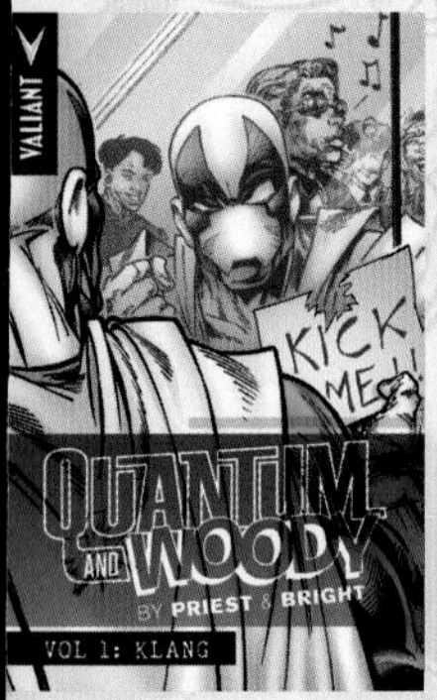
VALIANT
KICK ME
QUANTUM AND WOODY
BY PRIEST & BRIGHT
VOL 1: KLANG

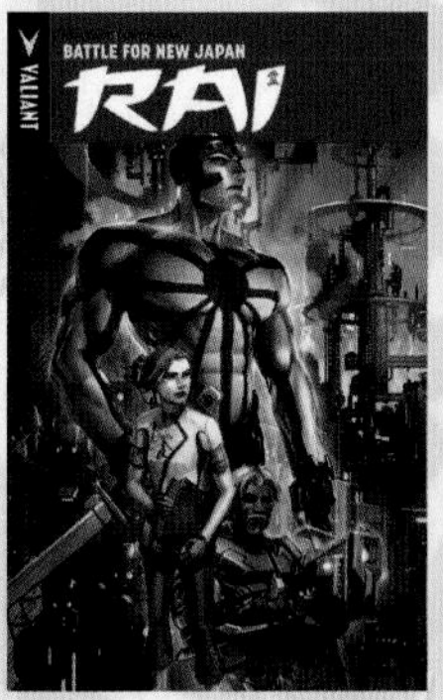
VALIANT
BATTLE FOR NEW JAPAN
RAI

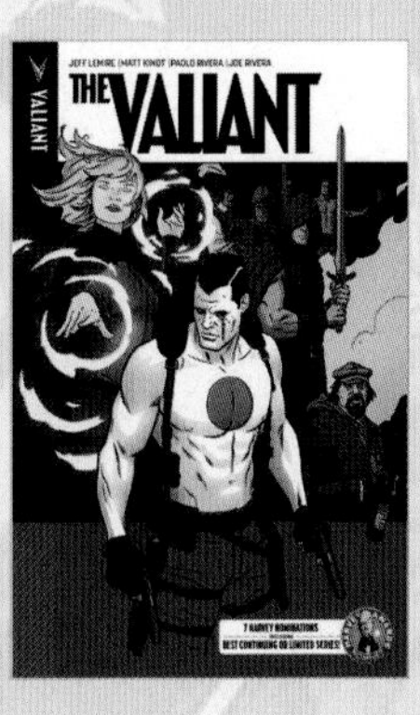
VALIANT
THE VALIANT

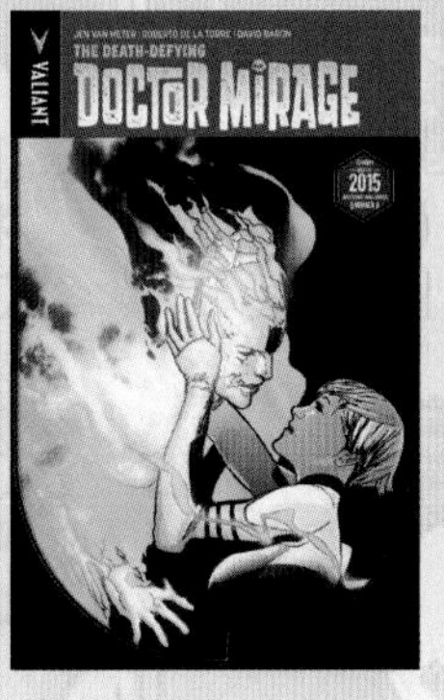
VALIANT
THE DEATH-DEFYING
DOCTOR MIRAGE
2015

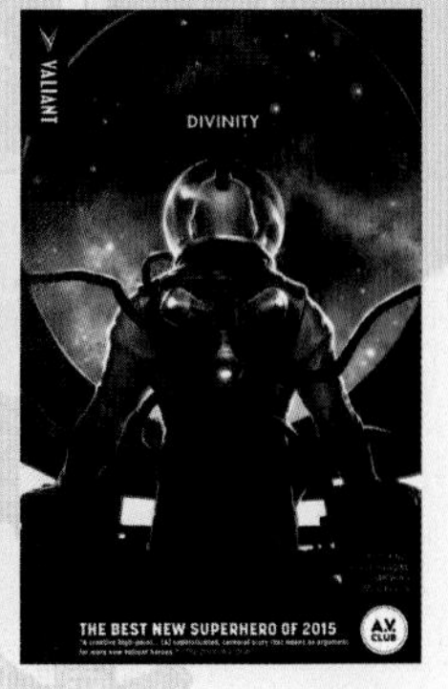
VALIANT
DIVINITY
THE BEST NEW SUPERHERO OF 2015
A.V. CLUB

IMPERIUM

Volume 1: Collecting Monsters
ISBN: 9781939346759

Volume 2: Broken Angels
ISBN: 9781939346896

Volume 3: The Vine Imperative
ISBN: 9781682151112

Volume 4: Stormbreak
ISBN: 9781682151372

NINJAK

Volume 1: Weaponeer
ISBN: 9781939346667

Volume 2: The Shadow Wars
ISBN: 9781939346940

Volume 3: Operation: Deadside
ISBN: 9781682151259

Volume 4: The Siege of King's Castle
ISBN: 9781682151617

QUANTUM AND WOODY

Volume 1: The World's Worst Superhero Team
ISBN: 9781939346186

Volume 2: In Security
ISBN: 9781939346230

Volume 3: Crooked Pasts, Present Tense
ISBN: 9781939346391

Volume 4: Quantum and Woody Must Die!
ISBN: 9781939346629

QUANTUM AND WOODY BY PRIEST & BRIGHT

Volume 1: Klang
ISBN: 9781939346780

Volume 2: Switch
ISBN: 9781939346803

Volume 3: And So...
ISBN: 9781939346865

Volume 4: Q2 - The Return
ISBN: 9781682151099

RAI

Volume 1: Welcome to New Japan
ISBN: 9781939346414

Volume 2: Battle for New Japan
ISBN: 9781939346612

Volume 3: The Orphan
ISBN: 9781939346841

SHADOWMAN

Volume 1: Birth Rites
ISBN: 9781939346001

Volume 2: Darque Reckoning
ISBN: 9781939346056

Volume 3: Deadside Blues
ISBN: 9781939346162

Volume 4: Fear, Blood, And Shadows
ISBN: 9781939346278

Volume 5: End Times
ISBN: 9781939346377

SHADOWMAN BY ENNIS & WOOD

ISBN: 9781682151358

IVAR, TIMEWALKER

Volume 1: Making History
ISBN: 9781939346636

Volume 2: Breaking History
ISBN: 9781939346834

Volume 3: Ending History
ISBN: 9781939346995

UNITY

Volume 1: To Kill a King
ISBN: 9781939346261

Volume 2: Trapped by Webnet
ISBN: 9781939346346

Volume 3: Armor Hunters
ISBN: 9781939346445

Volume 4: The United
ISBN: 9781939346544

Volume 5: Homefront
ISBN: 9781939346797

Volume 6: The War-Monger
ISBN: 9781939346902

Volume 7: Revenge of the Armor Hunters
ISBN: 9781682151136

THE VALIANT

ISBN: 9781939346605

VALIANT ZEROES AND ORIGINS

ISBN: 9781939346582

X-O MANOWAR

Volume 1: By the Sword
ISBN: 9780979640940

Volume 2: Enter Ninjak
ISBN: 9780979640995

Volume 3: Planet Death
ISBN: 9781939346087

Volume 4: Homecoming
ISBN: 9781939346179

Volume 5: At War With Unity
ISBN: 9781939346247

Volume 6: Prelude to Armor Hunters
ISBN: 9781939346407

Volume 7: Armor Hunters
ISBN: 9781939346476

Volume 8: Enter: Armorines
ISBN: 9781939346551

Volume 9: Dead Hand
ISBN: 9781939346650

Volume 10: Exodus
ISBN: 9781939346933

Volume 11: The Kill List
ISBN: 9781682151273

EXPLORE THE VALIANT UNIVERSE

VALIANT
HARBINGER DELUXE EDITION 2

VALIANT
ROBERT VENDITTI MATT KINDT JOSHUA DYSART JOE HARRIS ROBERT GILL DOUG BRAITHWAITE DIEGO BERNARD TREVOR HAIRSINE STEPHEN SEGOVIA
ARMOR HUNTERS DELUXE EDITION

VALIANT
JIM SHOOTER | DAVID LAPHAM
CHILDREN OF THE EIGHTH DAY
HARBINGER
VALIANT MASTERS
L8-AGIN

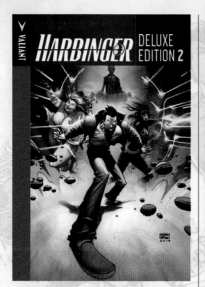

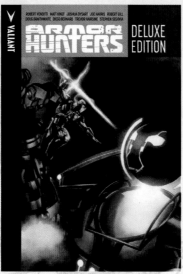

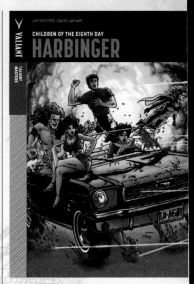

Omnibuses

Archer & Armstrong: The Complete Classic Omnibus
ISBN: 9781939346872
Collecting ARCHER & ARMSTRONG (1992) #0-26, ETERNAL WARRIOR (1992) #25 along with ARCHER & ARMSTRONG: THE FORMATION OF THE SECT.

Quantum and Woody: The Complete Classic Omnibus
ISBN: 9781939346360
Collecting QUANTUM AND WOODY (1997) #0, 1-21 and #32, THE GOAT: H.A.E.D.U.S. #1, and X-O MANOWAR (1996) #16

X-O Manowar Classic Omnibus Vol. 1
ISBN: 9781939346308
Collecting X-O MANOWAR (1992) #0-30, ARMORINES #0, X-O DATABASE #1, as well as material from SECRETS OF THE VALIANT UNIVERSE #1

Deluxe Editions

Archer & Armstrong Deluxe Edition Book 1
ISBN: 9781939346223
Collecting ARCHER & ARMSTRONG #0-13

Archer & Armstrong Deluxe Edition Book 2
ISBN: 9781939346957
Collecting ARCHER & ARMSTRONG #14-25, ARCHER & ARMSTRONG: ARCHER #0 and BLOODSHOT AND H.A.R.D. CORPS #20-21.

Armor Hunters Deluxe Edition
ISBN: 9781939346728
Collecting Armor Hunters #1-4, Armor Hunters: Aftermath #1, Armor Hunters: Bloodshot #1-3, Armor Hunters: Harbinger #1-3, Unity #8-11, and X-O MANOWAR #23-29

Bloodshot Deluxe Edition Book 1
ISBN: 9781939346216
Collecting BLOODSHOT #1-13

Bloodshot Deluxe Edition Book 2
ISBN: 9781939346810
Collecting BLOODSHOT AND H.A.R.D. CORPS #14-23, BLOODSHOT #24-25, BLOODSHOT #0, BLOODSHOT AND H.A.R.D. CORPS: H.A.R.D. CORPS #0, along with ARCHER & ARMSTRONG #18-19

Book of Death Deluxe Edition
ISBN: 9781682151150
Collecting BOOK OF DEATH #1-4, BOOK OF DEATH: THE FALL OF BLOODSHOT #1, BOOK OF DEATH: THE FALL OF NINJAK #1, BOOK OF DEATH: THE FALL OF HARBINGER #1, and BOOK OF DEATH: THE FALL OF X-O MANOWAR #1.

Divinity Deluxe Edition
ISBN: 97819393460993
Collecting DIVNITY #1-4

Harbinger Deluxe Edition Book 1
ISBN: 9781939346131
Collecting HARBINGER #0-14

Harbinger Deluxe Edition Book 2
ISBN: 9781939346773
Collecting HARBINGER #15-25, HARBINGER: OMEGAS #1-3, and HARBINGER: BLEEDING MONK #0

Harbinger Wars Deluxe Edition
ISBN: 9781939346322
Collecting HARBINGER WARS #1-4, HARBINGER #11-14, and BLOODSHOT #10-13

Ivar, Timewalker Deluxe Edition Book 1
ISBN: 9781682151198
Collecting IVAR, TIMEWALKER #1-12

Quantum and Woody Deluxe Edition Book 1
ISBN: 9781939346681
Collecting QUANTUM AND WOODY #1-12 and QUANTUM AND WOODY: THE GOAT #0

Q2: The Return of Quantum and Woody Deluxe Edition
ISBN: 9781939346568
Collecting Q2: THE RETURN OF QUANTUM AND WOODY #1-5

Rai Deluxe Edition Book 1
ISBN: 9781682151174
Collecting RAI #1-12, along with material from RAI #1 PLUS EDITION and RAI #5 PLUS EDITION

Shadowman Deluxe Edition Book 1
ISBN: 9781939346438
Collecting SHADOWMAN #0-10

Shadowman Deluxe Edition Book 2
ISBN: 9781682151075
Collecting SHADOWMAN #11-16, SHADOWMAN #13X, SHADOWMAN: END TIMES #1-3 and PUNK MAMBO #0

Unity Deluxe Edition Book 1
ISBN: 9781939346575
Collecting UNITY #0-14

The Valiant Deluxe Edition
ISBN: 97819393460986
Collecting THE VALIANT #1-4

X-O Manowar Deluxe Edition Book 1
ISBN: 9781939346100
Collecting X-O MANOWAR #1-14

X-O Manowar Deluxe Edition Book 2
ISBN: 9781939346520
Collecting X-O MANOWAR #15-22, and UNITY #1-4

X-O Manowar Deluxe Edition Book 3
ISBN: 9781682151310
Collecting X-O MANOWAR #23-29 and ARMOR HUNTERS #1-4.

Valiant Masters

Bloodshot Vol. 1 - Blood of the Machine
ISBN: 9780979640933

H.A.R.D. Corps Vol. 1 - Search and Destroy
ISBN: 9781939346285

Harbinger Vol. 1 - Children of the Eighth Day
ISBN: 9781939346483

Ninjak Vol. 1 - Black Water
ISBN: 9780979640971

Rai Vol. 1 - From Honor to Strength
ISBN: 9781939346070

Shadowman Vol. 1 - Spirits Within
ISBN: 9781939346018

4001 A.D. | READING ORDER

Read the entirety of the blistering comics event uniting Rai with the greatest heroes of the 41st century!

VALIANT
WELCOME TO NEW JAPAN

Rai Vol. 1: Welcome to New Japan
(OPTIONAL)

VALIANT
BATTLE FOR NEW JAPAN
RAI

Rai Vol. 2: Battle for New Japan
(OPTIONAL)

VALIANT
THE ORPHAN
RAI

Rai Vol. 3: The Orphan
(OPTIONAL)

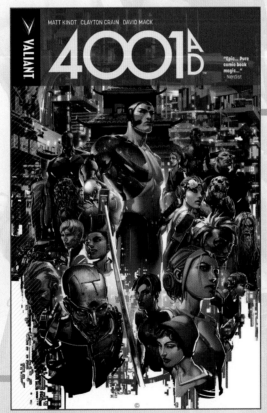

MATT KINDT CLAYTON CRAIN DAVID MACK
VALIANT
4001 A.D.
"Epic... Pure comic book magic..."
- Nerdist

4001 A.D.

VALIANT
4001 A.D.
4001 A.D.: BEYOND NEW JAPAN

4001 A.D.: Beyond New Japan
(OPTIONAL)

VALIANT
RAI

Rai Vol. 4: 4001 A.D.
(OPTIONAL)

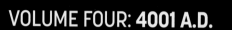

RAI

VOLUME FOUR: 4001 A.D.

ROCKETING OUT OF THE PAGES OF 4001 A.D...
THE ORIGIN OF RAI REVEALED!

MATT KINDT | CAFU | ANDREW DALHOUSE
4001 A.D.

For the first time ever, witness the violent foundation of Father's space-born utopia of New Japan...and, with it, the shocking genesis of the line of guardians that bear the name Rai! Born and bred by Father to enforce peace at any cost, follow the first Rai and his successors across two millennia as they chronicle the history of 4001 A.D. - from the launch of New Japan into orbit to the latest Rai's crusade to bring it crashing back down to Earth!

Valiant mastermind Matt Kindt (4001 A.D.) and visionary artist CAFU (UNITY) uncover the never-before-told story of New Japan's rise to power...and reveal just how the Valiant Universe of today became the 4001 A.D. of tomorrow!

Collecting RAI #13-16.

TRADE PAPERBACK
ISBN: 978-1-68215-147-1

4001 A.D.: BEYOND NEW JAPAN

ROCKETING OUT OF THE PAGES OF 4001 A.D...THE PRESENT AND FUTURE OF VALIANT'S GREATEST HEROES COME TOGETHER IN FOUR ESSENTIAL STANDALONE CHAPTERS AT THE HEART OF THE BLOCKBUSTER COMICS EVENT OF THE YEAR!

VENDITTI | LEMIRE | HOUSER | ROBERTS | VAN LENTE | HENRY | BRAITHWAITE | GILL
BEYOND NEW JAPAN
4001 A.D.

Blast two thousand years into the future as the never-before-told history of New Japan's dominion over Earth and the future fates of X-O Manowar, Bloodshot, and Shadowman stand revealed. Then, witness the battle-scarred debut of the boldest new hero of this century or the next when War Mother makes her history-shattering debut! The future starts now as all-star writers Robert Venditti, Jeff Lemire, Jody Houser, Rafer Roberts, and Fred Van Lente join visionary artists Clayton Henry, Doug Braithwaite, Robert Gill, and Tomas Giorello to bring the Valiant Universe barreling into the 41st century!

Collecting 4001 A.D.: X-O MANOWAR #1, 4001 A.D.: BLOODSHOT #1, 4001 A.D.: SHADOWMAN #1, and 4001 A.D.: WAR MOTHER #1.

TRADE PAPERBACK
ISBN: 978-1-68215-146-4